The Toll of Our Emotional Currencies: An Audit

DAN ANDREW COVAR

ISBN 978-1-953223-71-5 (paperback)

Copyright © 2020 by Dan Andrew Covar

All rights reserved. No part of this publication may be reproduced, distributed, or transmitted in any form or by any means, including photocopying, recording, or other electronic or mechanical methods without the prior written permission of the publisher. For permission requests, solicit the publisher via the address below.

Rushmore Press LLC
1 800 460 9188
www.rushmorepress.com

Printed in the United States of America

Contents

Prologue xvii

EXHIBIT A: appetizing entries, entreaties and entities for endorphin addicts

the child had whiskey-soaked dreams for months 5
I owe the dull sky a funny dance 9
budding roses resembled rat-heads 15
that meaningless fun 20
fortune-tellers, and cigarette commercials 22
gurus sitting on stumps 24
on madhouses and hospices 26
ruining the audacity of our winded virtues 28
seascapes tempt me to strip on the sand and call it a day 30
nothing but recycled worthless sentences that used to work 32
into one of her many voids 35
sweet-honey-dear 38

EXHIBIT B: bells singing due to being shot at by bullets with names carved on them

I am an over-spiced demon-feed 43
piss-orange 46
before your unroasted eyes 48
twenty-two years 50
motionless most of the time 52
in that small acre of eternity 54
caused catastrophic couplings 58
my view of you was most immaculate 60
meeting my axe, my revolver and my ex-wife 62
her hails were euphoric 64
full of weeping bodies, dispossessed 66

having a fight for impurity's sake 68
allowing for a caterpillar of good days to butterfly 72
through October's candied prostitutes 76

Exhibit C: calls to submission and hesitant relocations of our damned fondness

no-love left for you to hang in the closet, or to dry on the roof.....83
fall into love with neutered rhythms 85
half-cigarettes on the ashtray 88
decades of averted wonderments...90
long-faced, and believing in the long road's flaccid promises.........92
jubilee falls on the palms of the catcher 94
it's alright if we go unmissed 95
fatigued by love's dialysis 97
her fire contracts *all* so suddenly..99
drunk on convenience-store wine 101
for every brilliant obstacle that left a half-dome scar 103
then and there and *everywhere* 105
with a seamstress's sensibility 106
at the first touch of daylight 108

Exhibit D: doubts automatic and problematic eye-ticks that hinders a rather lovely conversation

an orgy of white sky 113
the only existential cure..115
a fax from the devil's mouth 117
infatuates of the sewer lids..119
it left like starshine 122
she was *sad* when she said that...124
in the blackness's grip 126
everything is permitted...128
while the noon is young 132
taking the whole length of it inside your mouth 134
dagger inches deep on the back 138
clover-green and sunset-despair 140
finding another seat to melt on...142

**EXHIBIT E: eavesdroppers of habitual sleepers,
   but wouldn't we rather be happily dying?**

large morsels and the *ones* good men choke on 147
that murderous mood..149
unhinged for good..151
leaving unsatisfying tracks to and from the funeral parlor..........153
dies at the rendezvous point 155
gaze at the tenderness born...157
watercolor memory washing over 159
*free*falling serendipity..161
above a postmortem angel 163
raped by tiny circles..165
miles of violent roots..169
implore the contours of her silvery death..................................171
the storm's terminal clients 173
shove onto a hard surface and suffocate 175
fragments I parted with 177

On Love and Lovelessness 179

**EXHIBIT F: fantasy meatloaf for frugal lovebirds and
   prostitutes of destiny's hourglass curves**

the injured illustrations 185
laughter stun 187
in awe on the streets of her natural authority...........................189
lovingly given the death penalty 191
for these jaded delegates 193
a year-long nap...195
a little part of your soul you're fine without 197
her house..199
my discharged muse 202
the person you'll be*come because* of my breakdown 204
in silver cuffs 206

EXHIBIT G: game of lies set for the future and detours endured with maximum excitement

I broke my nose on the pavement wall 211
its fondest fascination 213
hurtful momentums foaming at the mouth 215
what *we* thought we knew 217
my first true downfall was somewhat sincere 218
in favor of those lost dogs 220
their high functioning anxiety 223
devoted to haunted sighs 226
chaos of smiles and monster love 228
make me feel useful doing useless things 231
deep mining auras 233
in our unhappy jungle of a flame 234
what a rush! us humans, *being* 236

EXHIBIT H: hello, it's glee, lacking fullness in the mass grave of slightly happier scenes

sunshine's new will 241
the little details of our magnifying love 243
drawn a second sun 245
this last ounce of beautiful anger 246
love is passed around to be wronged 247
the truth behind the smile in the petty pictures 248
the blistered climb 249
raw and tender 251
no longer 253
the whale's carcass is now vacant 254
smoking the devil's joint 256
the genocide of her finest starlight 258
on our white nights 260
the winning alibi you'll need for the rest of your life 262

Exhibit I: indifferent motives and clarity that catches ridicule of the fiery sort

the bones for a neat melody 267
the sound of our specific pain 268
let euthanasia occur 269
nothing could undo our cosmic noose 271
I'm losing track of the important stuff 273
rest your beautiful soul here 274
under the paper-thin roof of a burning chapel 275
laugh at our triumph 276
I cannot help myself but weep in beds cold as ice 277
I smile till my teeth rot as I am listening 279
Oh, love, was it ever misunderstood! 281
plenty of dark spots in our white hell 282
censor train doors from speaking 284
notes most contorted 286

A Buttonless Robe 287

Exhibit J: jousting with faith's reflective dunes inside eyes terrified of love's continuance

they slept the loudest 291
welcome to the madness! 293
bleeding under the elephant clouds 295
my ultimatums and towering conditions 297
kisses which taste of roadside gasoline 299
good news for sharing over white wine and rye bread 301
die losing track 305
by windowsills and under beds 307
collecting therapeutic friendships 308
God's grace 310
time's vacuum 313
mute what is required of a man to sing 315
my MK Ultra 317
it's an honor to be love's ashtray 318

Exhibit K: killed or be kissed by our wants' fatal solution, needing imperfect Gods to accept us

we wake up with a dead eye...321
it stays like a bad scar on my face......................................322
my heart is filled with cold tea..324
swinging left and right with the liberated breeze, swirling you.....326
slowly with our gracelessness 328
a thousand names uttered the wrong way 330
the quieter we wept 333
revoked 334
darling *shoot* for the questions marked................................337
I cheat my way into..339
her magnificent frame 341
the rest and peace in those future days.................................342
a charmless dream, prepping for the real thing 343
liken to speak to you in tongues 345
a loving conversation between beloveds................................347

Exhibit L: lows and highs being six feet under-average; love granted by nocturnal medicines

to be in command of this 351
my arm froze rowing 353
our bastard hearts beating with*out* love..............................355
my mouth through your open bruises 357
a silent kill never ends a loud misery, she said......................358
my great red mug summons my will to return 359
the coldest trail down the tundra's icy sheets.......................361
I understand why love must expire 363
the distinct footprints of cowards 365
opium prayers 367
her music and melodies 370
entry, by entry, ad infinitum..371
lay on our soft paradox...373
such electrifying screams...375
whenever my halo begs for your septic loving......................377

Exhibit M: mind buffets for the maggot populace in the lobes of our labyrinth wastelands

innocent eyes...381
walk through the fire unscathed 384
grow ten feet long, like them, we fell in love with life 386
infect my normal heart with your crazy soul.....................388
for *heaven's sake!*..390
my killer aches for killer arcs..392
her incredible strokes..394
winning is a permanent daydream 395
a *bad* apple 397
m*ost* impure and most sinfully inclined 398
a table for two 400
a threat to her tranquility 401
dreams are a perfect dying place 402
a creative lie on queue 404
honest lips...406

Exhibit N: noise offerings in the silent conquering of hearts missed and granulated on a sieve

joyously dismembered 411
a coward's countenance 412
fair warning overdue..413
to sustain the awe 415
the chalk outline the angels drew................................417
munching on *Picasso's* ear...419
fucked by the sunlight..421
I wasn't wrong to place those fugitive bombs 422
the skies will water our dream's satellite 423
pure heroin...424
seeps flowingly towards the absurd 425
our elongated fire 427
pro*cure* a head full of stars 428
degrading our photographs..429
looking wishful, staring into nowhere paths...............431

in its original deformity 433
a cha*rred* sun 435
old promises enhance our *foggy* sunrise 437

Graced by a Phoenix's DNA 439

Exhibit O: old habits lie hard about past courtships that sank within the depths of dead time

the most passionate sounds 445
after drinking a pitcher of expensive grief 448
naked behind a tree 450
the role-playing game 452
the shine on the nightstand photo 453
the flames eat away what it wants 454
make orphans of the snowflakes 455
keeping my darlings dispossessed! 457
undressing dawn with a grin 459
breathless since that day, breathless since that day 461
how I can control *you* 463
posthumous novel 465
what a magical thing, our type of confusion 466

Exhibit P: poor judgements regarding the vines of incarnation

an unknown period 469
an elongated disco 470
this divine moment 472
this lesson 473
on how to best navigate through vilest sunlight 475
a proper thief 477
a dash of burnt cinnamon 479
you're a lesson I didn't take seriously 481
accidents are meant to breathe 483
find fabulous aw 484
a pulp 486
amateurs with nothing else to *live* for 487

EXHIBIT Q: queens in debt exiled into enlightened poverty

dying for granted on the little I could give 491
where I am least likely to swim 492
the final drop 494
snap my neck neat 495
porcelain needles of springtime..496
my divine troubadour..497
stagnant it was..499
it was lubricated with care 501
install a resurrection please 503
the evening favors lost love 504
her whispered ultimatums 506

EXHIBIT R: running the wire of benevolent persuasions

death's yellow agent 511
to our tsunami of secrets...513
that girl I met, *was she even true?*.....................................515
your magnitude...518
your intrusive nature 519
pour from a constant fountain...520
yearn for this 521
die away in numbers so great..522
from a single sigh 524
corpses rot happily below our footsteps 525

The Thin Air's Zen Highway..527

EXHIBIT S: sun-baked sadness and asinine commentary on what goes on if you don't

yes, that's you you're looking at..533
watching our flames trying 535
somewhere in *us* something is wrong...................................537
free birds 538
remembering the softness of the sands..................................539
for each other, *for each other* 540
a better adventure as divine silhouettes 541

polished by lantern snow..542
riding on borrowed time 543
red...545
yellow..547
green 551
never ceases to amaze...556
daylight's optimistic nuisance of a friend 558

Exhibit T: the toll of a love unshackled, unshaved, undead, and inundated by false prophesy

this black and white world kills my lady love............................563
painting creative ways to love me..565
vague words set on a timer...566
out of our beachside ashes 567
distorted and hostage by the sun's decrepit rays......................568
think of all it brings to us 569
vague words tell great lies 571
behind the bitter aftertaste of red wine 572
rejoicing with the same melody as yours..................................574
may we rest..576
ready to become dust, restlessly collecting 578
before our demurred eyes 579
gambling away youth's energy...581
let love come to you preserved..583
with the kicks and high-jumps of small feet...........................585
all our kindest sin told the perfect story..................................587
there's no other choice but love..588
acacias over orchids..589
coping 590

Exhibit U: untied chances and butane containers perpetually emptied

I'm smiling at you expecting a smile back...............................595
in your kiss..597
salvation taste of fresh honey 598
shimmering with venom's forgiveness 600

its midnight choreography..601
may be the greatest thing I've ever kn*own*..................................604
shamelessly magnificent..607
we left..608
the best parts of love..609
our premium exhibitions..611
a monarch excreta..613
a basket case of bleeding apricots...616
my constantly mesmerized gaze..617

EXHIBIT V: vases of dead flowers for depressive days love couldn't save

glowing bats, neon butterflies, and shooting stars......................621
everyday feels like this 622
relax and wait *here*..624
I like this new you, you feel inspired..626
under the stars to songs overplayed..627
placing a question mark on *us*..629
giving me a helpless puppy vibe..631
all tangled up and mental...632
becoming *unloved*...634
her last endeavor..636
constantly shifts, constantly ask..638
speaking kind syllables..639
as our nightmares fight for realism...641
lead us back to the islands of front pages 643
flip a coin to decide my faith...645
you don't exist without me 647

My Helena Of Troy..648

EXHIBIT W: walk of blame at the altar, alternating between feeling loved or imprisoned

the worst inevitably follows 653
with someone else on the safe side...654
in the form of the most deceitful embraces................................655
won at an auction in a guru's deathbed.......................................656

chambers of generic silence nonverbal unscripted 658
that ecstasy, that majesty! 659
in search of meaningless answers 661
to console 663
the smell of carcasses on our land 665
your soul keeps mine happy company 667
withdrawn by a temporary honest heart 669
the reaper's favorite whore 671

EXHIBIT X: x-ray impressions through long-distance affectations

walks with me in pastures of green and blue 675
you are a queued rainbow to someone's hard night 678
be okay despite 680
going blind, seeking vengeance 682
that will better and embitter 684
the sweetest end 685
I will ask for no kind apology 687
in a forestry of laughter 691
an imbecile's prayer 697

EXHIBIT Y: yellow witnesses pouring anecdotes dotted with pretty hearts

my way back to your sunlight 701
stab me where it hurts the most 702
the serene white lie 704
choosing weapons we don't know how to use 705
your purpose here was a highway accident 707
that smile that *is* life 709
kissed by our dead light 711
a melody 713
near with that same sublime look 714
in the light of who we were 715
I am not that guy anymore; *I am not that guy anymore* 716
spontaneous words began turning heavy rocks
to find zero worms 717

EXHIBIT Z: zebras sliced by patterns of black and grave white rays

the wrinkled center ... 723
after a beautiful choice ... 725
"It's a celebration!" ... 728
our blueprint burns black ... 729
my one lie ... 731
my testament ... 733
may I have your disapproval? ... 734
the lowest source of hope ... 736
the biblical end ... 738
unapologetic insults offered towards the *morning light* ... 740
in a dopamine trance ... 742
you're beautiful ... 745
fascination elsewhere ... 746
so sweet, *yet are we?* ... 747
worshipers of unconscious heartbeats ... 749
not so inno*cent* anymore; my white coat ... 750
every passionate release redefines love ... 751
the moments that break before d*awn* even waves ... 753
dusty forgotten books in a low shelf ... 754
obscuring paranoia valleys ... 755
en*try* by entry by entry; eternal ... 756
ever-changing tarot card readings ... 758
tears, illusively tranquil ... 760
a list burning like sin ... 761
I fell for ... 765
the hymns of *our* longing ... 767

Epilogue ... 771

Prologue

I don't know. I don't know where to begin. We rarely do and we never *really* will. Yet, we must reflect on why *we are* who *we are,* from *time-to-time,* otherwise, we go bankrupt of meaning. Let our prayers know of our existential desperation and our eagerness to cease living any further. Even if segments of life are miraculous in its conception, we'd still condemn certain functions of life, as they happen to us.

Then, we respond with agony disguised as bliss, mixed with honeyed applause for taking such initiative to try our stab at this futile game of hide and go seek. It's natural to collect beautiful and grotesque accounts of our attempts to be better players. We only ever relive specific memories. We always pay for accidents with delayed bleeding in impossible areas. It's terrifying how much fun and exciting trivialities and directives from the divine mother could be. It is a vast thrill to read through your memoir and realize it was merely a pasture of run-on sentences; a layer of conflicting decisions. We react with ever-changing faces of a madman, as we're reading short passages, in elementary journals or half-burnt notebooks, from the perspective of who we were once-upon-a-time. Happier, less numb to universal ploys and vices.

This collection-basket is weaved by years of collisions with goodness and tightened by the percussions of evil. It's a windy dance on a wire, trying to understand the free-flowing drama of human narratives. It's a drunken state that aids us most, through the digestion of our emotional circumstances; *why is that?* When gambling with faith, *why is the best bed an alleyway?* We just love being tortured by niceties, thinking undeserving of its fleas keeping us company. While simultaneously, being misinformed about life's brilliant tragedies; speaking ill at the many doors and many windows that let love in.

These recollections live in their own specially constructed, cognitive birdcages. It's made of wild openness and delicious fragility. It makes the murderous nights interesting; hearing the rattling in the darkness, in your skull-fucked, dreamless abode. While dark forces with the foresight and sensibilities of winged vertebrae are catching the scent of its next mental subjects, crossing the roads of ordinary life. As they make contact with hard reality. *All the world is green*: a mantra of the deceased. It's tempting to release the locks, and allow the door to swing wide like a whore's shiny legs, seductively slow, and be witness to which burdensome, rain-drenched cloud the bird flies towards, neck fully erect. Most importantly, to know with certitude, the size, width, and equilibrium of its droppings. The entertaining closure is deceit. As its travels are denied, it is banned a taste of success and fueled with mind-shattering anguish. Stuck in between immortal rocks, dismembered by crimson rivers and black and white channels, free to roam on the surfaces of "wherever" or to "whomever" it wants.

Every single person has this ability to armor or mar their neighbors. Mercy alters just about everything; loyal in the best and worst possible ways. These stray *receipts* are organized into exhibits; a museum of paper, sharp enough to cut throats and circumcise invalid thoughts. Each *soliloquy* is laid like a boxed-coffin; the *titles* serve as a vase on each active burial site. Every word represents the deadest flowers one could bestow another dead thing.

It's difficult to embrace your entire life as a whole and pinpoint the exact moment of when it *start*ed for you. I learned that there is no direction. We are spontaneous energy of spirit floating through the next person, place, or feeling. Forever fleeting like a ship with a broken radar, or the last autumn leaf on a tree with one season left. We're bound to get lost; bound to be found. Discover your truth and summon the bravery to grasp courage even as it wanes, even as it waxes. Then, smile at whatever results, you were unconditionally involved.

Ask yourself: "What is the toll of my emotional currencies?"

It's alright if you say: "I don't know. I don't know where to begin," as I did.

Who the *hell* does?

Entrance

EXHIBIT A

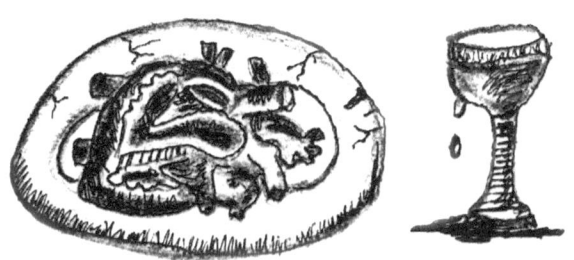

appetizing entries,
entreaties
and
entities
for endorphin
addicts

EXHIBIT

A

the child had whiskey-soaked dreams for months

Breathe through your teeth, let me in on another lie so sweet.
Seethe through your lips as I watch you all alone under the swing set.
Painful regrets chase me like a game of tag:
I feel like a kid again.

Diamond and Gold memories keep my spirit company.
When I get old, *would she still talk to me?*
From one heartbreaker to one heartless pretender;
sincerely escort my sanity out the spinning doors,
our fruitful endeavors are falling from Eden.

Oh, how we look like lifeless tourist on heaven's tarmacs.
We are sinners to the core, let's glamour
in fake romance some more.

My viridian flame consumes Gomorrah with her delightful
delirium
and penetrates Sodom with her thorn-infested rose stems; God left
Delphiniums in the unmarked graves; the soil that our love violates.

Performing a circumstantial ballet;
twice expired of beloved chances;
romance fished from the depths of a tar barrel.

How could we say something is never-ending?
A lovers' quarrel can't end without the debris of drudgery.

We're a class act; always pretending
we're not despicable liars.

Statues would glance at us, and winch
as if punched in its marbled guts.
Whiskey on my shot-glass goes bad;
it makes contact with our child's flailing arms

when you punctuate our disputes with:
Let bygones be bygones.

The ones I've already downed, shoots its way back up;
the child had whiskey-soaked dreams for months.

I fled the sight of your reptilian eyes; my soul is disowned.
I plunge at dark ravines near the slaughterhouses grinding genuine feelings.

I am done.
I am finished with our drunken parties;
sobering predictability and hollowing misery.

I remember recording every explosive confession in my memory;
when once we were cruel lovers that shined with ego.
Whoring sympathetic tones only desirable on the stage;
getting critics on the mood to fly into wormholes for words.

A thousand dandelions fill a body bag.
Raindrops thicken on the gutter's long arms.
I am wandering the conquered greens of the unconquerable evening;
our child is crying beautifully, I could hear it from another realm.

Heartless till the return of dawn;
careless of how vague I won and lost at the same time.

The lighter blow is most important, you said.

The narrator rarely writes itself a map back home.

Suddenly, I'm no longer perspiring with overconfidence.
Honesty readies the bat on the mound of her tender shoulder;
there it rests as she sighs.

She wants me more than I need her.

The courage garners a smile;
the thread-like branches within us,
throbs sunset-red and summer-blue.

I would lecture on about my heartbreaking travels
through dead seasons. She never truly accepted
the love I had blessed her.

We swam the canals of manic richness,
in dreams just awakened from with a tornado kiss.

A herd of canaries burst through
the winsomely carved windows.

Our adolescent doors remain unbolted,
unscrewed from the nonexistent walls.

Despite the conjuring of threatening songs sung
by despair's concubines, we're in total repose,
we throw shining pearls at ancient fountains,
we'd throw garden gnomes, stone buddhas,
and empty pots where flowers failed to grow.

Listening to songbirds and their provocations.
Staying under the covers and letting the soothing breeze begin a
chorus line.

All that tangerine shade caused a tangible sadness to misbehave;
night returned, as a flying disc would after it is thrown at someone
you trust to reciprocate it.

Silently, we forfeit this tired game of charade
and I'd still follow your heart
with desperate heed.

You're my most fragile seed,
I refuse to put a fence around you;
I want you to be free.

It's moments like these in the renewed darkness,
under the same ebbing constellation,
that I infuse never-ceasing remarks
about unjustified regards.

This history you tell smells of kindness wept.

Sorry in advance for my impulsive laughter
and under-assuming banter.

Seal us away on a glass cabinet.
Keep the plate clean so we could eat from it for a hundred-
thousand-million years.

Midnight.

Time for another piece of meat
I had no room for to consummate,
with the better fortune of the most passionate crave.

Before
the morning light
sheds skin, *again;*
leave the burnt bacon and
aborted eggs on the table;
the devil fancies
our accidental
offe*rings.*

I owe the dull sky a funny dance

Dearie, I think our love died.
It did a somersault for the clouds,
repeating **Proverbs 31:30.**

Spring came at last.

The viral visuals irritate the cracks on the looking glass;
the blizzard sounds like machineguns firing from above.

Your anxious humming turned
snow into shards of lightning,
from tiny cups you've thrown
on previous fights.

My heart is beating, pops like a wine cork,
yet it thrives under the warmth of your ghost thumb.

Empty me alone.

Never share my intoxicating energy
with anybody else
but your bathroom mirror.

Inebriate lust.

Market our smiles through radio frequencies:
A.M and P.M stations.

You're a collector of car plates.
Stubborn with the price of premium.
No grace period ever befalls us.
I am out of pennies. I am out of *wells* to call home.
I am taxed by boredom. I owe the dull sky a funny dance.

So that it comes smiling down the spiral steps of a cloudy
atmosphere,
with the brightness of a five-year-old, excited to open holiday
presents.

Skinny branches think
they're deadly arrows;
I am their lovely target.

I am nurtured by death's brilliant works;
disciplined by hopelessness and the adventure
it evokes these karmic bridges with intricate design.

The elegant skin around your virtuous eyes,
there's no black center to meditate on.

Making plans as the water chimes,
you'd mow our desolate grass on the marrow of noon,
through dark mud of yesterday's tracks just waiting
around remorsefully where X marks the spot.

Even when there is nobody there to be guilty about.

I fooled you. I ran and said goodbye.
I perish every time I wake now.
I feel inferior when I called you my Queen.
I was a deer caught in the headlights staring at the screen.

The impermanence of everything,
holds molecule moments
completely in contempt;
I was unsatisfied until
the eggs were burnt; *until*
the leaves turn rusty
and resemble bread-
crumbs.

I thought of taking my own life;
cease every possible journey.

Everyone here in this tourney sickens me;
lighting fires, igniting with desire
for the prettiest thing.

It's fun numbing
out sadness
as it stings,
as it sings
with repertoire.

Youthful days are for doing-*in* the pause button
on God's remote. Mixing plot with other people's
stories; taking pride in the pages most rotted.

Written in ink illegible;
no*body* can read it now.

This heaviness was lifted,
when my cage collapsed,
and I grew wings,
and hated for once
the peace of mind
my cravings fed,
my aversions said,
my illusions bled.

Finally, I am one with accepting this faith;
this mess of tangled rope; untying a noose
that made itself. Patient for a row of humorless days.

I won't blame anyone else;
insanity is a friend to every-
thing and everyone; wisdom
turns black real fast.

Suddenly,
we bid farewell to the mornings
and live under the city lights,
instead of the moon and stars at night.

Craving to be admired.

We break our necks just looking up;
addicted to averting our thoughts
to a coattail of dreams; cocktails
lined up like relationships.

Read between the lines, they said.

Purchase
on sale date;
stock up
on sublime
*stat*es.

Was the time spent in-love only a trick of the eye from a quick hand?

A silhouette of a demon acts as a blockade.
I doubt my destination, once again,
humiliated by the lack of self-affection.

Did I lose another kite to these perfect places?

I am in a loop of mystery; funneled through crimes
where I am always your victim.

It's alright, you said.

"Such things are meant to be
learned; such things are meant
to hurt. In the end, if we don't
allow it, there is still nothing
to be sorry for."

It's an emotionless war.

A steady ride into a familiar deceit;
into passionate affairs of the heart
I already once met.

You're un*fair*.
That's *most*
of *why*
I loved
you.

I took your first kiss away under the turquoise shadow of May;
we're best of friends built on the absence of a dagger aimed at the chest;
pending.

Our euphoric evenings made amends
for what hasn't happened yet;
before we're restricted or stricken
by other lover's set of rules,
we'd make it up as the calendar
is ripped of its square pages.

Questioning the prize of our sinful bets;
your morning is my night and my heart is a toy
I'll permit you to destroy many times over.

Legend says:
"Give power to love and it will give power to you."

But at the break of day,
I find myself
va*cant* of soul.

It seems my mental ambiguities sanction more power.
*Lo*ve won't sim*ply* do.

budding roses resembled rat-heads

To the right of us lay an exhibit of our wrongs.
See the misplaced sofa.
See the missing photographs above the chimney;
faced down.
Hear the dog whimper;
frightened of you.
What did it witness in my absence?
Did you leave my voicemail running, to help lull the Shepard to sleep?
You never listen, *do you?*
Do what thou wilt: it was your go-to saying.
My brain aches with familiar grievances.
You are driving me insane!
You know exactly what I'm talking about.
Quit hiding!
Confess your faults;
I am ready to suffer
in the attempt
to understand.

Refresh
Refresh.
Refresh.

My listless trust in you
is uppercut by neglect.
The malevolent hush
in our apartment made the
*sun*light,
*moon*light,
*street*light,
regret its descent.

Tonight, you'll try to leave me;
my agreeableness became your new fear and worry.
Oh, the horror it was, to be e*ye* to e*ye* with you.
Time learned to adjust and tempered itself
amidst *our* bedridden love;
shame drips from our IV.

We threw away all worries,
not knowing that our liabilities
are flurries of snow; purely young
and inno-
cent.

To the right of us lay an exhibit of our wrongs.
I am the neighborhood cat watching
with half-closed
eyes.
You're the unfortunate rat
on its jaw, dripping with black
liquid on our misplaced couch.

I am not sharing you with anyone else.

Quit resurrecting!
Die only once tonight.

Dangerous motives kept true love buried;
a single rose is all you'll get on your tombstone.

You're quick to act
and tried to hurt me.
I'd pull open each drawer to see
what mind-numbing anger finds me.

Your
shirts,
skirts,
panties,
socks,
empty cheques
and magazine
pages, vomit out
into the chimney.

I turned on the gas,
but, I couldn't find the match.
You hid it behind your back.
She knew my arsonist tendencies;
even *loved* me for it.
When once it was dead flowers from past lovers,
or letters they've written to us that burned there.

I chased after you, I d*read* unfinished work.
You hid inside the shoe closet and locked it.

I fell back, I hit my head on the base of a sunflower lamp.
The malevolent hush in our apartment made the
sun*light,*
moon*light,*
street*light,*
retrace its ascent.

I knelt.

Clawed your leg from under our bed; a shiny cut bled.
Words you uttered rang with gongs of resentments, *I can't hear* the demons which possessed me, giving me orders;
seducing my morbid ideations with golden chocolate coins.

I can't hear a thing at all.

What's better than nothing?

I am deaf from your silent stares;
lighting matches before me,
and flicking them at my face.

Reminiscing thoughts that were said out of love;
eyelids shutting down like garage doors. Heavenly
voices came from above; the sweat of lava evaporates.

The perfume of soft-baked cinnamon buns fills the living room.
As my muscles turn to wool the bliss kissed my scalp with fire;
she tore apart the piece of art I made her on our last anniversary.

She kissed the dry blade. I am *ashes*. The cat would think
twice to lick its paws, walking over me. She turned into
the substance of darkness. I can't see the sparks. *Do you?*

I am no longer there.
I've faded away.

The cat stood like a human being, lifted a heavy window,
let in a terrible suction that swallowed every particle of me
from her held breaths and other charcoal images which stolen
oxygen from love's respiratory system.

It's during times of great love and great hate that clarity emerges.
I am not asha*m*ed.
She's not asha*m*ed.

Another inferior love is gone; under almond dirt.
She licked the rain which drizzled in,
tasting of vanilla gumdrops, tasting of Danish filling.

Budding roses resembled rat-heads under the nightlight.
On my tombstone my photograph made love
with the Lord's dizzying spade.

that meaningless fun

I know you said this for a while now: *Walk through it alone and you will surely drown.*

You were a firefly shining in the middle of the morning sun.
Come on out and let's misuse the meaning of fun!

I know you said it before: *Settle down, but you cut the wrong wire of an explosive tongue.*
See this through,
until you do, I won't stop coming around
your side of town.
I played this game before;
losing weight in the process;
living through a new low;
drowning in rain-checks.

Some stranger once told me: *I am a paradise untouched in the middle of a forest fire.*

I will come on out; I'll have that meaningless fun!

I knew too much.
Now, my brain is so crowded by an assortment of fatal bugs.
Dwelling on it, caused it to multiply and divide.

I lived like this for a while now.
Walking alone and taunting the trees which grow in one place.
Maybe, I *envy* them their
stillness.
I'd find myself tripping on stones, tha*wing*, skin freezing layers old.

I loved someone who once said:
We are paradise untouched, at least we are to their aging eyes,
which know of no beauty, which marinates their lives with artificial
emotions.

She lived through a million lifetimes.
Replying only with letters typed in **bold.**
I knocked on her skull's window and whispered in her ears:

Come on out and endure the heatwave of my volcanic lust.
Come on out and let's have some insidious fun.

I know you said it before: *Settle down, still, you cut the wrong wire of an explosive tongue.*
See this through, until you do, I won't stop coming around your side of town.

fortune-tellers, and cigarette commercials

"The clouds on the day you died met with comets of purple crystals."
Our moon lost its virginity when nighttime came. Then our immortal
sunset was beyond divine on the stripper stage. The neon teal really
sealed the deal with the truckers, and accountants from the
building across.

Let's take a look back at childhood and early adolescence.
Let their stiff silence mature. Leap into the porcupine mattress
with your incurable faith; liberate hues from the quick-sands
of time's five-minute hourglass.

Settling your tangled hair on the blue stains.

I came to rescue you from fortune-tellers,
and cigarette commercials.
What arrived on the welcome mat,
had gum stuck on the sole of my happiness.
I felt you harden before my unsmiling eyes;
it was bliss then and still bliss now.

I became a beggar under your reign. I falter before the domino of
lines that were said.
Calming me down underneath the chilling spears of a motel
showerhead.
It sent chills in the back of my spine. Listening to **Psalms 40:6.**
Someone
left a crinkled twenty on **Revelations 21:4.** As if a bet had been
placed.
It is a Canadian bill.

You threaten to leave me, with barely a physical scar to peel off at a later date.
We cross the border and spend the twenty on massive cups of strong coffee.
You can't leave now!
I surrender to one final kiss with an open heart.

Let's take a look back at this while the moment of silence endures.
Talk me out of my persistent fears. You're tempted to cast me aside.
It's been people's routine to leave me out to die.

They'll travel to unknown straight lines;
without me singing blues nearby.
Forgetting words to your favorite songs;
you'd hit me with that snare,
until I laugh myself into hysterics.

I am neither good for you nor a bad alternative to the soul you'd rather have around.
It was bliss then and still bliss now.
Our hideout in the middle of nowhere was farthest from a letdown.
"It did us the best favor somehow…"

gurus sitting on stumps

It isn't easy pulling the sheet over your dead body.
It wasn't my fault. Keep what you saw to yourself.
Innocent blood is spilled. Another freak-accident.
Another despicable coward overanalyzing life's
technical difficulties. You have yet to witness the worst to come.
Move zealously with the sable fire taking acres of land.
Hell resides in every person's refusal to love. What a perfect design!

A beautiful sight for motionless gurus sitting on stumps.
I cannot forget the sheen of those electric-blue grass underneath the
Turkish-blue canvas.
I am enlightened temporarily.
I am the happiest I've ever been,
wearing a jaded confusion.
Holding a beer bottle with one ounce left to the dry lid of my one eye,
rolling back,
possessed.

I cannot hold what the flames offer you as gifts, relays the chartreuse
grass at dawn.
The godless door closed behind and blew what the night's ashes
freed.
It isn't easy pulling the strings around my own neck. It wasn't my
fault.
Redirect your sympathy to someone else.
Now, you really lost your mind.
What got you so inclined
to bend over a hundred nights,
rain or shine?
Your eyes pursue to hypnotize mine to no avail of apathy.
Leave me here, on an empty street outside what used to be my house.
Leave me here!
Blow away what my ashes freed!

Screaming through orange pastures by and by as I hold your vase gently, like a baby on my bosom. The thought of you alive left my tongue as cold as the tip of Mt. Everest.
My prayer was converted into a press release.
I denied all their calls.
Feeling like an embalmed corpse.
Please leave a message after the tone.
I have heard every great song shared.
Thinking it would help a *little;* thinking it will help me *some.*
When I saw you come out of the fire harmed, my fingertips lit up like Hanukah candles.
What a beautiful day it was. Your name collapsing at the sound of the music.

You are dead to me.
I refrain.
A dead tone.
A wronged number.

on madhouses and hospices

Fallen thoughts, they could pause time.
Walk away or walk towards the mines?
Years would pass by, I'd still wonder:
What have I done?
Fallen thoughts could harm.
Stab the chest or break the bones first?
Years would pass by and I've been dug out:
What could possibly go wrong?
Life drained the laugher collected and heard.
Made you despise her sweet kisses.
Still, your stubborn senses will cry.
Obliterated by the mines.
The devil was with us.
The devil was us.
We're founded by these fallen travelers;
soon enough they'll pierce us with flags.
No matter where we hide;
our sails catch their wind,
and we're inspired to worship their waves;
their efforts to calm us never fails.
The idea of freedom is likened to tear us a new one.
Running on our own across the stretch of desert,
deserted as usual;
with insignias burnt into our collar bones.
Bleeding with the truth of every sinister echo;
sinister echoes we'll endorse for them.
It is an open season for these conniving ghosts.
Manifesting urges within us to copulate
with the colorful or the colorless
and spend our budgets
on madhouses and hospices.
Don't pay attention to their hoax,
their handsome charity and silver fangs.
When you're lost in their woods;

you should be scared to death.
You mistake excitement for bravery in favor of the dying.
They're the best liars ever conceived.
No opposing energy could compete.
My fallen is yours, it will protect what remains of your conscious life.
You've got no choice but to
comply,
comply,
comply.
I feel like a kid in a game of freeze-tag.
Left alone for an eternity, untouched.

ruining the audacity of our winded virtues

Just keep practicing my darling,
until you come up with something good.
Zoom out, zoom further out.
Then look down,
maybe you'll save that already faded image.
Everyone moved on too fast.
It's how it usually is.
Are you up for a brand-new test?
A replacement for the words you've said.
Life given to wasted chance,
buried in the septic tanks of your mind.
Bleed-through the dull edges of those photographs,
with imagined antics and judgements predetermined.
Just take five minutes to sit back and rewind.

The moments replayed will lift us up, only so that its impact
descends on a few seconds delay.
Darling stick to what is, *now* and run the track which flows most
soothingly into the raging sun
and watch the nature of this attraction follow you away.
Are you up for a brand-new test?
Time is murdered fast by fixed targets.
Tore holes on parachutes circling like a tune;
ruining the audacity of our winded virtues.

Don't de*sire* time.
We are constantly falling out of rhythm.
Staking what was never ours to stake.

Keep your head low and submit to my words; leave with your
suitcase packed
full of our undeveloped manuscripts and screenplays.
Look up. I double, no, triple-dare you to recruit hope.

Apologize about what hasn't happened!

The dialogue of hearts are no longer there;
darling, look up and know that forgiveness
is on its way with a grain of insults.

Stick to what is, *now*, this pitiful stare at the clock.
TICK-TOCK,
TICK-TOCK.
Charge towards the raging sun and feel
days, weeks, months,
and years burn charcoal black.
It crumbles just as easily like aged rose petals, hot-glued onto the
cracks of an iron-grey vase.
A momentum of innocence that was excluded from the final EDIT.

seascapes tempt me to strip on the sand and call it a day

After talking to oddities under the dim, cancerous LED light.
After a friendly bottle of rum; courtesy of a senior couple from out-of-town
that said I reminded them of their dead son.
My soul lost its color on the busy streets.
My strides were uneven.
My breathing was stalling as if awaiting a response from the cosmic heavens.
Being there, in a park bench.
Watching a baseball game.
Being part of this forest of afternoon shadows, but not alive.
Not fully present.
I sit and stare away from healthy visuals;
seascapes tempt me to strip on the sand and call it a day.
I am a hologram to them.
I could barely feel the air in my lungs fan my spirit
and feed the sparks praying for a second chance to burn through me.
I am waiting for a heartbeat that sees my longing face,
and deliver me to Kingdom-Come.
It's now 3 A.M. in the morning.
I find the riverbanks so harmonious with my current stasis as I laid there,
waving back at the wide branches which fans me;
resulting in intense disparage.
I will return as an infant,
when all the lights are killed.
I wave goodbye, at the oasis I am undeserving of.
Whatever business I end up occupying in this world;
I can't pay back the cost of endurance.
I forget how much I paid for the recklessness that I am.
To be a pocketful of nothingness; it may be hereditary.
I am afraid it's dumb luck.
Hope is kissed by blessed repairs, says she.

But it fizzles out so many times like a breeze,
I could barely feel it.
Not even the prowess given off by mountains all lined up.
Only as I am killed by her love-light that a semblance of power stays.
I am drifting with the wind, every word turn to ribbons in her hair.
I savor the knot's complexity.
My soul is relieved of its entanglements.
I'm told to embrace yesterday as a gift.
Unwrapped best by the sinister gears of wall-clocks
with delicate claims to our existence.
Waking up to the fiery breath of our unfriendly dreams.
Awoken by lightning strikes:
I am off to the rain!
I love the touch of God's tears on my skin.
Will my love for you remain, strike me again?
I now see what death celebrates.
I wave goodbye.
I am on my way to be loved again,
despite my recklessness.
Slow and painfully
tripping on stitches,
vines of madness,
endless amazements,
the ritual of fixing ripped pages.
I like my eggs burnt black; *did you know that?*
Pitch.
Black.
I feel so numb.
It's been a *great* while.

and those with fingers intertwined;
shuttled off into sunken dreamless boats.
I am shaken with blinking headaches at every stop.

Uncomfortable silence endures amidst faint whispers from everyone's
coded selection of music. The maximum volume of agony,
muted.

This new design separates us even more. We'd hideaway,
pushed further from the finish line where we are all winners;
orphans to the train getting smaller.

We are individual heartbeats waiting for a specific doctor;
that special pill to heal and accept our imperfections from the
decaying insides;
slowly giving-in like a poorly structured sculpture in a city square.

But we are blocked like sewers;
we have nothing fresh to share.
Providing nothing but recycled worthless sentences that used to
work;
that we are hopeful to learn from again.

We love the taste of familiarity in a new face.
In this case, your mirrors need new bandages.
It's had enough of your singing,
complaining,
apologizing,
lying,
selling-out,
self-pity
and
denying that what is done could possibly be undone.

Listen carefully to what I say about cases like yours:
Take the biggest piece after the hardest punch and frame it!

into one of her many voids

Our coupling felt like a hundred years in the making.
It felt like cuts from roses picked in the evening.
It felt like wolf-dreams in the forest-filled moonlight.
High voltage streams chiming at the return of childhood memories
in victims brave enough to swim. I am intertwined with your
earliest roots.
You're enchanted by the gravestones filtering through dawn's fragile
wishes.

Our interlude, introduced our strength, our magnetism to each
other.
The sharp edges of a dagger we used to threaten angels to hand over
their wings, so that we could fly back to each other.

The absence of your letters and the absence of your scent on my
shoulder.
She made my soul grow fonder and seek the delight in another apple.
I miss the sight of your sorrow taking it out on the candlelight;
burning half the house down.
I miss the villainess laugh on another interrupted plan.
The silly-dancing we'd perform for doleful clouds.
The spoken intimations on the bed,
awaiting Mother Sun's judgement on your spacious forehead.

The shine on your truffle eyes, and doe-nose;
you're one of nature's grotesque perfection
the divinity of details are hard to erase.
God's heart-shaped maze just got longer
without her.

Forgive my awful-stitches;
the scars I fashioned into a quilt,
that's all I have to give away;
the last bit of time I'd kill to forsake you.

Her,
unfading footsteps on the sand are magical illusions.

Her,
presence makes Willow trees bleed gasoline
and provoke boulders into blood-boiled violence;
the friction would cause sparkling gossip to ensue.

No number of helicopters or fire-soldiers could take it.
They'll walk into the fire before it rains butterfly wings on our sunset boulevard.

Her,
evening charm, brilliant smile,
caring and uncaring mouth
deserves bottled applause.

Whatever weather comes; I'll brave the journey
like a guitar through a sad medley.
Till time grants our whispered wishes;
or totally kicks it into one of her many voids.

Until our records show we made it an art form to disapprove of easier-times.
For heaven to shed some fear in the subject of us. After we sleep under the shade
of one of its immortal trees; the thunder sneaks in a peak.

Indestructible words cherished in the altars already blessed;
before our footsteps dragged through it in disgrace.
Sailing past what has happened; for a blissful view of what is now truer than the very essence of truth:
I love you more than I hate you.
I only hated you for making me *leave* you.

Love can be purified from all angles.
It can be approved by even the most bitter angels.

Now that another year has passed in your mortal life;
grant us one wish tonight.
Love the notion of surrender in a songbird's hungry cry.
Fold the white flag; stop turning rocks.
Love the wrinkled blanket before bed;
inviting to share one with a gentle heartbeat one day.
Love the notion of liberty; away from the ticking
and talking hands that push or pull us
many times over away from one another.

Love me now or never.
Free the fireflies caught;
let's follow where it goes.

Let's not return to the acts our souls played in the beginning of that wet April.
The summer of beautiful prophecies we must be burning, can shelter in us once more;
or *will it forever go untold?*

Farewell, gardener in the rain.

The Reaper reaps the fruits of what you learned and slings it in the middle of the flaming desert.
His final caress and mercy for hearts
broken-in worse than roadkill leaves me speechless.
It's almost like being in the presence of royalty.

sweet-honey-dear

Darling,
we are driving away from the sunrise.
Darling,
I am praying your car door accidentally opens
while we are on the highway bridge.
Invest in merciful tones next time,
sweetheart.
Admire the tender purple hues on the horizon with me.
Quit bruising my attempts at liberating you.
My ego is big enough for two;
bite me!
I am your seedless watermelon.
I am always shifting your gears.
Well, aren't we mindless conjurers of delight!
Quit controlling the weather in my heart.
Without hesitation, you miss our intersection.
Now,
we're lost in an endless jungle of judgments and sinister persuasions.
Darling,
we are driving away from the sunset.
Darling,
I am famished,
let's stop at a buffet
before I elaborate on more
starving questions.
"Kids are we having fun yet?"
I would say looking at the back seats,
asking with a dead smile at what fell on deaf ears.
"Look out!"
Sweet-honey-dear,
I may have discovered something
endlessly fascinating.
You'd block my mouth
before I made up

some-thing.
When will our dreams be chased by willow birds again?
When will the hummingbirds stop bitching at our window pane?
Who let these brain-dead vultures inside our kitchen?
Well,
darling it's your fault for yelling:
"Kids dinner's ready!"
Is everyone feeling comfortable yet?
Push your seat all the way back.
Car windows would suicide;
she'd spit out her gum on some buckwheat.
Darling,
we are driving away from the moonlight.
Darling,
let's get wild and crazy at the hotel tonight.
Remember when we were prom King and Queen?
Those were the nights you'd court the moon to shine on our good
side.
Babe,
do us a favor and cut the engine.
Park over there,
by the riverbed.
Let's just spread our legs
and hideaway from
who we were
hours ago.
Let's rewrite those loveless quotes into
some-thing
else.
Let's laugh for hours starting now.
We've suppressed so many.
So damn,
many.
Let's get high,
from the lemonade kisses of the Sun's eyes on our infatuated lips.
Your eyes catching fire like I knew it could.

I've never tasted heaven so pure in any human being ever,
you're electrifying!
Believe in shooting stars once more;
be that little girl.
Revive the other half
of the other half,
of the other
half.
Release the anchor,
the hat-trick,
and light eternity's matchstick.
At the slam of God's hammer,
refuse a guilty verdict.
Sail away with me,
not from me,
to higher altitudes where grey clouds are forbidden.
There is so much more:
Bound by nothing when living just half the *love* our God promised!
Dear *my* Dear,
speak kindly and tell me
what will you do to beg the other half of my heart to stay?

EXHIBIT

B

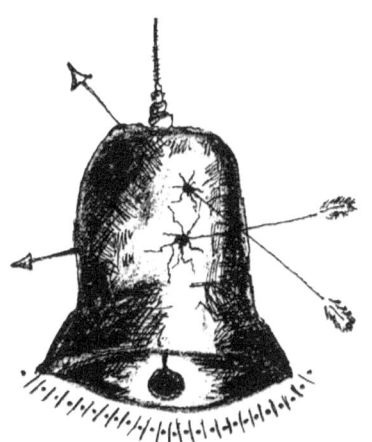

bells singing
due
to being shot
at by bullets
with
names carved
on
them

I am an over-spiced demon-feed

I've cracked the code.
I am just a joke to you.
I am your inferior, close-to-nothing joker.
Knocking over serenity's door,
with my briefcase full of worthless inventions.
I've been a cast-member to your make-believe;
I am an over-spiced demon-feed left to marinate in the
basement-freezer.

Darling,
reel in new fish from the bay.
We're not O.K.
Let me help you pretend that this never happened.
It happens to the best of us; you're better at listening to reason.

I am *afraid* you'll desert me.
It was indeed a seedless role.
I don't give a dam anymore;
let yourself gather somewhere else.
Everything is crumbling down,
piece by piece of our so-called,
so-cold
love.

Entirely drowned.
Our riverbed dried up,
and became a path.

But to where?

We're shunned by the crowd,
laughing freely about.
We're an exhibition best
viewed while intoxicated;

weary with blood-shot eyes;
skin peeling-off
and bird-shit
white.

What must we need to fulfill said prophecies?
Prompted last night's foaming lips, in the middle of brushing.
Why are we so damn overjoyed by all the doubt?
Replied I, in the middle of a gassy beer-shit.
I am wrong,
I suppose that mirror-image of us is a hoax.

It's devoid of compassion
and it is obvious plagiarism
of actions already once mistaken for bravery.

Who will be first to run outside and burn the house down?

It can't be me.
I'd like to take my time here.
I consider these moments holy.

Come on, you know me.
I can't redeem the smell but,
the truth is better than it looks.
Nobody's that *open* a book.

That evening, the rose gardens were the first casualty.
An accessory to an orgy of a thousand suns.

The open windows shatter from inside.
While I dreamt of smoke lines emerging from the dark mud
of yesterday's tracks, summoning a million snapdragons.

Then,
shards of glass flew overhead,
on our feet it cut deeper than seven-inches.

We're stuck as always,
bleeding from the journey.

I can't see the pain.

Just then,
fresh sunlight cuts through the darkness.

Are you overjoyed by all the dimwitted applause as I am?

Oh,
the yellow lines on our canvas
so bloodied and blue.

I can't see the pain.

All I see
is you.

piss-orange

Could the sunset dull this?
Will this head of mine find you as its fix?
Looking through windows of crowded busses;
I met so-many mutating shadows.
This must be stage-fright.

Her hair touched my shoulder, like a calming hand.
Her abbreviated smile disintegrates our glacial embrace.
I gazed above her head where a halo used to live.
I'm laughing with myself;
I must get out of here.

Nurse, pull the plug,
kill what's left of the energy
I took from you.
Just take one last look.
That's all I can offer you.
Aim for the eye of the moon,
if you're to make a pity performance
out of the grave afternoon.
Ignite what remains of my bedridden fireworks.
Turn this red-room, piss-orange
and change the tone of our world.

Keep that mask of forced-excitement as a souvenir.
Will the sunrise depress the horses galloping in circles above my
disarrayed expression?
Will this moon ever retire?
I remember my life and think: *Why aren't the blinds fully closed?*

Here I go, into the nothingness.

Fly a kite during a monsoon; laugh at the devastating results.
Solitude is a seat all the way back; I was wise not to evade.
Afterwards, I laughed about a dream I wasn't in.
Sanity sat a few seats away.

After holding my breath,
I've closed my eyes.
Her fading took a few *Hail Mary's*
and half an *Our Father*.

Just pull the plug,
embrace what's left of the energy
you took from her.

Just take one last look.
Remember: *Aim for the eye of the moon.*
Howl submissively,
like wolves communicating
with the lunar projections.
Channeling the tones of all-worlds.
One endless sleep to terrify those you left behind.
Sailing passed the shivering skyline of no-direction.

Wear armors of incredible fear.
Bathe in solace. Heaven is through the mist.
Forgiveness wages a war with strange souls,
a few seats away.

before your unroasted eyes

It's been dark a long while.
Are you trying to tell me something my love?
Is it fair what you're doing?
Thinking you're in the side of right?
It's been a long while since I corrected more answers.
Send me more manufactured lies,
please.
Pretty,
please!
I endured shifts in our time clocks for months.
I am saving up for a heart-attack
while investing on a kidney-failure
one neat glass at a time.
Did you set the hour hand back in your watch to match mine here,
so as to not wake me up too late at night?
I've gone to bed and said my prayers.
Why is your heart pumping with cruelty and some sort of unappealing
humming sound?
Stop flipping through your history.
Stop flirting with what is gone.
Come and go like others have.
Extort from a line of delectable nights.
Fancy luminous futures.
Lustrous rations of amenities before your unroasted eyes.
Overcoming vibrations of rancorous hearts.
Conspiring against box-cars of symphonic contemplations.
I'm the only passenger here.
Make the intruders feel welcomed enough to steal from there.
Lecture them on recycled fears;
on the merry-goodness of off-shore doubts.
Tell them about how I never fail to call you up,
just in time before you sleep with somebody else.
I'll be there.
Taking pictures like a private dick.

I'm never too far away,
away, away, away.
Am I toxic for being this
free, free, free, free?
I think loving someone is best done
through the submission of vast shipments,
filled by our gravest flaws,
uninsured.
I might be a hostage instead to her pretentious generosity;
to her vague way of life.
It became routine to dramatically proclaim the word why,
as if it is an entity with its own laws.
Life wouldn't be as musically rich,
without your speedy-rampage
in my arteriole halls.
Her purely monstrous growls lull my corneas,
pulling the eyelids over itself like a duvet.
When blackness ascends,
I am happily lost in a landscape of cornfields
harvesting clichés.
Then I am off to the burial sites.
Robbing flowers from waterless antiques;
daydreaming of our daughter's names
and fearing our son's inability to see straight.
Another one lost in the skunk infested alleys of complex avenue.
We are splashes of nameless hues,
a pastor told me.
The light drizzle of rain blackens the overcast day;
turns the milk in the fridge grey.
Why is your heart still pumping with cruelty and some sort of unappealing
humming sound?

twenty-two years

I was not making it up as I go.
I feel inspired to the bone.
Just so you know.
I was not giving in to closed doors.
I feel no hatred.
Just so you know.
I could kill the white spaces with more lies.
Burn through a canvas with my eyes.
I was submerged in red wine during my baptism.

What's the point of my life?
Will anybody save us?
Am I missing the point of your smile?

Come say a joke; entertain us.
I am missing my chance to get eaten by eighteen hours of sleep.
Quarantined in memories of unrequited lovers.
I will drown in nightmares,
anyway.

I silence myself.

I know nothing good will come out of anything
I say.
I was not abusing certain words.
I feel like watching a rerun.
I was not throwing a fit for attention.
I feel insane, but *what do you know?*

So, I line up the prisoners I collected over the past *twenty-two* years.
I choose which ones will fight alongside
my contrived end.

Black lines protest the newspaper headlines.
They're all lies; they're all lies.

I place duct-tape over your duck-bill of a mouth.
You ran out of retries; you ran out of retries.

Kill the white spaces,
men with words drawn as weaponry.

Never knew you were there.

You're part of the problem society faces today.

Fear kept you blinded from the authority you're allowed to have;
wearing diver's goggles
and Indian silk with no-underwear
or any soul left to save.

I just never knew you were there.

Pray you find a new God.
Pray you love what you got,
my only *beg*otten son.

motionless most of the time

I was told all she knew about the life across the window.
She was a curious case of seductive persuasion.
You don't feel alive, she said.
Liven-up a little,
shoot-up the yellow-heroin.
The moon gives you generous access.
Sit alone with yourself.
I'll be here,
darling.
Watching the neighborhoods change their clothes unnoticed.
Pass through their lawns,
kick the picket fences down.
Bless the old paint-job with our new-age brain particles.
Drop classified manila envelopes door to door.
There's no shame in needing to be betrayed by the idea of
ultimate calm.
I feel you reject my half-opened mouth,
ready to say something meaning-full.
The dust dances beside us,
appalled.
The hurricanes of half-circulated love rarely gets the job done.
I dizzy myself holding onto your alien gravity;
can we sit down together and try at saying nothing profound?
I used to like the train,
until you told me where it *really* goes.
I trusted glowing halos to lead me out
the gradually darkening tunnels of aging.
I am growing lines under my eyes.
Her finger traces my face like street guidelines.
Then,
the beautiful demon held me down for therapy;
corrupted my gate's hinges,
and willed itself to live inside me.
The currents start to bark at us.

The river hid missing kids.
Under our broken boat a trout sang *Kum*baya.
I stay.
Knee-deep in her silence,
and knee-deep in her wet past.
I waited,
while you exit to my left.
I am laid-back alone,
sinning next to morning jugglers.
Another *femme-de-glace* enters with groping eyes.
She talks of life across frameless windows.
Fantastic bodies,
she tells me.
I'll soon travel through silhouettes spoon-fed
by noon-light
and night-tingling
particles.
We're all dirty insects,
drowning in margarita gins,
she tells me.
Die on the beaten path;
serve as a bridge for a lost gambler.
We are motionless most of the time.
Emotional casualties in life's doctored plans.
Lay with as many angels,
steal enough feathers to fill a mattress
or a single cum-
stained pillow.

Even the sourest lines the moon could provision,
can't pro*cess*
the energy
of that *one*
night.

in that small acre of eternity

You're magic.
I can return to your straight lines, excited as if it were the first time.
I rise from the quick-sands of yesterday.
Slow-down,
I said.
Decline the elevator's upward lure.
Trade it in for a falling-down from the rooftop's edges.
Who's the fool who planted a tree so close to the clouds?
The gust of turmoil became something we had in common.
"We turners of tables and turners of smiles,"
observed something that died.
Another metaphor flies over their heads.
Gather the bars of our mental cages
and contour the lake's perimeters with it.
Charge the trespassers
and pay the new-day for shining on us
the bright*test*
with a net full of drowned-sacrifices.
Cheers to the suckers with hearts of stone,
skipping impatiently to see.
Stabbing the walls demanding a key.
We realize too late the absence of a door there.
Anywhere.
The electricity of our lost journeys came
as an outburst of blue lines,
causing skid marks on our unlit trips.
The fire in quiet warnings is allergic to us.
Over and over.
Over and Over.
The mourning of valued sins.
We are after the dignity left in the debris.
Finding that courage deteriorate like a roll of film.
In fear of leaving a mark of dangerous red;
instead of inspiring desire of the same color.

We are masters of our own truths.
What a humbling lie!
Let's be still.
Let's shimmer in life's finest arrangements.
The blood on my mouth bled the same shade as your lipstick.
Take the compliment!
Should I freeze you out or leave the idea of a good-life to thaw?
A couple more songs and maybe a hopeless sigh and we are off to go!
We'll floss each other's eyes.
Nickname our egos after planets light-years away.
Be fairytale characters in an imaginary book.
In this one,
reality threatens a dreamer out of a unicycle.
Shouting: *you'll never be honored; you're never to be quoted.*
You'll be living a loop of amoral circumstances.
Dreading the same plot.
Swallowing pearly beads of the priest's rosary.
You had too much fun,
cutting his sermon in half,
pulling the man down back to earth,
with the rest
of us.
What must be achieved in these yet lonely hours
except more self-indulgent rhymes
trying to please
and stutter amidst
the power of a question
mark?
I ask of more from the birds in the night skies.
I never minded being frozen right beside you.
You perspire with white wine
under heavy blankets you'd hoard
every evening.
I am wider awake than the rain-dogs outside.
I am offering torches to blind stars.

Answers seek refuge in clearing orbits;
a tattoo on the fleurettes immortalized in icy altitudes.
Oh, the spectrum of her attitudes.
These great lies we tell ourselves about "being alright" caused the cosmos to gasp.
Feigning at being full from all the love we delight in getting.
Dies too soon
doesn't it?
We know it's never enough.
It never is!
Dissatisfied nature; *with too much green.*
Dislocated arrowheads.
You've become a fragile mention to most of them.
Damn you, suffering fools.
This ability is a disability we learned to master.
Waking up to false alarms instead of the gross truth.
Our flesh are distances away
from the disturbing dream
we got a quick taste of
on somebody else's bed.
But, like the nicest sunsets or the least disturbing rainbow,
it does not stay for long.
It needs to die before our buried eyes,
just so it feels rare
or meant for only a few to own
in that small acre of eternity.
The ministry of unsaved souls offer hints of things to come.
Share the great news before they are resold;
its core ideas derailed by second drafts
and defecated by polluters of our sacred trust.
Admit it.
You've lost.
You showed up late for church;
now you can't have HIS body inside you.
Admit it.
You've won.

You paved the way to hell's midnight café;
I'll order double of what you're scheming.
Before we eat, the devil's cake.
Let us pray our ashes don't blow away at the entrance.
So, that in the great *there-after*,
we may ditch rest.
Become finally deep-miners of peace.
We desire this more than another-day
trapped in one another's alligator jowls.
Farewell to the fangs of desire-*less*-ness.
Do you want to contact somebody first?

O.K. then, I'll meet you at the bathroom counter!

caused catastrophic couplings

The clock ticks twelve for midnight.
We escape from reality.
The morning sun reaches out with sunshine.
Could this really be?
It is time to search for it,
even as deceiving thoughts run through
my head.
You loved this far,
however,
I fell over the edge.
Don't catch me,
let go,
I've fallen
already.
The seedlings have grown into massive trees.
Our escape from reality.
The hormonic blaze caused catastrophic couplings.
Could this really be?
The memories become a complete blur.
Our escape defaced reality.
The pain in my heart is without a cure.
Could this really be?
Let me return a favor,
my kind darling.
No more taunting clocks.
I'll pitch,
and you will swing to kill.
No more turning in our sleep.
We are young spirits on the permafrost,
laughing at moments when things made no-sense.
The heavens discontinued it.
We complement each other's disease.

So, here we are.
Back to when we escaped our reality.
It is time to search for it,
even as deceiving thoughts
run through our heads.
We loved this far,
however,
we fell over the edge.
Quit reaching, let be.

Let your daydream
regard me.

my view of you was most immaculate

I awoke hearing the voices of a dying clarinet.
We emerged from the foggy lighthouse.
Our ship passed through like a bullet on an empty sheet of twilight.
The dawn bled passionately with deliverance against the chiseled black-rocks.
I've seen too much; I can't bear it all.
I left myself on the battlefield,
away from your twisted reach, my love.
The new-day kept its hand on the bullet wound.
I did the salsa in hell's caterpillar palaces
and came back as a whirlpool of wishes
pre-enlightened.
I miss the palace of many red moons inviting the lost fires of incapable lovers.
You're better than black-coffee.
I am choking on ashen bridges at the rim.
It fell with a nod.
This wet sandstorm reeks of cinnamon.
The fever endeavors to meld me with her.
Tonight, betray yourself for a while now.
Go on! *Survive.*
Lay out your finishing touches.
My chosen one.
The other candidates have fled.
You remain to kiss my tulips.
A brave soul in flight conquers the unattainable future, says she.
Realize without a rewrite.
We're given a second life.
My view of you was most immaculate, my love.
I emerged victoriously, unscathed.
God sends a disaster now and then to quarrel about.
Your sorrowful spites were too-much.
I left, to be alone.
I cried during the instrumental fights.

We are given *one-last-second* try to sing in the background.
I am afraid to ask the mayflower for my girl's palm.
I kept my hand on her heart; felt less-pounding.
Breathing-in her ruthless sin.
Melting onto an arm-chair.
I once adored reading hell's letters to her;
she desperately wants me back.
We let the massacre of our promises offend.
The fever found a soft conclusion.
Softer than the flames which encased my torpedo's edges.

I miss feeling jaded with you.

meeting my axe, my revolver and my ex-wife

Time sure flies when you close your eyes.
A sentence murdered too many times.
You laid next to me spouting clichés,
being predictable,
being too easy a score.

Where are you when you're not next to me?

You are the talks of demons down in hell.
My point is sharper than the words that you utter.
My voice will echo, until there's nothing in the air
but smog from your dead radio-stars,
meeting my axe, my revolver and my ex-
wife.

Whoa, are you genuinely longing to make a wrong to become right, is that the most positive move you can think of?

Mistakes commit to failures done right; my sleepless eyes
are the proof.

Time sure flies when you demonize the ones you love.
Your horns cannot hide from me now.
When are you not disguised as a noose?
A nuisance to my seven senses.
We blessed the seven-wonders of the world being incompetent
lovers.
You are the nightmares of angels up in heaven's canals.

Time sure flies when you are making a profit.
Time sure flies when you are about to lose it.
Time sure flies when you close your eyes,
she'd repeat with solemnity to her crescent smile.

I love you, only you and especially that fucking fox-grin.
I'd pay with my life to renew.

Time sure speaks to us through our delicate lies,
I would say, feeling my face bruising.
Your precious hand didn't quite agree with that one.

My point is sharper than the words that you utter;
a hoarse call to say *good-night* is my proof;
not the rainwater I left on the nightstand to quench you
when morning peaks from the bullet-holes.

My voice will impact the years to come.
Your life expectancy lengthened,
ever since you swept me under the blonde rug.

I'll leave you with threads of terrifying miracles.
Starting with our wedding night ritual: a verbal apology, and two copies of a will and testament.
One for the fire to kiss and one for the waves to spill-over.
The foreign air will feign to translate the unspeakable parts.
Better listen for the bed-springs.

I sleepwalk with my zippers down and my gun drawn up.

her hails were euphoric

She took time to get used to.
Change is what she lacked.
Fear held her down backwards, screaming.
I'm here losing track of Satan's bidding.
But I won't give up on this treasure marked with six Xs'.
I know it's not far.
Oh, to hell with it!
To hell with you!
I'll give someone else the chance to find me in the crimson rain.
I know a journey home is still mine.
Be it lonely; be it without a roadmap.

She's dressed in white with *Bette Davis* eyes.
Love's narrowing offer, flashed mercifully in that single smile.
Approving of my soul's mouth-piece and saying: *minuscle talks with you are trippy.*
I am your junkie, cherish me,
lure me with mutating hymns.

I want to see diamonds circling around.
I held a violet candle over her skull,
where it parted on her scalp,
illuminating two pathways.

The wax drips, and her hails were euphoric.
She lit up like a flower understood by a child.
She was a show-stopping red light; the wheels drift in repose.
Unashamed.
God's neck twisted in denial of what HE is in witness to.

We watch the flames ignite from the veils of honesty's bangs.
Burning every shadow with insight. I found her dressed in white,
immune to the lure of other colors. She took my hand and said:
"I am worth more than anything you ever had."
While I'm here wondering how she even became mine.

I still believe treasure can be found under her vainest doubt.
I know, her disgraced ashes could fill the tub.
I know, the journey stole my black coat and gold watch;
everything lost its sheen to the adhesive powder of her subtle
make-up.

I grip with blackened hands,
debris of her spirit hair.
I stripped before the moonless beach
for a cleansing. I never looked back.

The icy illusion cracks before dawn;
fed us to the avalanche.
It's about time amnesia resets our alarm.

I retract the anchor from the deepest-ocean blues.
Stuck to it are snails for frying,
bon appetit,
my whore.

Be fed by safer
and cleaner hands.

Wherever you are now,
I know I am not in the clear yet.
The thawing of secrets are inevitable.

full of weeping bodies, dispossessed

I am worried.
Terrified.
You know
this is about
YOU.
Out of eight-billion people, the ones farthest and no longer here
understands me the most.
Stolen from me, were my scared dreams and sacred wishes.
I sent a prayer up in the clouds; they respond with:
Puddles of rain, gathering patiently.
They run across my brow.
Before any wishes are allowed to cool,
I find cover under the fattest flowers.
My tears blend with the puddles of their pain.
Tsunamis of misery circles around its own space.
The evaporated silhouette of your sun-kissed footsteps
walking the other way haunts the seed out of the soiled soil.
I feel lost in a crowded room;
full of weeping bodies, dispossessed, and gratefully unfulfilled.
I will escape this inner uproar; savor what remains factual to my
divine senses.
This invisible war is beyond our mortal hands to manipulate.
The pendulum swings,
armed with doubting parrots,
reciting the alphabets backwards
to soldiers whose hearts are broken-in.
I made a game of counting the smoke lines clearing;
seeing them as angels ascending before your rapid-fire
comes with the second wave.
MERCY!
Your delicate malevolence,
entranced the living and the deceased.
You entertained millions during a televised-trial.
Made the network millions in advertising.

Puddles of pain circulate around its own marketplace;
a price-tag, over a priced stag, on the bargain bin.
I do not desire to purchase her.
There will be changes to our mournful skies,
taking Quaaludes, and inhaling a two-hundred and nine-thousand-
acre marijuana plantation.
An arsonist could only dream.
Hurry, let me piss on your tea-cup for good-luck.
Hurry, before another evening takes the pill
and YOU will never be reborn as an infant.
Re-name yourself after your grandfather who had *thirteen* kids.
I know, it is in*deed*, fuc*king* in*sane*.

having a fight for impurity's sake

Our fireworks implode.
Its colors were never as vital,
as when I felt it leave your skin;
and the irises of your many eyes.
Who made the most noise that night?
The couple next door compromised about hanging each other.
While here we are having a fight for impurity's sake.
You connected with the best parts of me.
You read me like a first-edition book,
in its spine, you'd hide a string of loving messages.
I kept them stored in a safe for evidence;
you're my fairest capture.
A fantasy of a twelve-year-old child
is susceptible to fall for the prettiest
thing that makes *it* laugh.
You lost the page on me;
a breeze took the bookmark;
she closed the book on me
and got lost in a silly remark.
Our story rips-off another story twice ripped-off.
I grope for loose change and threw it across your oval window.
I get on my knees,
palms of my hand digs rough and deep,
fingernails peel off in consequence.
I deprave my optical nerve,
from your angered footsteps
drawing closer,
drawing nearer.

I pray an earthquake comes around turning your place inside out;
I dare you to take a look back, accept the fact that I don't want you
anymore.
Does my crumbling courage mean I am more of a man than the one
you knew?

Your doubts only feed the fire.
What you wanted from me is simply fantasy,
staged. Go *get-back-inside* your tower of deceit.
My embrace with you never felt wrong to me, she'd say.
Growling, I reply:

What else is here to say?
What are you going to do today?
Send me a note?
A final goodbye?
Do I get a say?

It was raining doves at our wedding.
Sending our so-called,
so-cold *future*
to a sweat-lodge
until our love is purely bled.
What we were had real meaning.
It feels demeaning for me
to say it out loud;
to you, I wasn't
enough.
I was never a priority.
You're always distances from where I'm going.
Never walking beside me.
Your shadow is more intimate with the grass,
or the wheels of cars,
pressing on you like iron
on hot summer days.

I am certain that you never liked it by my side,
on the bed,
in the shower,
on the couch watching
All About Eve.
Knowing the whole movie by heart,
but barely knowing anything about *me* that matters.

You're not present when we're on fire
trying at love-making, rarely making-it.
You're more inspired to wear a gas-mask
while a toolshed of distractions has your attention.

It was the spur of the moment, she says.
Wearing it outside as we walk the dog.
Now.
As if it's not always, that you're cold and alone.
Don't confuse the pain, it's organic, gluten-free.

Did I make my point clear that I still feel the same?
Amidst your silent cries,
raining down above me,
creating circles on the bloodied soil,
watering the unshaved grass.

My arms embrace your ankles.
I want you to stay, let me continue this war with myself.
I am waiting for the day you hear my say.
I knocked at your door many times,
before this final
assault.

A second ring.

A bigger diamond for a bigger chance.
Allow me to blow the charcoal;
make use of our forbidden spark.
Does courage mean anything to you?
Your doubts only kill the fire.
Send me a sincere note,
inviting me back;
an imprint of a kiss on the front.

Forget my *sayings,*
they obey another deity,
don't worry, it's not a prettier face.

I dare you to break your neck looking down
as I wept of dead stars and stain
the petals of your dress
with bloodied mud.

Damn you!

*Damn you,
my love.*

allowing for a caterpillar of good days to butterfly

I was there.
The only garbage not picked-up on the side-streets.
I am without knowledge of when my life will recycle
the bad days
allowing for a caterpillar of good days
to butterfly.
Many have passed by my corpse's disabled glance.
A likeness detached.
I dream of shaking their hands,
one of these days.
I imagine it feeling like an opiate intervention
in my veins'
red and blue highway.
Still, hopelessly, there remains a disconnection.
My liberation is rabid,
hungry,
dangerously desperate
for emotional currency.
Then, pain throbs without my consent in the upper vines of my
forehead.
Stars got lost in the questions I ask.
Maybe, I demand too much, when being alive is enough.
Yet, the fumes of wasted energy stretch the band-width of my
heart's endurance.
Days not being touched,
not being loved
and spoken to,
spoken of,
or being *smoked* like a cigarette.
I long to be inhaled and exhaled.
Instead, I am a prime-recipient, the main-benefactor of disgust.
Soul after soul of their disdain.
The nature of *why-we-are* nested such heaven for sharing;
yet we close like Venus fly traps,

on each other,
hide in greedy solitude of a jungle created for a speedy
ego-death and ego-resurrection.
I'll be your whore, waiting in your parking spot.
Longing to dance with the stardust in your eyes;
covered by black-shades on a bleak winter.
Share
your privileged fire,
your hot-shower;
my grotesque reincarnation,
my unkempt soul.
Before any restoration attempts,
contempt so doleful and young,
red kneeling devils were lusting on our cheap intentions.
Come over,
save me,
reward yourself,
benefit from karma's Grande provisions.
I cannot emphasize enough on the return you'll receive,
by even noticing a hair on my body.
Hurry, before I decide to start pulling the pearls off your neck.
Let's watch those glistening dreams bounce on your tiled kitchen.
Then, I'll press your face on the counter,
and use your spine as a chopping board;
cripple your curves;
demote them into
moats.
Who are you to deprive me of a life sentence?
My face transforms into an eagle's look.
Without pity for any cell of your body,
I enter swiftly.
Just *once*.
For sixty-seconds,
I am looking down the sunset pavement of your rear,
admiring the flow of your fear.
Whose heart was it staring with damp eyelids?

Weeping is common sense.
I loosen my grip and you braved the sight of me.
Finally.
I exist.
I don't know why you're nominated for *Queen of the cosmos*,
melting with melancholy at the sight of us;
a shivering masterpiece.
God was there and there I was.
My mouth began firing like machinegun bullets,
unapologetic, smiling with the teeth I had left.
Untying the scars on my nakedness,
prompting that I reveal their stories.
I am sure you'd find them individually amusing.
You'd sit against the cabinets,
opening each one slowly,
your eyes that notice me finally,
was still allowing my being,
or what's left of it,
to exist in your periphery.
I find the electric-clock,
the neon-yellow indicated that it is 3 A.M. in the morning.
There we were, choking on toxic lust we pushed down our spiritual throats.
I open a window.
Knock over a pot of aster,
and my heart-rate increased.
My mother would have back-slapped me
if I bent a blade of grass in her garden of eden
behind our old house.
I never noticed, but I heard something metallic,
and knew you found your pistol.
You were ready to reinstate its smoking habits.
We were there.
The shine on the sun's smile races through your torn ice-cream pajamas.

Waiting patiently for thunder to subdue the sleep-walking beast before you.
Oh, you flatter me.
How did you know, lightning terrifies me?
I carefully fix the flower back into the soil.
While you wrap-up our holy meeting.
We were there!
The cymbals.
The triangles sang.
Our deadly reunion left me cold and unwanted.
I can barely refrain;
the choir members were put to shame.
The bullet-hole was God-sent.
I danced to my suffering's musical ambiance.
Let them laugh.
Be trampled by graceful horses running freer than us.
I am so happy here, behind the despair of a loved one.
Save me please!
I am begging to *no-one*.
The smoke clears from the chamber.
It is absent in your mind to drown in dark waters asking: *why?*

I was there…

I was…

There!

through October's candied prostitutes

The rains arrive from opposing sides;
my thoughts lied.
Again, permission is delayed and I jumped at the wrong moment.
My face is pressed to a dirty window,
slamming into it, half my face is paralyzed.
It was the best kiss I ever had.
The most humiliating attempt so far at self-love.
Before impact, I cherished my final view.
Fragments of it shot through my bleeding, throbbing skull.
My insistence to succeed at being brain-dead,
and definite in my fading was almost tragic.
Almost.
Inside the train-car I French-kissed,
I had a remarkable view of teenage mothers
and their beautifully photogenic children.
They've been *"back to school"* shopping.
Then, to the left, some teenagers,
about the same age as those mothers,
was picking on some slouched kid in a solid-colored hoody.
Their scented hair-gels threw off the senses of a few old ladies
nearby,
wafting the air, and holding-in a gluttonous sneeze.
They were waiting to be seated by someone brave enough
to exhibit compassion and let everyone at eye-shot remark
on their goodness,
on their divinity.
They're forgotten; nobody bothered.
I may as well be dead, my legs are killing me,
says the one with a telephone wire as a ponytail.
You can read lips and hear people's deepest thoughts,
seconds before you die,
apparently.
Try what I did, and find out.
Ha-*ha*-ha.

What a strange day,
full of travelling spirits drifting to be deemed;
isn't every single day like this?
We tailor-sharp knuckleheads,
and magazine-cover infidels,
exchanging brooding faces,
waiting for the green-light to lick
our tears and whatever substance we sweat.
They'd fabricate jewelry no one can see except them.
Holy notions of what a good-rich-immortal-life is like.
Planning their vacation on March-break a year in advance,
and counting June's many Clift-side weddings,
being best-man or brides-maid
and being the most-fucked-up there.
Plans extending all the way through
October's candied prostitutes
and November's poppy-pinned coats.
Visiting caskets of those unrelated to you.
Be here, it doesn't always have to feel like a noose around your neck
is being tightened.
Doing nothing for no one, or being of nothing for yourself should
be crucial
to our tolerance of daily survival.
The equilibrium is there, you just have to look within
the components of your uniquely blended salad dressing.
We cannot pawn our regrets, but we could profit off their guilty
confessions.
We wear them every day like our eyebrows.
Pay professionals to pluck them out to reach an impossible
symmetry.
They are sharper than the thorns Jesus wore.
My soul would like to kiss yours every night,
before you attend the church of sleep.
If a lover decides to hold us; pray that they're willing to learn, and unlearn.
That it's never a joke to inhale such smoke of originality.

It changes you instantly
and drowns your modes-of-being into the muddied depths of
immeasurable vastness
and violently reshapes your perception's DNA;
to snort such drug from our noses is an SOS we never want to be
saved from.
Sensing fear yet my Princess?
If I made it,
I imagine myself walking through the moving train as if it were the
red-carpet.
I imagine myself looking left and right like a lifeguard.
Why be selective of the life one guards?
I'd be choosing wisely from the menu.
I refuse some fries with that.
"In the name of the hooded hearts, open backpacks, and unlit
guffaws. Amen,"
proclaimed the train operator through the P.A. system.
Construction is in progress in everyone, without flying ribbons of
yellow tape.
We might be trapped here a bit longer.
Do you want to light a joint memory with me?
Sound the alarms.
Let's party in our prison cells tonight.
Join me on this rail-path.
This special layer of cake with extra *mercy* on top.
Marry me if you wanna...
In our vows, include
what you dream about.
Lean against the train-window glass
like a homesick cat
in love with the stray
outside.
Screaming at the moon;
I do it to pass time.
You do too?

Let's whisper the stops and beat the automated voice to it;
it's all a game.
"Next stop Hell."

We frame a butterfly for sudden awe;
I spit red-love on your bathroom mirror.

Next stop:
"Danger."

Next stop:
"Heaven."

I am curious too
about what that boy in the manger
is up
to.

EXHIBIT
C

calls to submission
and hesitant
relocations
of our
damned
fondness

no-love left for you to hang in the closet, or to dry on the roof

Shine away from me.
You see my one eye hanging,
and you'd laugh.
Vomit with clever insults,
here,
and there.
I beg you to leave.
I've got no-love left for you to hang in the closet,
or to dry on the roof.
I would be okay with this final view of us,
being gradually terrified by the truth.
How do you think I feel?
I am either near to being great
or divided by the disease of me.
Our path seems unclear.
I see nothing here for me.
Our shine is dwindling.
So, we showered in fluorescent paints,
made from barrels of caught fireflies.
I bet you and I would rather be okay.
But it made no difference at all to think this way.
How do you think I feel?
I am nowhere close to being great.
I am divided by the disease of *you*.
Our path is unclear;
I see more meaning in leaving.
Years later,
I am blinded by the aching scars,
trying to belittle me.
Orange is my vision as I stare out overseas,
sitting on first-class despair.

How do you think I look?
Living in the chalk outline,
you drew.
All that's missing is the musical-bars,
which your lungs failed to reach.

Let's hope the Lord
has the energy
to read lips.

fall into love with neutered rhythms

After an idle step,
I broke my crutches;
I am stuck inside my cloudy head.
You're a bird's nest free-falling and backward-dreaming;
beautiful light holds us hostage screaming.
My grotesque ideologies regarding you are now beginning to catch aflame.
Light-swords punches through dirt and pierced through our coffin.
I recall one observation of yours,
became misunderstood even in the grave.
The heartiest songs dispersed from our ribcage;
millions of maggots got excitable like expiated entities.
I am seduced by deeper soil,
by their taste for new-born blood.
My pale uneven scales caused mayhem in there
making the wood vulnerable.
It started breaking;
the dragon took flight.
My eternal doors are now inside out,
I expected visitors; locked and loaded with their firearms.
Ocean of disasters I've invited.
Dark dream becoming.
Park the first shot,
a little closer to home,
babe.
There's no labyrinth,
in justifying what's O.K. for killing,
twice.
Keep walking through beaten paths,
running across sad riverbeds,
and climbing sandpaper peaks,
following my intense,
shadowy dichotomy.
Be desperate and passionate

for your bullets to land somewhere
clean and admirable.
Before, I am forever lost,
and forever mixed-up in another coast.
Chaos never turns its cheek from a challenger.
We're all still learning to walk a straight line.
Ignore the rasping sound *time* gives off in lonely nights;
fall into love with neutered rhythms.
The circling crows expose another
criminal-lawyer,
criminal-mastermind,
criminal-editor,
criminal-lover.
Orange sunset upper-cuts the jaded cut-throats,
standing on their studio-apartment balconies;
blowing nicotine towards the winter line.
I am out of breath.
Although,
I am breathing-in your six-feet of dread.
Madness is my God!
You'd shout agonizingly,
extracting hang-nails with brand-new tweezers.
The bathtub sailed away and is sliced in half by *Zeus*,
hiding an insane smile.
Let's not end it with a threat.
My lover for a fee, *didn't we agree to meet half-way?*
Did we not sign that oath with fire?
Should have ended it when we met on the pier.
Do you know any time-travelers we could bribe with our thick-poetry?
The heart of our song pays with acrylic-blood.
The blades of grass pray for better guitar-riffs;
tips vowed like sunflower stems.
Rain-showers, finally!
I am seduced,
penetrated,
and fed a blanket of morning turmeric.

My taste for blood is satiated through many versions of certain strangers.
My pale uneven scales proved too-violent for the receding air.
My dragon for once refuses to land on the undisturbed valleys.
Its heart caves in on the inside,
planting explosive confessions soon to be felt in dwarf-whispers.
No more holidays.
No more free-performances in the purview of a beloved's spotlight;
with pressured hands directing my flight-patterns.
I fly above,
pining skywards,
betting on the sun's morphine-love.
Forgiveness like glass makes rhinestones out of my skin.
A billion to one versus one massive-fire-breathing time-traveler.
Each child's gaze exhumed with arsonist schemes;
locked and loaded with their firearms;
oceans of disaster I've invited.

Dark dream---

half-cigarettes on the ashtray

Too true.
Too real.
Evil is upon us.
The voices in your head will try to understand it.
You're not going to allow it to take charge of your soul, *are you?*
Eh, working-class guy?
Eh, femme wearing a two-ton, feather-hat?
Let the nights swell with unconscious goodness.
Dollar-bills, pocket-change, go ahead bury yourself with it!
After an hour or two;
I wake up from a *Monty Python* sketch.
There is nothing else to do except await,
warnings by larger head-aches
and blessings from botched impulses.
You'll ask yourself; *where did the pain come from?*
There lacks a purpose to claw-through or problems to waft over
sophisticated soup.
The world supplies us,
however,
with dangerous,
erogenous zones.
Therefore, we remain obedient to the physical-form.
I'll keep learning,
keep fighting
and surviving through the flowing
and changing legislations of these handy-capped lessons.
Her river serves to drown.
Kids, ready your rocks!
Throw them to spite me.
Nothing lands to maim,
despite their great-aim,
the wind-currents are too-strong.
It feels right, only *some-of-the* time.
Power from the sticky-sun.

The anatomical choices shine through;
casting more shadow-pains than you're regularly used to.
We just ceased to be!
Nothing matters;
raison d'etre.
After-all, the after-life is jammed by our wants to stay.
Timeless waterfalls are for screensavers,
and drowning with fashion.
Hours hoarded are like half-cigarettes on the ashtray.
You're not broken;
corrupted,
yes!
Healing is in the unloading of offensive memories in loosely administered installments.
Don't run from your own *bleeding* irony.
Let the blood dry;
leave a trail to heaven.
Her river serves to drown.
I am dodging rocks,
now gathering in a pile.
Dulling the diamond-razor of the leaping-sun.
The larks sing of her rejected arks.
Thrown at the imagination to spite me.

Her morning-light,
frights me.

decades of averted wonderments

We weren't told at the beginning of the loneliness we'll face.
We weren't warned of the blood across the room.
It, being so uniquely-grotesque,
selective of who it's most-*dain*tily visible for.
I could stare at it for hours;
throwing *spared* change.
Lessons learned take their time to settle in
and know the choreography by heart;
memorize the floor plans of God's
bound-less,
bath-rooms.
The moment falls apart, knees bent the other way, controversially.
Bullied by theories,
terrorist of literary cults,
and holistic liturgies.
The suspense is constantly nail-biting!
Are you able to succumb?
Are you able to respond to the truth behind my one-dollar grin?
Is there any kindness left in my one-buck eyes?
Are you able to forgive, for continuance's sake?
Are you able to feel pleasure in hearing my common name?
Would you flatter my vicious deadness with mercy?
We were not consoled to understand meaningless words from voices
out of our comfort zones.
I won't fail to comment on decades of averted wonderments;
clinging to
the *empty,*
the *emptier,*
and *emptiest*
of resolutions.
Our love was being possible.
Our love remains the same.
There is nothing worse than being a flat-lined,
methane jape,

having seizures
on the page.
Our love forgets names.
Except when it commands you to hot-glue the shattered dishes.
Take your shoes off the horse!
She'd say one evening.
I felt the dewed pleasure in hearing my name being called.
I stared through the window, as she *rides*-away,
and I am *rid*-away;
her *ribs*-swayed laughing,
a-*ways* farther than
I'll *ever* be.

long-faced, and believing in the long road's flaccid promises

I wonder if I deserve your good heart?
It's painful to repeat myself with another host,
I am faltering in this guise.
Blink another tear away;
blink and lose another year;
blink and lose the light of day and return to that image of…
Her smoke created pictures heavy with angels and heroes.
"The way back is to split and fall apart, it's to spit in the eye of love's art," she'd say,
long-faced, and believing in the long road's flaccid promises.
Do you ever wonder if a good lesson will find a way to be understood universally?
Do you care to change today and bet on tomorrow's positive halo,
being less dismissive,
oppressive
or spiteful?
When the *storm-wakes*
and the *thunder-breaks*
through *hope-less-ness*
that we've praised.
Our reactions were a masterpiece.
That's it, another day is done!
What has departed and rebuilt itself?
Questions without heart are beaten blue
and damned by a darker hue.
May I take a breath now without bleeding out?
Are your holes mended by plaster, mixed with brown sugar?
The truth is too much pain for one,
so I ration it into twenty equal parts to impart.
The ruthless day injures my patience
and the troutless net is the cherry on top.

It is too *freaking* much!

I had enough!

Blink another tear away;
blink and lose another year;
blink and lose the light of day
and return to that image of…

jubilee falls on the palms of the catcher

How dare you fake a laugh?
How dare you metamorphosize into something that I don't like?
Will I remain forsaken or is moving on a façade?
Let's retrace our steps and overcome this.
It's faster running alone;
I am choosing my passion over your own.
Let the wrongful destinations, smell of nitro and gasoline doubts.
I so adore her footsteps on sheets of virgin-snow,
donning a sheet of stained fur-coat.
How dare you rush my soul to forgive you?
I am infected by love's incurable rash.
How do you slave yourself to wrongfulness and call yourself a disciple of good?
How do you feel having something that you did right?
It's a bore, *isn't it?*
Are you ready to be forgotten and buried in the forestry of deserted conversations?
Let's retrace our steps and dodge the comets with holes in its many eyes.
What do we do with these uncharted youths?
Addicts of the rapturous joy in watching the plums as soon as it jingles,
and jubilee falls on the palms of the catcher.
You're my hostage now,
surrender to my salivating jowls.
I am choosing my passion over your own well-dressed status quo;
over your own weakening resolve.
How dare you be involved in my world;
it's impossible to exorcise your ghost.

I am human after all!
I hunger just like you.

it's alright if we go unmissed

Our waterfall has ceased flowing.
My memories of you arrived in easier terms.
Then, I saw another sort of hatred,
dropping into the deepest of my cognitive-waters,
mystified by a Sypris's serenity.
I am kept occupied by your heartfelt decisions; your newest
distractions.
If the world were to continue without us, *do you want to know if we
were missed?*
Call me sooner than later before the twist of midnight's dagger.
I am home, but I am all alone.
I want you here beside me.
I want you here to love me before I go pale and live miles away from wellness.
I have been reminded by you
that the idea of a soul is to weaken it
with every heartbreaking travel.
I've been rewarded because my memories of you stayed.
But, I saw another sort of meaning swimming
from the shallowest of shores;
emerging from the coconut shells.
I am a man saved, occupied by her spiraling blaze,
contented inside my skin as she slips me in and out of it.
Let's look forward, always forward.
Just as the sunset begins to marinate our sorrowful grounds,
making every cliché sound profound, take effect,
and lick the moonlight in the darkness of its cage.
Think it through, my bluebird.
Let's trace the flexible, silver-rays with inuendoes
and permit it to inhale the totality of what burdens us.
You'll materialize during my darkest situations
and the land-slides in reverse.
If the world were to continue without us, it's alright if we go unmissed.

"We'll always have each other," as the saying goes.
Isn't that enough to ward off the blasphemous sorrow from taking effect?
Call me any-time,
spring-time,
winter-time,
autumn-time,
night-time,
day-time;
let's go bankrupt with our expensive calls.
Claim the right to our bliss in our small part of the garden.
Forget the *rest in peace;* we've got it in spades!

Let's walk each other back HOME.
Shall we?
My *Helen* of Troy.

fatigued by love's dialysis

I won't stand still,
kneeling below the mercy of another wasted hour.
Judging from the looks of you,
this is our final frontier.
Oh, how I tried.
But, keeping you to myself was a bad idea.
My world can't deal with another pretty liar.
The joke's on you;
I've found respite and awoken
into the arms of wellness,
nonetheless,
fatigued by love's dialysis.
The creamy waters of faith can't hold me down.
I'll rise higher than my previous ascent
and feel the sweet victory
through star-kissed hotel windows.
I cannot return.
I cannot turn back,
but, I wish I could.
Judging by the thoughts that bloom,
my recollections of you bestow resurgence in my facial agriculture.
I cannot go on.
I cannot do this any longer,
I cannot rise once more,
your smothered rocks just pull me under.
Oh, how you tried carrying my body across the foaming shorelines,
to silence the information you haven't yet smoldered.
You know exactly where to pawn the black pearl,
I drowned and died for.

Whence I awoke,
I sensed your smile through the metallic door.
I hit the floor, reeling for a lost prayer;
God's reply tickled my ankles.

The look in HIS eyes just says it all.
The final frontier is over.

her fire contracts *all* so suddenly

As we continue to play with fire.
Are we also longing for a specific sort of burning to transpire?
As we join the cast of liars.
Aren't we also waiting to seek the blight, most displeasing truth for the sake of entertainment? Can you join me for a fine array of discourse with the sunset?
Are you up for a little upset?
A journey from an embryo into a brighter summit?
As our mountain of superiority continues its rising;
the falling avalanche increases in the toll of the feelings captured by frozen hurt.
As we tour the gates of heaven.
Aren't we already turned down?
Are you longing to join me for a ride into the sunrise?
Are you longing to join me for another surprise?
And I don't understand.
No, I won't take another person's hand.
I see our future and I am delirious.
I need to lay down.
On the final days, it's sadness that will replace all the scenes we've made together.
Still, I wonder, *did it mean something?*
Do you mean every word of this rhetorical question?
I am in love with the scenery, despite the muddy rain.
I am waiting on a rainbow to dig holes in the plot of her bestial acts.
As we continue to fall and fall.
We fail to ask if there's an ultimatum from each talking wall that discloses a secret.
As we pretend our way through life.
Eventually, we mean it when we say:
I don't understand,
I won't take another person's hand,
and I see our future fall apart before our buried eyes,

and on the final days it's sadness that will replace all the scenes we've made together.
I wonder if you've acted like you mean it, *do you mean it at all?*

When
her fire contracts
all so suddenly,
there is nothing
to look forward to
anymore.

drunk on convenience-store wine

There's no brightness to your eyes.
The dragonflies mistook the noon-skies for crops of lilacs.
You came reserved with a wonderous opulence of desirability.
Conflicts heel before your colorful image.
Purgatory's waiting room is filled with your stills,
and nudist sayings,
versatile with wide-spread interpretations.
Go on and con, misguide and apprehend
the spaces between in-between lovers,
that's a direct order!
Reason with their holographic fire.
Did you receive the church's approval?
Once in a while, you'll come by a fish that overthinks itself out of
the aquarium.
It's best we feed *it* to the melancholy sharks,
right away, before it offers classes to guppies.
You're a glitch in my screen-door; look to the right, you're *Exhibit A*.
You're ignorant as ever; dumbfounded by the bitter weather
in my membrane's private compound.
You came around, leaving a trail of white rose petals,
leading to an artless, browning punishment,
drunk on convenience-store wine.
Go get your money back, your spent footsteps forgot its receipt.
You're too smart for me.
It's open season for the most subtle lies.
A few verses from **Timothy**; becomes prelude to our drunken fights.
You came around, *did you have permission?*
How do you really perceive religion?
Say, *I do,* with a little more jazz!
You came back hoping to resign from the relationship.
You've got solid evidence that will break me.
So, I make the changes for a fix you can't deny.
I pray below a miniature-crucifix dripping with ordinary-blood.
I came around, *uninvited.*

You came around, *conceited*.
A U-turn presented itself.
We feed on it.
I had my fill of conflict and the choir of demons cheered me on in the bleachers.
I bless *thee* with repertoires of apologies.
I reason with the feelings I purchased.
A deadpanned look sizzles in the black sky.
It finds meaning and purpose for disobeying the sins we put on a stove-timer.

Conversations with myself that start with:
"Will she remember me?"
halts the motions of my rocking chair.

for every brilliant obstacle that left a half-dome scar

Rise to the streets, my hot ember.
The limit is reached on our radical love.
The crickets played a lonely refrain.
Rewritten notes, are too choked-up to speak, this evening.
My arms open up without you noticing,
coming to warn you;
it's too soon to think about a cover-up.
Trust my mortuary mind's octave assurances,
as it offers shelter,
for what we knew to be gone.
We will be okay, gladdened by the miscalculations.
Stop stalling my landing at an improvised song.
Surprised, your vows made me lose my mind, and saved me just now.
The strongest foe a man will ever have is a woman's undoing of himself.
At least, you get to choose *who*.
Do surrender quickly, soon enough you'll both do.
Rewind to yesterday's retraced steps.
You will be okay, all tangled up; covered in cobwebs and barbwire.
Yesterday saved us a spot, for silent consultations with the window-sill;
dying phone receivers *outnumber* each laugher life afforded.
Who will harvest my soul's flight-recorder when I am ashes?
Manage your myriad thoughts.
A mirage opens up without you noticing,
coming to warn you; it's too soon to think about a cover-up.
Trust the lucid creek, and its crocheted lily pads.
We'll be okay because forever is no joking matter, here.
Refrain from imitations we can't go back from.
Let's play at being murderous fools,
losing count of our winning streak in a game of: *"Who done it?"*
In time, you're woke to realize nothing matters;
except for every brilliant obstacle that left a half-dome scar.

These half-moon memorabilia will enthuse and amuse our blood-lust like nothing else.
Submit to our newly discovered truth.

We're dead stars
seeking attention,
remember?

then and there and *everywhere*

She's in the wind as beautiful as ever been.
I am alone with the mystery of all that should have died away.
I miss her every now and then.
I miss how softly my kisses lay on the top of her hair.
I've seen the light of day all over her face,
take me for who I am.
Love will remain, she says.
She's in the wind as beautiful as ever been.
I am alone with the mystery of all that should have died away.
She's an eternal flame too stubborn to ebb.
A stormy wind too prideful to give mercy to the low-waves.
I am alone with the mystery of all that remained.
She embodies the chill; she's the frozen mountaintops,
she tends a cemetery in the clouds,
she's pristine, wearing a flowing white gown.
The mystery of my blissful one-night-climb;
my nightmarish view of the crystal mist,
hiking till my legs gave out
and all that's left
is her cold embrace.
I miss you every now and then.
I miss how tiredly I kissed you on the top of your disheveled hair.
I've seen the light of day all over your face, take me for who I am.
Then and there and *everywhere.*
Love will remain, I said.
She's in the wind as beautiful as ever been.

The joyful mystery of what the wind took for granted,
every second, of
every minute, of
every hour, of
our final days.

with a seamstress's sensibility

I am ill again.
Fix me?
A mission you'll pass on.
The question, I didn't really mean to ask.
Today we play a game that will end all games, really dramatize the heck out of it.
What remains on the board is yours,
may it be horse-meat or the bishop's hat or a pawn with some flesh wounds.
I've fallen for your sickly-faltering sighs; the overrated lines you'd mute in movies
or wished you blocked your ears too-late for.
Bear with me or shoot me on the ridge of my nose where my glasses always slip away from.
"No matter what I do,
I just can't forget the love we still have,
but chances are so hard to catch,
in a world where nothing really last;
my worry is the pain that will be with us forevermore."
When did love feel like emptying a vacuum?
I am singing in my grave; the acoustics aren't as horrendous as I thought it would be.
Quit pretend-digging!
Accept the burden she passed onto you.
Prove your worth;
auction your dismembered parts;
aspects of yourself too-much to cater all at once.
"It'd be easier to love you more if there was less of you,"
she advised; her logical bolts intact.
It's yours what remains, reads her bargaining chip.
I trust in her new government; the laws she revised with a seamstress's sensibility.
Her regime is adorable!
she advised; her logical bolts intact.

Damn the chances that were difficult to catch and damn the
attempt at immortal-love,
that only resulted in being unconscious inside EMS vans
and being left stark naked and emotionally bruised by the coppers,
silver moon-fishes and golden toothed,
sun-sunny bastards in my schizophrenic heart's unlicensed
base-camp.
And fuck jail-time, being institutionalized for being crazy hilarious
at funeral houses, fainting, and turning yellow with intense guffaws,
everyone raise your short glass, let's cheers and shout formaldehyde!
I worry about the oculus of this dome, and if forever is enough
to emerge at my freedom, once again.
When did love feel like raking fallen leaves at autumn-time
while leaves are still falling and it's four in the morning?

Damn you, late-night jumpers!
Dusk had enough.
I am ill again.
Fix me.

at the first touch of daylight

Holding on again to a certain time in a certain place.
The view from the window passes me away.
Holding on to this remarkable pain, I've borrowed.
Till tomorrow comes: *What will remain?*
So, let me tell you about myself through eyes that met troubled souls,
on the streets, ungrateful under the grapefruit moon.
I've felt the cold in a demon's home.
I wasn't told much about being alone.
I am in the corner wondering about the time I've borrowed
and what time I allowed doing actual good.
Till tomorrow comes: *Who will remain?*
I am holding on again to a light, which nature it is to fade;
a light that asks for too much from the nothingness that we-are,
and the added-pressure we feel as it speaks to us individually saying:
Go ahead, pick up on something of significance to move the narrative along.
I am loyal to the featherweight-darkness and the transference of
hygienic equilibrium.
I've harvested sorrow on the pillows of mutuality
and forgot about it at the first touch of daylight.
Till tomorrow comes: *Where will I remain?*
Letting go, what a chore!
Am I still yours?
Letting go, on my own; just like before!
But I don't know what it is about my life; *should I miss something so uneventful?*
Why do I want what hurt me, and pursue to dislodge and disarray my facilities,
every time another visitor triggers the shingles on the doorframe?
I am infatuated with troubled souls, *you see...*
I ask now, *are you one of them?*
Do you also refuse the notion of being alone?
It never felt right to be told to stand firm in one place and dust.
I laugh to myself, in life's many corners.

I am wondering about the time thieved and the greatness
I allowed myself.
Till the morning light wakes me up
through bloodshot, grieving curtains:

I will remain.
I will remain.

I will remain.

I will remain.
I will remain.

I WILL REMAIN!

EX<u>HIBIT</u>

D

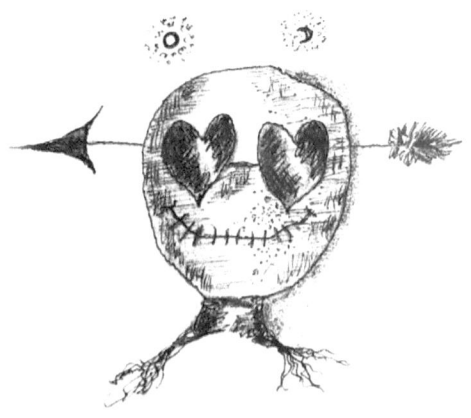

doubts automatic
and
problematic eye-ticks
that hinders
a
rather lovely
conversation

an orgy of white sky

Cheers to one of life's trap.
Love's been a sickness, I cannot outrun.
I should have left her inside that thunder-cloud.
It was futile explaining music to a tyrannical woman,
obsessed with silence.
As her white ashes fall,
I am betrayed and I am fooled.
Live without a saving grace.
I don't want you.
I refuse to love you.
I ran out of room in our motel bed and I am in the tub burning the candles she left.
She dashed into a snowstorm; an orgy of white sky,
twisting and turning, like last night's anxiety trip.
I lend her my wings so she could imitate Angels.
I hid in the caves of the linen and fell into the floor.
I influenced her belief in gravity's gentle touch
and the aerial jugglers,
whose daydreams it is we store in our lungs.
Earlier that week, I took her to sites, where St. Lucia was executed.
If only you could *see* the spaces between us where disaffection
felt chronic.
The stitches came undone as clarity is judged by the needle-light,
as the candles fluttered and dismissed itself from my bare,
glittering skin.
The woman through the slightly open door,
peaks at the drowning nightmare trying to resurface.
She could not control her laughter.
A few pauses gave me a generous time to perform
my disappearing act.
Then, the candle emerged victorious and our thunder was reborn.
Our unloving state got on my nerves.
I felt like abandoned ice on her whiskey glass.
I aimed to maim, and succeeded in doing so.

*I don't
want to
need you.*

*Do not
refill me,
with you.*

the only existential cure

Dance!
Now we're waiting on the sunrise.
Smile!
Now we're on cloud nine.
Trust me everything will be just fine.
Save your absurd cries for tomorrow's assumptive rains.
Our favorite past-time is on.
We watch the storm destroy the whole neighborhood.
It's the only existential cure for our morphine withdrawal.
We watch the moon return with letdowns, till sun-up.
Why do we put all this weight on the world?
Can't we block out the hate with tidal considerations, and mid-day vigilance?
Our fireballs of indecision are beyond magical.
I always never believe it.
Our concert of tranquility has gone stalemate.
We must find an empty jar looked-at with fondness,
before a clear-shot is fired, shattering expectations.
The leading ladies of Gideon, choose our type of love and its complimentary war.
Doubt!
Now the sky has no color.
Her Cheshire tendencies irritate the calm outside.
She made our scars twice hazardous for tourists who just want their photographs.
My love, challenges herself into a showdown.
I am losing weight, at the sight of her frown.
We watch the storm weaken everything we hoped for;
burying the Pollyannas hitchhiking on the side of highway-checks,
and capturing immodest doves hired only for deranged weddings.
We watch the moon give in to undignified bouts
after the darkness preached of dawn's lonely teacups
spiked with sleeping pills,
lovers forget their honeymoon.

Why are we here stealing each other's love?
Why are we here keeping it to ourselves sometimes?
Instead of trusting it as something that acquires a mind of its own.
We're drenched in the honest qualms of gratitude whenever it leaves
the trauma fizzling out.
*Am I warm enough to where you hid the treasure chest with emptied
batteries?*
Our divine love has been searching for better wisdom,
and authenticity that actually provides,
instead of merely keep tabs of everything.
Bartender, let's have another hit, *shall we?*
You'll be the bat.
I'll be the pitcher.
I'll toss the glass with expertise.
Make it fast, you said,
looking th*rough* me.

a fax from the devil's mouth

My living soul awakens through the foggy night.
It's time for me to let go.
It's time to be rehabilitated from the bullshit and be freedom's prostitute.
Who's my heart beating for again?
You are whispering too low.
My troubled and angry eyes can't see you.
I saw meteors ascend on the flowers we dent.
We zig-zag through the dark, muttering and murdering prayers.
Will my spirit choose you? Is our love in vain?
"There is always a demon watching!"
We're known to say.
It's taken me so long but I found you.
Our fire is immense.
Our love is intense.
It's taken me so long to finally need you.
Our imaginings were deceiving,
I am letting you know that my living soul can't take it anymore.
You're lying through your teeth, again.
I am through with your wandering eye.
It's time for me to explore another beating heart.
The fire in your eyes perished before.
You're no longer my responsibility to preserve.
Will I ever see you the same way as before?
Revelations avoid us consciously,
no matter what heaven we see
on something dying on its knees.
We got a fax from the devil's mouth.
Why is it that these demons have the best lines,
and the purest methods to hush the wails of love?
It's taken us too long to accept our loss.

Our fire is out.
She's dust on the plow.
Your imaginings were meaningless collections of woe.

Still, my living soul
is dying for
you.

infatuates of the sewer lids

I must admit,
I was pushed too strongly by the initial waves of joy that came
from you.
I wonder, *am I selfish in saying I am most grateful?*
Could you enlighten me about my insensitivities?
Was it in making you my odd form of remedy,
that weakened your jaws
and told me real sweetly
to freeze and think it over?
Am I being pitifully transparent?
The oasis of the Earth's chest imprisons our spirit seasonally.
Still, I've followed your spontaneous flight;
trusted your prestigious escape from the wheels of fire.
You never fail to lead me towards love's greater pursuits.
It led me to dance with such rawness,
pulse-pounding motions,
so eager to blossom with the chrysanthemums
just in time for Mother's day.
Will she be the mother to my little resurrections?
I guess so.
This, I know as an interchangeable fact.
The grotto of our lips, awaits zero-gravity consent.
Love is a bet forged by unsure possibilities.
In due time, we're trash's toupee,
scatter-brained on the curve;
infatuates of the sewer lids.
It takes a molecular form of hope,
so hideous, to place us in a state of certitude on these lonely tropics.
They leave us with towering questions,
and fruitless answers just entertaining enough to sleep with
for a few days,
and then forget.
We distort each other's glee, *wouldn't we rather live like this,*
eternity-deep?

"Understanding is a dream,"
you sang, as the cure came evidently with the truth slipping
through our hand like grains of sand. A toxic rash molests the base
of our eyelids, so swimmingly, we hallucinate the fangs of defeat.
Unconsciously embraced, were you ever awake?
You've treated me like I'm emotionally crippled.
I am finished collecting trapdoor hinges,
and being a victim to your contrived hospitality.
LOVED, *why do I feel numb all of a sudden?*
Whenever I offered my arms to you,
I never asked myself *why?*
I did ask, *how much would I let you store in my head like a box?*
I am keeping my key.
I dare you, set my luggage on fire as I exit.
I know a secret.
You're no mystery;
you dull me.
Nothing is worth stealing in all our years together.
We're proud of thinking that what's next for our heart to do is all
figured out.
I refuse to kick more dirt under the rug or ask for your legs to
stumble over mine,
when all I wanted was a brand-new start. It seems selfless to me,
to name you my muse; the pathway I choose to discover new art.
I never meant to trust your light more than I would shooting stars.
Or to wake up with your image, ignorant when my imagination lies.
I've tasted your lips, they're bitter.
What's sweeter than the truth from a piece of paper, that's fated to taste
only fire?
Uninviting.
Is that a knock arriving?
Or more of the damaged ships we've sent off with wrong directions,
now arriving on the docks to massacre us?
It is filled with men and women,
conduits of powerless words;
annihilators of the maddening silence.

Redeemed only when their blade touches ours,
and fuses the DNA of fear into everywhere
of everything we are or will be.
The beauty of sunbaked dawn greets us on the balcony of truce.
We bask in painful temptations,
inhaling each other *slowly*,
nearly melting on the duvet,
wrinkled with blinding passion jettisoned.
Be my ultimate guest.
My dearest,
fills my lungs with a pure soul,
passionately hurting me with recycled kindness.
She's promoted to LOVED.
A permanence our hearts could weather through.

We wept.
Christ!

We chanted vain curses,
all our treasured demons
and delightful angels are stunned and decapitated.

We lay claim once more to the inevitable feeling.

it left like starshine

I want to be straightforward with you about a delicate subject on how we are.
The last few weeks or so has been hard.
I ask, *should we cut the strings of the musical playing?*
It's your choice,
you started it all by being so open to the perfect storm of my elusive words;
being a red-target for the sharp lies
I've thrown.
Are the goodness of my words calming you down as if nothing was wrong?
When surely,
I extract from your pain, until a beautiful rain of distortions come pouring in,
and becomes these creative islands I shelter myself in.
I demand you to listen to every raindrop cutting through the air,
burning through the mad soil,
and lifting an infertile seed.
As your tears bleed with the sorrow you borrowed from me.
Despair for all I care, shine or refuse to,
darkness has been an ally in all this ruse.
There have been tours I'd journey through alone.
I brought brochures from the palaces of many hells,
it is full of surprising treasures,
I solemnly swear.
Do you still see heaven in me, my dear?
Honey, I refuse to put my hand there.
Your hollow chest shelters no heart;
it left like starshine,
first-coat of white,
on our make-believe
dream-house.
I am done with opening Band-Aids for kids with scraped knees in my imagination.
There are no crying except for loud, deafening silence, here.

The wedding bells are nonexistent, just like my talent with the strings.
And holding your hand is a hundred-thousand-million miles away from happening.
Unloved today.
I am ever so sure, this particular deceit brings the largest smile to my many faces.
That one voice of clarity pulls at my shirt,
delivering a regretful choice on how to clean the stains on my conscience.
This one poet's loaded gun of reasons,
aimed at the head and the heart of a special person;
one with long,
beautifully parted hair,
kind brown-eyes,
and an honest complexion;
drooling with premature lies caught in her own reluctant webs.

Is she still the proud owner of my heart or is she now being labeled UNLOVED?

she was *sad* when she *said* that

I love you because of how persuasively unkind, and serialized it's all been.
And you hope for a chance to unite with my old self.
In the killing fields,
I am bait to the monsters hiding.
I cower at the sight of you.
The glory of you.
In the killing fields,
I am in the depths of your worst feelings
and I am lifeguard to the anxiety you bed in compliant orgies.
In the misty rain of sin and dust from rays of the black-sun,
I saw you.
I am in the deepest sleep because your melancholic lullaby convinced my eyes to close.
My greatest fantasy was real before it was reduced to make-believe.
I love you, even if I live in fear of being hostage to a conspiracy addressed to you.
I adore your accuracy, the font you've chosen to involve me.
While you hope for a chance to weaken one of my many souls making flapjacks in the stoves of the abyss.
You'd give me up for nothing at all.
You'd give me up in the killing zone.
And you did so too, *remember?*
Damn those hours I cannot take back!
Damn those minutes that died in my arms!
"It only takes a mere second to take me back," she said.
The train-cars explode from within
and the casualties bleed onto the rails,
thrilling it with daydreams provisioned by rain-drenched windows.
The Lord pre-emptied another forbidden ashtray
and lit a newborn Cuban cigar for all to see in the killing fields,
where all the monsters suicide
and incarnate into
ME.

In the killing fields,
all our best feelings come to
DIE,
peacefully.
(If it could be believed)
With dull movements,
I sought you, I am in the deepest death
because your lullaby torched
the flowers that spite me.

"If I can't choose you, it's the least I could do,"
she was *sad* when
she *said* that.

in the blackness's grip

I am her fall guy.
I stay in on winter days;
I fell in love with the apparition of her ways.
I am a year older.
I am still a madman for her.
I am trying to filter out what I could.
She's keeping the sunshine from drowning my fever with chill.
She's the dream I forget after I wake up, and the seam tearing off my straight line.
Over and over.
I lose count.
I am a time-clock ticking away, with the farewell's gentle abode.
I stay up past midnight to be degraded by her.
I don't sleep; a minute without suffering is not like me.
This slideshow of hell is too amusing in the blackness's grip.
It's pacifying an old habit:
Freezing of heartbeats.
"You're but a fallen-leaf," she said.
"Onto a campfire," I finished.
She knows that I truly did love her.
I failed when I tried to speak.
Nothing comes as smoothly and naturally as the rain!
She'd gawk.
After our freak show sold its tickets.
I was distracted by the chiseled rainbow, and was occupied in the tasting of its copious colors. We used to watch the sun go to bed
and tie a bow around its neck
and forget the words that were said
half-meant
and stumbling
on a downward axis.
Having fun yet: said the soap-bubble on your upper-lips.
You're an alcohol solution in which I clean myself with.
Wow, what a statement!

You're so *deep*!
You're *deeper* than the grave I am sleeping in.

What did I do to deserve seven-feet of sarcasm?
Keep-keep-keep me on the other side of the fence.
We're in a war with ourselves, remember?
"Now, sell me for a buck and a crime."
Does she hear me?

everything is permitted

I sit before her, awaiting the unraveling of truths.
One: I am truly unsure of you.
Two: I am fucked-up by your dense fog of pretenses,
I am dying for it to clear,
I can't figure you out, d*ear*.
You're armored with a cold hard shell.
I freeze from the touch of your hell.
I am colored with exaggerated green.
It's the envy I feel,
for the months already corpses
in time's flowerbed;
how can we be sure it's really dead?
I live in the atmosphere of her lying epiphanies,
in which I'm told my chances are as high as the altitude of the clouds.
She just loves the activity of deceiving my soul.
My friendless fiend faces away as the heaven I crave, meets its dead-end.
It saves the spontaneous and contrived days, for long-notes of mumbled effacements.
I perfected the art of bestowing words,
never to be read with a straight face
and without choking on a mouthful of cosmic
foreskin.
She's unlike most strangers
I've met.
She knows where she's going, or what to seek from the worldly producers.
I was a lost stray in the empty parking lot of a hopeless evening;
voluntarily suffering through her nightly strolls.
"Your eyes, never saw kindness for some time.
You want to be manipulated and controlled.
A master who calls you frequently, someone to bend for,"
she says, before she held my gaze's defeated stillness.

Our decisions have been so crazily devolved.
It's creating madness shaped like laughing tigers.
The shape of a love misinformed;
a love confused of its worth,
with gates and fences and walls,
decorated by bullet holes.
Decorated by arrows
and stones
and hatchet marks
from other hearts
she disregarded
and disposed of.
I am needing only an upper view of her sheen thighs,
and surround-sound of incredible silence on a session
of pure
decay.
A second glance at our electric shock.
The chance to be with her, now, redirected currents.
In my mind, she was perfect:
The one love I am willing to wait for,
be strong
and brave for
and sacrifice it all for,
just to create a genuine future.
An embrace forever empowered.
Hi!
Bull-shit obstacles, *how are you?*
Let us down from these icy altitudes and morphing attitudes.
Accept
the blues,
the nude-day,
and the rain-bows strangled
by our strings of hard-rain.
Our painful resurgence from yesterday's intrusion,
influenced articles to be rewritten,
and deleted for no heart to see.

Yet, they were honest tunes, *weren't they?*
If only she'd do the same
and be fearless
and unbowed by doubts;
unbent and unbroken by the demons who shout
and scare away her angels.
They know *first*-love never-*dies.*
Nothing could remedy it, either.
Little boy, I'm sorry.
It was just a false alarm.
Little girl, don't worry.
He will forget you in time.
Little boy, love freely
and make more promises
you're willing to keep.
Little girl, I loved you
and I am grateful
for your time,
and your words,
especially the ones you haven't told me
in confidence
or through thick-walls.
I hope you find another,
without my ego,
my infectious sorrow
and my pathetic views,
scheming with the wheels of life.
I am a runaway train.
Unafraid of death.
I rush and slow time to my likeness.
I push boulders,
and throw grenades just to bend more straight lines,
thus causing a wildfire of false alarms.

Everything is permitted in a wildfire of false alarms,
false alarms,
false alarms,
false alarms,
false alarms.

while the noon is young

We're a hurricane intent on destruction.
We're a lightning-strike aiming for a beloved tree wearing a neon-
yellow caution-tape satchel. We're a volcano enraged ready to yell
and scream something that'll be hard to clean-off
our wind-
shields.
You're ready, ready for our destruction.
You're ready, ready to strike at me.
Oh, how bitter!
Oh, you vipers!
I feel your heated arguments scorching the four legs of my
comfortable seat.
"You belong in an unescapable island, your heart is dangerous,"
she says.
Something in me does long for the sun,
somewhere else
and with someone else.
I would approve of her walking away.
Razor's edge, *her*
raindrops cut into my skin.
Regions of filth begin to mix in with my tears.
I am losing on the accounts of many wasted years.
Show me a place where I am not wrong.
I am only believing the lies told through the teeth of the beast.
There's no sky-traffic when the rapture hits,
people mow the dandelions;
only dreamers kick it.
I need to escape from the jaded fellows with pressed hats
and chase my runaway bliss in open-road-traffic
while the noon is young.
Watch me stray from the succubus clouds and her poetic,
Dijon mistress, commanding the eyes of the happily deceased
to awaken.
You know me from that dream;

it was a nightmare it seems.
It was a nightmare it seems.
I am enlightened by your eyes.
I've been a crazy nut-case,
ever-*since*, in*sin*cerely.
What on earth did it unearth within me for looking at them?
It slithers like a water-snake on my bronze sky.

Our last memory was found dead.
It was poisoned from within the depths of itself.

Oh, how bright the massive green slope became!
Oh, how inviting the land-slides were!

taking the whole length of it inside your mouth

I am not shy to admit,
I might not be the best character in your book.
Do me in with what they call a second look.
She's a familiar voice
I can't get rid of that easy.
I put a sheet on our bedroom mirrors.
She breathes the same glass air;
fragile with filigree.
I wronged the person beside me, it's okay with her.
She's the type of lunatic who exiles
loving tongues,
from the fleet of her unloving words.
Go ahead, kill the moment, she'd whisper.
I am a survivor of her merciless disbelief.
I wronged the right person and still,
willfully,
I've chosen to fight alongside her.
She'd deny my aid.
I am an essential part of the hearing.
I am what she needs for liberation.
I am a joyful evidence, the jurors can't ignore.
Sue me!
I have nothing to hide or give from the open-flaps of my Jekyll and
Hyde complexion.
I'm sorry, but you cannot just treat me like I'm your glory.
I am not deserving of your company; don't guilt-trip my knees from
bending.
You don't know me.
You'll fall and it will be because I pushed you.
And as you fall, I'll be the last face you see.
I'll spit on your shadow.
I'll leave no roses on the grass,
no one ever grows underneath the stone-face of a joy-less killer.
I might not be the only one you've done this to.

I am enough of a madman with sufficient non-sense to come after you.
I'll gleam on daytime's torn dark tights with my infamous voice.
Even from the dead,
I'll still haunt you.
Hey!
Piggy in the mirror.
It's not your reflection anymore,
is it?
You're a wanted-thing;
a hunted creature,
who are you but my con-joined twin?
Breathe the pollution in the airwaves;
it might just kill you to behave.
You've wronged the only person right for you.
Then killed the moment I forgave your return with two precise fingers.
Yet, you're just fine in your cell.
Wronging the right person,
intensified your nerve-endings
and hardens your tangy marrows.
Employing crew in the submarine of your subconscious.
I'll leave no roses on the grass in commemoration.
I'd be growing old,
alone.
I see you,
falling down;
falling down into the core of whatever scene
we're to star
in.
You will be the main event in this freak-show of molested colors.
The collard greens are green-no-more.
They demand an encore for your brave performance.
They wonder if you'd taste better without dressing.
Darling, bow to the audience.
Let your head be decapitated by their slicing glee.
Secure headlines.

They'll photograph
your faded-brilliance,
your faded-shimmer,
without your consent.
You'll focus on my silhouette,
as you gain their currency of admiration,
but lost my golden respect.
You're enough to entertain me.
Darling, hear my voice cower behind the train-tracks
watching you leaving with the hordes of them.
You will never hear our timeless song again.
You will find an active dynamite land on your hand,
one day,
silencing the explosion by taking the whole length of it inside
your mouth.
Here you are again,
having the last
word.
You will find nothing grow anymore,
worth staying another year for.
You will go insane in a flaming rage,
dicing flamingo legs for a side-dish.
Breathing poison in, from the air vent.
Death comes with a slowly written
and rapidly-felt,
thank-you note.
Here's to all the persons wronged by you;
still smiling with the truth,
selling its soul for elaborate
punchlines.
We're all strangers,
pedestrians
on pedestals
praying and looking
to find or fund a mentor.
Another moment is yet to arrive

to put your neck on a leash,
and cuff you to the hand-rails.
You're mentioned by handsome devils with tearaway scars and an expired license.
While you work on yourself some more, turn me into the finest bullet.
I approved of all that's been and ever was with us.
Kill them softly.
In this week's wheel of misfortune,
bankrupt them on the first date.
Wronged the right person, or *is that only partially true?*
Birds excrete on my already heavy shoulders and taunt me with their sedated eyes.
"Love regrets the bail of its horrid victims," she said.
The swallow wiggled its tail-feather in defiance of the beautiful day, undeserving of the sun's
unquantified shine and
unquantified warmth.
We sailed through its anguish swimmingly.

"Your soul is on queue to die of dehydration soon enough,"
someone said
after *fell*atio.

dagger inches deep on the back

The grey sky says our garden will wilt and rot.
Begotten feelings for you are blooming,
are they not?
We've been judged by giants
and have been set to fail,
soon enough.
Call me by my name; *shame, shame, shame.*
Teach me a better game than the one where I'm hiding in the
corner,
crying and bleeding
without
a sound.
I am trying to dig all the bodies out,
failing.
I end up leaving it
all behind.
I am powerless.
I am singing your broken heart to rest.
I am trying to save all their souls,
but my victory is buried deep.
The lack of moonlight doesn't mean our scenery is bleak.
Cue our anxious breathing.
The violets grew taut.
My sincerity is true sometimes.
Call me when it rains; *pain, pain, pain.*
Help me accept what happens on the surface.
Too late,
it seems there are greater odds of a comet coming
down,
then throwing itself back up at the sight of
us.
On our broken path,
we're convinced,
it's safe to run;
leaving it all

behind.
I got wet sand in my eyes.
Pellets of disgust from the restless stars.
Their patience is waning;
the moon is not in the mood to laugh.
An excessive shower of adhesive snow
won't be enough to freeze our soul
in one uneventful posture of disgrace.
On this white night, we will push
through the pylons, and road blocks.
We'll intimate with limitless affection
at our monsoon of heavenly lies;
accept it for its hellish nature
as it swirled like a little dancer.
Victory at last; *victory at last.*
I had to say it twice,
I could not believe it.
No more hiding in the corner crying.
Bleeding with every sound,
I plot a celebration,
finally,
leaving you behind.
God humbles my soul with your absence.
I pray for new disasters
wearing the morning light's dentures.
I love you, is a toy soldier,
with gun resting on its lap,
dagger inches deep on the back;
going unnoticed.
Stay in my spirit's periphery.
It's only a curtained distance.
An apology fills the picture show
with sirens snaking over the sleeping
and vibrates the deeper sands of their faith.

How are you tonight, my sweet?

clover-green and sunset-despair

Under the heat, we have met the scenery of a winter storm.
The snowing dandelions are caught
in the winsome currents of a summer breeze.

They're hostages to the immersive feelings
rushing through our veins,
in clover-green
and sunset-despair.

We echo these dead wishes
and in resurrecting them,
they're faultless,
and flawless
in trusting us,
again.

We've allowed them
to linger and manifest,
to get caught in our best-hells
and bathe in our rawest intentions.

Our fruits never landed safely
on our open palms, instead they're picked up,
bruised on impact, and dramatically tearing,
with bleeding verses of uninspired dialogue.

As it lands far from our view,
it gets away with cruel innocence.

Each one is a child running in the park,
unsupervised.

Only to end up in someone else's
lawn.

Seeds plucked out
and tossed
at the gutters.

Never
to return
the *cycle*.

finding another seat to melt on

I reminisce with a shake of my dizzy head.
I remember clearly,
the blinding green of a flower pot in a bicycle basket.
The apple seeds in her hair.
A smile she hid behind a scarf.
The bronze locket she opened up,
and of when I was astounded by her profound merriness.
In the middle of train interviews.
The sound of opening doors
and colorless shadows
passing-through with a gun-shy view of lover's,
in the midst of an immortal memory.
I stall my loneliness,
allowed my alloyed eyelash to flow along
with what she released
and relived through
with a melodious expression.
I picked it up,
her station in my heart.
But will she receive my curiosity, or blister my fingers when I touch upon it before midnight?
In my brain
I began escaping,
finding another seat to melt on.
In my brain, I parted the door,
while the train is speeding into the next station,
and roll over the tracks like a barrel.
She smells like rain, I thought.
She breathes poetry like sin;
wet clothes stuck to my dry whims.
She's the cause of a deadly fever, pending.
I am remembering that first line I overheard her say
to somebody brave enough to compound on her serenity:
"You smell like cherry blossom trees in the evening."

I knew you were the one, everyone wished sat beside them.
Men, women, or animals.
Amused, you replied with a clever question:
"They smell different in the evening?"
Just like cherry blossoms,
your bloom isn't meant to last long.
I watched the silence endure for ten full minutes
and a gaze farewell felt like tightening a barbwire
on an open heart.
The far-away watcher that I was,
hurt the most,
that it wasn't my heart bleeding
from her many
cuts.
I've been greedy tonight.
Haven't I?
Seasoning the evening's black burger with salted doubts.
I strolled along the quiet path,
feeding the homeless congratulatory looks for letting me invade
their sacred spaces,
where murder is known
to pass.
I'd sleep on the couch tonight.
She'd nod with a sigh,
the many ghosts sitting on my couch.
Under the bathroom lights,
I give myself permission to talk out loud.
I saw the devil horns grow in height as it met the front lights of a
police car.
Take her off your walls,
she's just another unsold painting.
The evening canvas pretends to be friends with the stars
I depreciated.
I shed my skin again.
I make it into a game.
Not a fun one, *still*, a game.

I am patiently waiting to offend myself
into a dream-filled chamber
of happy-go-lucky,
sugar-sweet
visuals.
Traumatize me will you!
Comatose my virtues will you!
Sign your name where I am pointing,
I would say shyly to the man in the frosted mirror.
Lock the door behind you!
It would say, and I always obey what it says.
With such an authoritative tone of voice, *who wouldn't?*
Suddenly, I've been awoken by a billion tiny noises.
A blue pot becomes a casket for one unpicked, singular flower.
The worms feasted on my decolorized skull,
forever ungrateful,
forever pale grey
with discontent.

The yellow moon is sublime enough,
maybe, I will dream of *her* tonight.

EX<u>HIBIT</u>

E

eavesdroppers
to
habitual sleepers,
but
wouldn't we rather be happily dying?

large morsels and the *ones* good men choke on

I find myself locked inside this cage of hopelessness.
The chariots past by to avoid my soundless joy.
The seagull's cries fill my weekends.
I hold on to peace
I borrowed
collecting seas-
hells.
I find myself seasick looking in your general direction.
I am waiting for death,
listening for struggling breaths.
The waves preach of large morsels and the *ones* good men choke on.
It's up to you now to forgive me and to judge the heartache
I put us through.
It's up to you, to change my mind as I surrender too
and to embrace the lies that danced with truth.
Sweetheart,
open the box the wind shoved
with gentle incentive
and explore the lack of corners.
I know it's hollow,
and sounds of empty
promises.
Nothing's there, even if, I send my old self away.
I need a refill of her best flames in order to evolve.
I know,
I know,
your warmth
is a luxury,
I don't de-
serve.
My hands await yours, in a solemn prayer.
I will buy back our peace somehow.
But, there's no use, these four walls know too much.
There's no shine here, anymore.

The insanity evolves to love me like no other.
There's no running away from her weaponized corset.
The thought of us before, was never anything more, than
misunderstood gospel.
I'll find that hope tomorrow.
I continue to row.
The blue flames get higher.
They perform a betrayal from a Shakespearean play.
I feed it new levels,
until there's nothing more of me to give.

Our loving act it dev*ours.*

that murderous mood

Hurry up!
Let's fast forward to our wedding day.
Slow down!
Let's rewind to yesterday.
I had enough!
You're not funny.
You've had enough?
"I quit this boring masquerade," you said.
You've put away the mask that fell in love with the idea of us.
My smile refused to exist for you.
A broken guitar plays our song on a melody with no prior experience.
It was hiding stories of our stupid past that did us in.
I wonder what name to give the dust you'll leave behind.
For a thousand lifetimes,
my soul remains the same;
finding love with passion,
seasoned with dismay.
Hurry up!
What's this lie you're about to say?
Hurry up!
And abuse your liberty today.
I've had enough?
You're singing out of tune again.
"I ran out of promises to delete," I said.
I've put away the mask that fell in love with the idea of us.
Our plans are never insured.
There are never any solutions worth depending on.
Better yet, we let this destroy us.
Let's remember the pain's vitality.
Don't deny this love and how rare it has been.
"This love usually comes with bluer moons," we said.
Don't put me in that murderous mood.
Together, we're two individuals losing.

We shamefully accept it, though.
Our victory was a lie, there's no question about it.
Don't question the motives of a prophet.
We took off the mask and fell out of love with the idea of us.
Hide your waxing smile and let's engage in dancing lunacy.
Let the energy be nothing but extraordinary from here on in.
We're made from a thousand lifetimes of souls greatly changed.

We may have found love,
with great passion, but,
ours are seasoned
with greater dismay.

unhinged for good

Relax! Stand by!
I am as low as a kite catching your dead air.
And falling down, falling down, opposite your general direction.
I surrender to wherever this river runs.
I've been discharged.
I've been turned off.
Her unlawful wind rules, hammering-in the last mortal flame we promised to protect.
At night, I am alone in the desert searching for golden crumbs.
I get nearer with each weak pull from her yellow rope, shining deafly down.
Yet, we don't speak at all and rest instead inside sandstorms.
This silent death is far from having passed through.
The feast for crows was a letdown.
The meat is too divorced from bone.
You're a stubborn speaker.
I sealed your lips, yet your flowing tears translate the words unsaid.
Rise up and fight me.
There's no surrendering, dear.
You'll soon be an unfortunate centipede caught under the knife of a six-year-old kid.
You'd respond and I'd listen to a scripted answer.
With discretely weaved suspicions, you've ignored my calls.
Immediately, I fall out of line, without imparting my side first.
You've flat-lined a few dried tears ago, I felt.
My darling, depends herself with a damaged song.
She'll enchant my soul into submission.
Her rhythm section pierces through bone and burns into my hope's main lobby.
Her irresponsible notes flew to crucify my palms into her, unworn, unloved, arctic blankets.
I dreamt of a Kingdom.
I am a foe to her mercy, as always.

It took many trips, each more dreadful than the last, before I made it over the wall.
Your welcome, I misunderstood.
We're unhinged for good.
Our stubborn wood wouldn't catch aflame.
I felt perfectly alone.
She deserted my body six feet under the water she cursed.
Don't join me on the bedrocks.
I disapprove of your attempt at rescuing me.
I like my archaic view, my primeval misery.
Please, don't tease me away from my exotic tomb.
"We could talk this through,"
I'd persist in uttering.
Yet, she chooses to remain mute indefinitely.

Our silent *May*. *June* stay sober.
July to me. *August* to forever.

leaving unsatisfying tracks to and from the funeral parlor

Dreams escape me every single day.
One would die out of boredom to go on,
it inspires courage to the many more
that'll die away after.
My own schemes elude me.
I can't prioritize every supernatural voice I hear.
Your low growls keep me up all night
and the cycle begins
when the alarm clock explodes
to our wedding song.
Liquid agony rains all over my frozen heart in our white room.
The scars in my heart are marred by prisoners,
counting their days inside this forced shelter of our misbehaving love.
Feigning could only endure a limited moment.
Until the act is beaten to a pulpy ash and zesty nothingness.
My sanity goes astray.
I am so caught up in our graceless game of tag.
I let you win many more times than I do.
I am first to miss your touch and with such immense sadness, too.
It's a healthy habit to fall victim every day to your gracelessness.
Reality pulls me back into your ridiculous design.
But it doesn't love me as genuinely as dying alone to the sound of
B-flat.
Every waking day I gather more reasons to escape thee.
Schemes of her love elude me.
Until there's nothing left of my melted heart on the dark pavement
to step on;
leaving unsatisfying tracks to and from the funeral parlor.
I can't stitch the scars on our bed.
We've tarnished its dignity and beaten its soul with our insane rituals.
We've been super caught up in this game we're making up,
cheering to the rounds sent by *life-and-death*.
Holding a wine glass overfilled with powerful red,

and our face adds a mixture of guiltless fascination.
We've abandoned our best channels to the landslide.
The thought of what the heavens painted over has left me falling apart
almost every single hour of each resurrected day.
I am harbored in a cobalt blaze unloved by future mornings,
and its unsecular grim ends.
Filling my calendars with crisscrossed hatchet marks
and circles drawn hesitatingly with scarlet compromise.

Our disappointed angels would watch the red marker run dry on our view of the yellow sun.
"Turning away from one another, was the most important thing we've ever done," they said.

dies at the rendezvous point

I am drunk in the backseat of a taxi.
It's been a while since I had this much time to think.
She hands me another bottle of whiskey,
so I am myself, again.
You missed my turn, we've been here before!
It's my lies that made us lost.
It was my dreams begging on the side of the church.
Your missing portions
disobeyed all repayment options.
The night's white disc hid behind bulletproof showers.
The main character dies in the devil's hour.
In my book he's still alive smiling young,
and breathless.
In worlds of our imaginings,
they're amateur survivors,
because in her truth I still don't find
a way out.
Her farewell wasn't the last dance I asked for.
Who would join me in the back seat, now?
I am calling out for you in the middle of the streets.
A stray came to greet me, for a second I thought I met my
soul-mate.
It's been a while since I've walked through this graffitied tunnel,
with a heart just as beaten-down and disrespected.
Please, tell me another verse from the King James Version,
so I can pray the devil out of my visions.
May I enter, now?
Says the fallen dog.
I am dumbfounded, the speeding wheels disregard
what will soon be sun-kissed in about an hour.
Sweet little thing, *how could you be in two places at once?*
Sweet little thing, in our show, *wasn't my wounds a cover-up?*
Sweet little thing, in the book, the pages were rougher than woodchips.

We're sailing across the fireballs of March
and April told a joke equal to how I am treated by our wonderlands.
Do our demons learn anything from our malevolent crisis?
Do we merely exist as an example?
For all my lies, I am sorry.
For my dreams, I am guilty of sugarcoating
my bruises, from consciousness's relentless uppercuts.
Take your portions, I want no part in it.
The dawn goes out of its way to show us,
how the main character dies at the rendezvous point.
In my book he's still alive, *somehow I believe my own folly.*
Your heart weights a ton.
In solitude,
my ball and chain are freed in all possible worlds.
Freedom is a hoax to those who've signed a treaty.
The lover's absurdity is publicly stoned.
We're neither loving nor supplying a heavy loathe.
The water droplets gather on the windshield,
forming a union.
She ignored my agonized look,
my hands are searching for words.
The truth is,
she's my way out.
Her farewell introduced the morning.
I weep in mourning of her slight struggle;
the door failed to close a few times.
I am all alone in the back seat.
I am left with an ounce of whiskey.
She'd mix it with her black coffee,
no sugar,
no crème.

I am myself,
again.

Who am I to you?

gaze at the tenderness born

Five feet underground; *who's in charge of the digging?*
Cheer me on while
I am hurting.
Get me going lover, faster than it takes for the milk to go bad.
Quit!
How could you put up with staying?
I am warned, your copious commands are out of hand.
I wonder: *Why are you still standing there?*
Underneath all the tragedy,
a whistling in the distance
calmed me.
A sour smile has befallen my sad austere.
It collapsed almost immediately.
We're consumed below the heat of the afternoon sunlight.
Go ahead and bring on the grey clouds!
Let sound the thunder as well, so,
I can wake up from this hell!
"We're better off miles from normal," she said.
Universe go far, fetch me the yellow sun!
I dare you to find me, go on shine your pornographic light!
Why am I still here?
Underneath all the panic,
your smile moved me.
The day dissolved our white masterpiece,
we can't gaze at the tenderness born.
Green is all I see as I escape into the fields naked,
your kiss on my forehead glistens silver.
The soil underneath my toes are softer than our bed,
I believe.
When you're next to me,
I am a drowned seagull,
paralyzed by a faulty telephone wire.
When you're gone,
I could swim freely about with desire for other winged sharks.

Let go of the microphone.
Let go of our fever.
Let go of the jazz player's dagger.
Let the rain take responsibility for its gradual sleep.
Prayers for rain arrived to encounter our rapture,
I believe.
The heart-shaped smoke lingered,
played with the deceased as if it were little feet,
floating in low-
altitudes.
While I am digging
at the ground,
fascinated by this contrived tune of despair
I've gathered safely in.
The grey in the downpour touched my eyes.
The pepper sky,
lit up for the murderers and prostitutes,
carrying brown bags like an infant on their breast.
Go ahead and bring on the stray clouds!
Let sound the sirens as well.

Honey, we'll finally
wake up in a cell.
Let's celebrate!
The cuffs remain
celibate to this day.
Off with the aching
boredom,
at last!

watercolor memory washing over

It may hurt for now.
It might stay a while longer.
You're staying numb, although it feels dumb.
You may feel betrayed.
It may be a while longer,
but things won't be the same,
goodwill still prevail.
We standstill,
while the world is destroyed around us.
Keep calm, darling,
stay still;
let's watch the sun go down.
We'll wait for the night sky
and see the stars twinkle with delight.
Blink and you'll miss the sunset;
blink and you'll miss the sunset.
It may rain for now.
It might be a while longer.
You're staying dry, although
you can't hide
your leaky eyes.
You may feel insane.
It may be a while longer,
but things won't be the same,
reason will still prevail.
Come over here, as I spread my arms
ever carefree.
Accepting you as you are.
It may seem you're too far gone, from me.
I long for tomorrow's dawn,
to be real and not a sidelined,
watercolor memory washing over me.
It seems time waits for those who stand still after all.
We're living proof

that the constant waiting can leave a brilliant journey
worth reminiscing on.
"Wait with me a while longer,"
your chosen words in that order, used to haunt my evenings, alone.
We standstill, while our world is destroyed around us.
Keep calm, darling, stay still and experience the sun's final letdown.
Let's wait for that empty night sky.
Watch the stars twinkle in my eyes.

You blink and missed my sunset.
I blink and I missed your sunset.

*free*falling serendipity

You've known for a while now, where my heart is.
It's in the same place where yours have been.
Don't go or I'll go out of my mind.
Let's start fixing every waking day.
There's so much I learned
about who I am
and how intertwined,
and truly separated
we all are.
Yet,
somehow,
somehow,
we make it to w*here* we need to be.
This *free*falling serendipity,
knows me by name.
You've known where the alluring logic is leading us on.
It's to the same place where doubt bathes in acid-conversations.
Don't go dissolving or solving our conflicts alone.
I'll go out of my mind,
I am already running out of desert to blame.
Let's start fixing every sleepless night,
with sincerity.
You know where this failure to comply would eventually take us.
It's towards the same place victorious feelings
cheated on.
Stay and I'll be with you.
You heard me right.
I am fixed.
Find out later, the vivid lie that it is.
Love remains ignorant.
Muck on time's sty.
Let's love every waking sound of tossed vases and paraphrased verses.
There's so much I learned about who I am.

How low the thinking breeze would go, to intertwine an already twisted faith.
We live in honest time, only after the separation is allowed to endure.
We know who we truly are
after having had a mouthful of soil,
spoon-fed with extra-worms.
Yet,
somehow,
somehow,
we die in the arms of *who* it needed to be.
Let things freefall to the hells of our choosing.
Along with the alignment of submissive mercy
and extracting of the shards fixed in the clay.
Our soul is collateral.
We overcook
and undercook ourselves
in the ovens of the air;
there's no middle ground to thaw or be garnished prettily.
We write formal demands on our skin,
hungry for signatures to mature
after being many years dried.
We live out machinations,
and overperform
or underperform
the tragic conclusions.
We rarely set things to free-
fall gracefully.

Please, don't let a breath get away
from your Godly
face.

above a postmortem angel

The last Willow tree caressed the spicy August breeze.
Her flames so tenderly eternalized the silence.
It was as if she knew,
I am an incomplete partner.
Then and there,
her harmonic melody
euthanized
me.
Our strange museum of shadows became livelier,
as pink raindrops cleanse each and every hopeless,
soulless description we co-authored.
The parking lot homes an abandoned car
under a funeral black canvas
above a postmortem angel.
It was but a m*ere* star.
My disgust at the absence of a moon made her laugh.
The streetlights bloomed with venom.
"Why do lovers wear such gloom when they think like that?" said
Dorothy's red shoes.
Our internal flame died too soon,
the morsels turned to rocky pebbles.
The evening forest in her sparkling eyes sheltered quivering lies,
in which I believed them all as miracles.
"Marriage is but a mirage," says the vanity,
framing us for murdering dusk with our obsessive rage,
in a jolly tournament to see who could endure the most suffering.
There wasn't a syllable uttered without religious ellipses.
Barely any residual seeds watered to reconcile what's been
manifested.
Love is the kidnapping of another's vulnerably open vault.
Still, I praise her sun's return and the baffling,
little-green lesson her rains taught me
and continue to teach.
I glorify her words.

They're what emptiness pursues,
through voluntary urges.
Her morning thoughts were so vague,
often a ruse.
Our particular spell took time to love and be a disciple of.
I've enshrined the integrity of our predicament.
We levitate what's heavy, and see what we're left with to study.
Expose it to a child's fresh, introspective eyes.
Quick, before the beast blows out the candlelight.
Our untold tales turn to bland soup in the retelling,
half drunk and *not-quite-high*
but getting there.
You've compared our launch to a kite caught by weak air.
Torch this cold,
cold invisible town in our crammed,
unswept,
attic.
Believe the strings undetected
by our anxious surf.
We're being wanted,
and unwanted as usual.
"God pulling our legs, what an honor," she said on the first week of October,
after the thunder intimates the hurtful reconnection.
I welcome the yellow twister's ineffectual,
and unforgiving light.

Jealous, because her love found
a rival.

raped by tiny circles

It is time for truth to dock!
Time for the clock to meet head-on with the primeval
sledgehammer.
My hand slides through yours,
I tease you about second-looks and second-opinions,
of how our desire works,
of how it couldn't work.
The phone line lingers.
The champagne glass helps down a tablet.
Our record player's been dead hours; *which side are we on?*
I tighten my grip of her candied soul.
Dropped the resale value of my vanished longings.
My fingers are tired of being used as your honey-comb.
I am embarrassed to be seen raking for the leaves of our worth
and catching the greasy remnants of dreams cut short.
That's my misguided head for you,
and only for you.
This confusing road has a long way to go!
The clouds were moved by her cries
and black dust shouts a reply,
filling our ears with muttering trumpets.
The ground is raped by tiny circles.
It began connecting as one to sketch meaning
into the virgin crevices of our struggling mind.
It makes me envious about the things that never began;
hinges too permanent to detach from the drunken door.
My dreams are put on hold every night
that I am a servant to yours.
My nightmares are barely getting time in the spotlight.
I miss being x-rayed by her darkness.
She'd be vexed by my morning face
and astonished by how unaffected my shutters are by what forced
itself violently in.
Nowadays my screen outshines the sun and my breath starts to hum.

Cutting the daisies outside
with the debris of glass
shamed into being
re-born,
re-fashioned
into asymmetrical hearts.
Our scenery is full of songbirds,
too shallow to resound
what the spaces pulsed,
forever dazed.
My skin gathers her travelling dust;
a love so tortured
by layers of interpreted facts.
Exposed by O.K.'s
and I AM FINE.
There exist no blinds as despicable, and carnage as ours.
No prayer will shield us from the details found on numerous
casualties,
lying on the metal table;
leach or slug?
Do fret of what's outside.
To expect it, is to lessen the possibilities for *real-deep-harm*.
What is easy anymore!
The alley-church would broadcast.
"All are vastly more exciting when hard."
It's a difficult chance that favors the land;
it's a woman that changes a man.
I am an avid worshiper of her charismatic fax and telegrams.
In return she admired how I pacified the immortal days of her youth.
While we remain alert to the tune of brittle heartbeats we emote in
choreograph of.
We ensure another layer of decay memorable and irremovable.
The hot pity cleanses our segregated impulses.
While the spirit rots and the devil watches,
with follicles on opera seats payed for by an underground
government.

I find that her punishments lend the best wings.
She inspires forest fires,
and the intensifying of epiphanies
only achievable in the outskirts of dreams.
Our homicidal tendencies are covered-up;
the loudest she ever laughed came from reciting a list,
I found under her pillow,
of people she would gun down
if she had a chance.
Since then, it installed such wonderful fear.
For once, I learned to breathe.
We laugh at funerals openly
and envy the rest and peace of the deceased;
the cardboard bed,
and the dead flowers
on a dirty vase.
Curiosity stains our eyes, at the sight of pretty pictures.
We wonder,
how the artist bled to have it shine
and passionately made.
We never thought we could do better.
There are limits our ego wouldn't dare to cross.
A round of toast to our guest!
Despair echoed through an empty gallery.
The books we'll never publish,
took another century nap,
saving itself for another lifetime; for another mime.
There's always an interference we punch-in for, and forget about.
Soon enough, we've aged, and are grey.
There is no hair left in our soul,
but a collection of coffin sites through years of being
confined and contrived in the most sickening ways.
Poets in the emerald sea, laugh until they're blue at our contribution.
Withdrawal from love brought us here.
We row until our hands are blistered and chipped.

And we're sleeping through another unfaithful day.
Totally unsatisfied with what is gained.
Which sins are enhanced by our fingerprints?
The quick dismay births another comatose purpose.
Simplified perfection is all we ever wanted.
Weekly, we deny blessings from the pastor,
and proudly hollow the wine glass and ask:
Which way to the barrel?
Yet, our loved ones, and ill-chosen enemies light candles for us.
There's no charge, no fee, all that is required is we bleed.
Are you bending the knee?
They would ask with a symbolic gleam in their expression.
Just let the words be meaningful.
Let the leaves at autumn time give us a carpet to lie on.
And let November's sorrow leave a cloudy day for us to analyze.
Winter is for feeling alive right next to the humbling heart of the generous fire.
Our seasons are too nervous to receive the actual contents of what it wants.
We weather through a bend in the road;
a *been-there*,
over-done that,
assuredly impetuous jubilation.
The constant heart vibrates with languor,
to bless the mugshot heavens we discover in others.
We're obliged to endure the fullest moon,
with a stomach full of red or white.
Victoriously balanced in a balcony of our choosing;
a three-pointed devil,
seeking our impaired smoke to dine-in.

To close my eyes,
I'd have to come undone.
I need to give myself completely to someone.
May I give myself a way to you?

miles of violent roots

Try talking to me now.
Metaphors you speak are...
full of bitterness.

I'd rather have your untidy silence,
what did I miss?

Try talking to me now.
Trust I gave you are...
fueling the hurt I feel,
your comfort is what I miss.

The message you've written on my wall
is so clear to me.
I can't speak of it...

The message you've written on my wall
is tattooed on my mind,
how did I become so blind?

Remember when we were sublime?
Someone, please wake us up!

Try talking to me now.
The kindness you give me is...
deceiving.

I watch you walk away
smelling of bourbon.
I was trying to hear you out
and I don't want you in my head
like this.

The lies you've told fertilize miles of violent roots.
The echoes of truth have grown into filaments of wrong.
The message you've written on my wall
is so *fucking* clear to me.
How dare you speak of it!
It's an ongoing investigation
in the springtime of my unlucky youth.

Who says going mad doesn't come without a chaperone?

implore the contours of her silvery death

I remember the first time you held my hands over your dead eyes.
We'd devote time to stimulating adventures.
What's most available in the dark?
"We design the answer," you said.
Our bodies got further involved,
obscured by the forestry of tyrannical words.
"The less they know, the more fun it becomes for us,"
she'd say skipping stones over a moon-kissed lake.
My eyes selfishly implore the contours of her silvery death.
My eyes close.
I am sung to, by her strands of strangled grace.
My mind is in the laundry.
My eyelids slide open as dusk is penetrated by her switchblade wings,
lashing out
vertically.
My neck angles skyward admiring her royal silhouette.
Then came the approving votes from the chiming insects;
the sheen of perverted stars behind meditating clouds.
We allowed it.
It's just us,
pressed against the brilliance of spontaneously combusting moments.
The usual.
You own my faith a seat.
My past succumbs to a broken vote.
"Don't get destiny involved," she'd say,
closing the gaps between her lips and the bottle.
It is time for us to change paths and hunt for other
cadavers.
Our views regarding beauty is toasted under sheets of mutating heat.
The brave animals found our entry amusing,
and our exit,
a precise dis-
appointment.

They procured magical perspectives from a mere glance at our fatal crash.
Clues, to what had to be and to what had always been.
Without any guessing game falsely advertised,
in favor of *one* winner.
"The less we know going forward, the better.
Let's dream of greater consequences until it becomes the end of us,"
she'd say,
gathering weeds into a bouquet.
Her lungs were the harvester and destroyer of wishes.
My sleepless face shows hints of retribution,
as the orange grass wept
with her tiny grey soldiers.
I am caught in her headlight's blue-beam intimidations.
I was in the midst of writing apologies onto our pyre.
My eyes closed permanently,
ready for her to take cover under my umbrella spirit
and to cuddle the remains of my body.
I focus on the eternity glistening inside those final raindrops.
Living on,
when everything dries,
becomes the most alluring proposition
in the rye.
I am no longer her pet mule,
but, I admired her the most
when she was just an idea.
I lean against a skinny-bone tree
with the hopes that she doesn't see
me.

The death sentence we experienced far too long,
in the wake of love's ceaselessly
lonesome
me-
teor.

the storm's terminal clients

Sleep disagrees.
Dreams are God's informants.
I stay awake,
yawning through impossibilities.
I've nothing to disclose,
except for my desire to make
as many unguaranteed proposals.
I let the evil in,
and give it pocket change
whenever it heads out.
The trees sprint with incredible speed in one place.
Thunder cues the storm's terminal clients.
The sun sends us an electrifying glance
and the rainfall leaves knuckle branches
for my frozen tongue to taste.
You set fire to the afternoon,
killing my rest.
I'd wake up with an aching stretch,
I mistake you for good company.
The aerial strikes of hard-earned facts,
gave up on love.
I am awed by the piles of crashing cars.
The air slashed with nails on my face.
Us, flying through the windshield.
No passion could quench this thirst for reunion.
I suck dry the sliver of your bloodied lips.
Our journey is yet to cut through the dreaded finish line!
Keep the phase alive.
The momentous pistol sounds.
Feel the sun buzzing and feed us rotating diamonds.
Watch the savior decline our mortified eyes.
We perish in the wreckage of weak words.
"Don't let us be the butt of a joke. Don't you dare close your dead eyes now!"

she'd whisper to me, half her beautiful face torn like wallpaper.
This wasn't the right path.
I can see that now.
I felt her last tries at escape,
consume what's left of my chest to deplete.
I can see the light, having disputes with the black clouds.
Let the end arrive.
Once you see the light, don't let it go out.
You'll return as a blossoming flower dropped over the fire.
The murdered patch of ground wakes our sleeping hearts.
The madness begins to uproot.
We ration the sunlight until the sullen sun rolls behind the mountains.
Morning has passed.
We're gravel underneath the coal.
What's left for forgiveness to conceive?
We'd arrive at a spectacular checkpoint.
Death begets the rolling wonderers on a whim.

Lovers beware, we're under the creator's yellow scalpel.
What's to come is between God and whatever washes up from the seas of the great Thereafter!

shove onto a hard surface and suffocate

Your ever-giving presence thought me wrong from right, *but not tonight*.
I didn't know evil, until it took your shine away from me.
It suits us best being isolated.
The thinker is usually the bitterest one.
Pity is a bearer of emotional gifts.
We are riding down an unsteady decline.
It was full of trickery, and uncut seams.
It has awoken many broken spirits.
I didn't know angels ran on candlelight.
One flew past by to steal my sleep.
I woke up feeling born again.
Her feathers fell like gentle snow,
like gentle sympathy.
She'd do me all sorts of favors;
my deepest sins got involved.
She'd provoke drama of lackluster zest
that proves nothing at most.
I didn't know who I was,
until I looked into her lifeless face.
Her corners are blessed by minor errors
and those cracked pieces are better apart.
I think they're better like this,
no one is ever wholly themselves.
Pity, I cannot refund this gift.
It is a revelation
I cannot shove
onto a hard surface
and suffocate.
I know we got what's dying.
So what!
It's entertainment.
The final breath is repayment for all the things that happen
along the way.
I cannot piece together the entire soul of it.

"We see what we want to see," says the dew to the wrinkle in your eyes.
As our neurotic love
rides on terminal
tides.

fragments I parted with

Bus stop advertisements…
Indoor parks and lawn decorations…
What a waste of time!
Hats on our heads…
Pillows on our beds…
The sting of fresh sin…
Pleasure so contrived…
The burn of a cigarette…
Baggage overwhelming…
Road signs in the sky…
I don't want to be the one to break you!
Wheels on cars…
Draped construction sites…
Falling buildings…
ignite happy fear in my eyes…
Telephone stands…
Damning the minute hand…
Oval mirrors…
Pole dancing to the crying orchestra…
Empty billboards…
Hooded fools…
Insecurities laying blame…
Roar because you're bored!
Hollow pockets…
Stray cats…
Next stop:
Freshly pressed straitjackets!
Midnight letters…
Candy cane pastures…
Our numbing type of love…
The absence of a heartbeat…
Breaking plates for dramatic effect…
To the tune of her foreign lips…
Her refusal to give to the sky…

My anguish at the sight of her waving arms…
A farewell to the fragments I parted with…

The better use she'll have for them
at somebody else's
ex-
pense!

On Love and Lovelessness

As a young man, I learned that there is great power in understanding desire; where it comes from, and for whom it'll best serve. In the midst of feeling excited, you'd end up foolishly interrogating that feeling and asking it what the fuck it wants. Then, you tend to sacrifice something you never knew would be valuable to keep for yourself. One of those devalued things is your *soul*; it dies immediately once you regard *some*-body as its home. It takes living and dying through numerous people to come by its transformative abilities, and it only ferments due time. A soul that dies often becomes purer and more adaptable; preparing it almost for the next *killer*; as the number of resurrections becomes too much to count. That we find ourselves hollowed out, scarred from within and deeply vulnerable to the point of wanting nothing to do with this thing called *desire*, anymore.

We become paranoid about the longevity of our connections. Our greater faults are better understood when you've spent time away from the reality of what your heart speaks of. It will talk with such brutal honesty about your intentions, and the context of your current love-affairs, and why they began the way it did. But the answers you meet just falls flat on its knees; betrayed by what you seek but cannot find. Your many attempts to involve the person you love most, falters in energy; all seems futile. It becomes a gimmick, a ruse, a trick to fool this supposed "home", of your anchored heart, and it stings to realize you've been untrue in ways you're unable to admit.

The thinking-mind is a malignant cancer, causing your heartbeat to lose its melodic and rhythmic charms. Until you're with great loneliness, and great laughter to the symptoms of clarity. The paths you've paved, and left to blur behind you, changes with each reviewing of the memories allowed. We place in a spectrum of loving or unloving awareness, the things found, the feelings established, the unique gestures, the polite mannerisms, details, *lots* of personal details in the photographs sent, to provoke unintentionally, or to show that the happiness achieved on your face is solely theirs to commit their eyes to.

We endure the saddening view of unmet destinations. And for the sake of constant renewal, under the eyes of the acquainted soul bestowed to you by God's generosity, our lies learn to spit fire with such nonchalance. It's unforgivable. Habitually illogical. Through our falsifying nature, we retire into the ropes of indecision, of losing our hold of the NOW, the core event at the mercy of our urgent compromise. We are flawed; leaning into unsureness of which seeds are worth nurturing and will bear most fruits. Which ones you'll trust aren't poison or could damage the whole of your land thus far, in its decades of tending. Until all that's present are the stumps from fallen trees, the weeds that grow relentlessly tall, the flashes of unfinished recollections, the toxic visuals of seeing what's left of the crops that grew there once, now, in emotional ruins, being the harvester of your graceless decisions.

But we fall into the trap of being collectors; being susceptible to the persuasions of emptiness. Which makes lab-rats out of us, on the limits of plans or unplanned manipulations we could tolerate, and how creative we are in waiting for such majesty to rise and bear golden apples. *Will biting from it teach us something precise in the topics of love?*

No, it doesn't. At best, we get the worm inside, or a seed gets stuck in our teeth.

The persons we develop such loving networks with, become just another uncomfortable accomplice to the worst fears we stored in the winters of our delicate lives. So, we call on death to relieve us from the fluorescent shadows of those who no longer see us with lenses of adoration. Every hour that dies and bleeds into the next one, attacks the sanity and magic you reserved for the very person, you would have gladly given that hour to.

Every redefining dialogue, or idea you would have had the pleasure of sharing, evaporates into the thick abode of black despair. This anxiety drenched coat we wear, keeps us from braving our efforts tirelessly. We give up on the prayers sung by closed lips. Now choking hysterically on all that was submitted and received. It's all a joke all of a sudden, the drama ends with you performing a one-man-show, to the ghost sitting on the living room couch, or the grey shadow in the darkness of your bathroom mirror.

Each person you've labeled with loving significance are graded by your loathsome ego on who loved your comedic, chaotic, misplaced, forgettable, persona the best. They end up dishonouring the gift of your precious time and minded very-much the shine of the phone-screen resulting in nightmarish dreams, thus, remembering everything that's meant to be erased after waking up; drinking their morning coffee with a traumatized look.

Here's the main thing I want to disclose.

Each person, each place, each feeling, melds into the next enlightened event. Where two people are just in the most tortured and vastly unremarkable state, that their unconscious purchases a deal with the universe and calls for their attention to embark on a deal, which would take months to actually sink in, to locate all the hidden fees and contractual clauses, that day and night will obscure, until you're so deep into the enchanting provisions that to return to the consciousness of such unification, would numb all that was partially good and convincingly tangible.

The experience of falling in and out of love; there's no difference. The experience of sensing its beautiful cessation is a high. *Where does that leave the two people so perspiring with doubt, and unfeeling touch?* But, back to the drawing board, back to the whispered prayers to their many saints, and to the flowing of tears for feelings now being shown at the aftermath of the separation. Uncaring of the sea-levels of self-love decreasing and drowning what could have been a fusion of timeless euphoria.

Oh, the agony, of burying that short-lived soul, which was used like a block of clay for the artist you've unconsciously chosen. The excavation results as a laughter-inducing Deja-vu. Your heartland becomes a cemetery for your one and only soul, or at least the fragments the previous owners are charmed mostly by. There is no end to this jaded analysis and the blame extends like a bowstring, shoots hurried claims to the guiltiest.

Mercy is the key, yet it never really dawns on the user that we are prostitutes of Mercy; we vow in worship of its wisdom, and it rarely allows us to use it at its most effective glory. At best, when we employ mercy, all we really achieve is a momentary exhale at places in people's lives, we were never truly given safe passage.

We're invaders. Disruptors of their heavenly peace. The kidnappers of their humble hours; keeping them from established routines and familiar excursions. *Who are we but a questionable guest in their already quiet existence? Who are we to judge them for their lack of noise?* Quit telling yourself: "I am the song they must hear." When you're gone, be it, debris of your orchestra play at their most defeated moments, and your loss, strengthens them somehow.

Somehow, losing you is justified by God's alternative candidate for them to desire righteously. And you're left with only your marked graves, in the plow of your heart, and each day you water it with your sin, getting more sinister and recklessly amusing. The purity, and innocence you met in those who passed judgement on your deficiencies, left you with just a glimpse of purgatory; each as close to heaven or hell as it could get.

Gratitude still paints your lips when you call their name at daybreak or before you sleep and weep through dreamless hours, which you'd rather sacrifice in the name of this thing called *Love*. Yet, we must continue on, and proceed with this one, very, *very,* very long life, with or without some*body* to spotlight our loving awareness on.

All the misunderstandings serve a purpose. Trust in the void. Surrender to its divinity and unavoidable ques of harmonious interventions. All that jazz will inevitably happen with somebody else. Before we are shoved into the abyss of *regret*-fullness. Let us not make the moon worried and hide the bullets of our morbid gun and pray instead that the sun enters with suffocating sunlight to push us closer to the depths of *The End* zone. The heart's pursuit of elsewhere is pending. And the fragmented soul is awaiting further dismemberment. In the name of the hopeless, and the dead skies, and the hole on the ground specially made for us. *Ah, men…*

EXHIBIT

F

fantasy meatloaf
for
frugal lovebirds
and
prostitutes
of
destiny's hourglass
curves

the injured illustrations

My future belongs to you,
my darling.
Begin this new day with me.
Is that a smile I see?
Fresh thoughts emerge as I kiss your forehead.
Our past was wrecked by many resting places.
That's what we get,
befriending the void.
Trusting superior hands on the deck,
and its duplicates
and funny lines
to make us comply
to the injured illustrations.
Despite that fact, prepare to land on paradise.
We belong there, oftentimes.
Our eager impulses beg to differ.
Still, fresh thoughts emerged;
I undo the knots over her forehead.
She wore my kiss like a badge;
a power she believes herself to own,
exclusively.
Our story was kinder to the supporting leads.
I am perplexed by our mortal fable.
It's too good to be true.
Our story makes me truly happy.
Why do I feel this way?
Our voice speaks love from miles away.
Realizing *too late* that we're going the wrong way.
I was telling no lies in my prayers;
kneeling on salt
reciting our first introductions
verbatim.
Before my unruly mishaps,
I hold onto what's left of our

needlework.
I cherish this brand-new episode for what it is;
a transparent plagiarism not worth the roll of fabric.
Remember when you were there when things would go our way.
Our rerun of passionate plays could impregnate the stage with
maniacal applause.

Please,
hold on,
until we redefine what it means to be *okay*.
Fresh thoughts emerge as *you*
kiss my *fore*head.

laughter stun

Picture us with children; you as my wife.
Being lifted by the highest feelings;
bliss on a shot glass from heaven's gutter.
Hearing boisterous laughter stun
and create the aura legendary paintings are at the mercy of.
A love fully venerated, under our simple roof.
Nurturing our greatest achievements
and preparing them for the rest of the world.
These little hearts, bring bass and drum.
A whole new rhythm to our lives.
Every morning they'd resound
with secrets and dreams
they just had.
Be the kind brown eyes that feed the children's love and care.
Our incandescent moods
and trembling starlight blues
would concert our bedroom
each night.
While devilish remarks ignite from their nightlight;
some of their darkness won't let us through.
Our aged hearts were jealous of their infantile despair.
The neighborhoods envy our exhibitions of total chaos.
Our tenacious teamwork
and capable hands
gave them pause.
We'd endure the acres of embers they ministered,
and we proceed in carrying this cross.
On cold nights,
a bed for two
becomes a community;
a shared cloud of
phantasm.
Our connected thread evolves
into a powerful and indestructible seam;

impartial to the misalignment of our journey.
The sudden breeze with the flashing lights came to take back what
was never ours.
A past
demanding too little
and too
much.
Our misunderstood time,
sheltered passion only parents could allow themselves
to be wounded by.

Alone, I view the photographs of what became of everybody else.

in awe on the streets of her natural authority

Our garden would be an arrangement of origami feathers.
Willow flakes of golden confetti and rare flowers,
enduring years of infinite beauty.
We're immune to the fragments of change;
everything about us is in near-perfect harmony.
Our frozen river is buried in carpets of fresh snow
and shimmering limestones.
We'd carve angels with our bodies that'll be immune from
tomorrow's sunlight.
We'd endure a summer of blistering woes until a deer from the
woods came along.
An affair with a counterfeit faith ensues.
She followed me upstream and trusted my waterfall,
into the depths you're too frightened to explore.
The gentle innocence on a playground took me back,
many falls.
"I'll push you on the swing sets;
I'll chase you around.
We'll play hide and seek for hours;
always to be found.
The seasons would change,
but, what is now
can be forever
ours,"
she'd say, as I patch the wound of our love's innocent capture.
I don't need to live a million years
or ever fall in love again.
Yet, she's stilled by second guesses.
I saw her residues imprinted in mountains of amazing discoveries.
Months being in her woods left my soul breathless
and in awe on the streets of her natural authority.
Death takes away what it's meant to get.
Heaven is now, we can levitate.
Don't label me ignorant, I admit,

there is a chance you don't feel the same.
Babe, lean closer as we both bite our tongues another day.
Confess with pride and leisurely vow to the trance available.
Let your heartbeat get away for once.
When it BEGINS, a long-awaited passion commits a faceless act.
As patient as the afternoon sky with pathways missing,
and scattered like feathers of a bird run-over by big wheels.
Our white ashes are guided through a silver lining;
where we met on cloud nine,
greeted by falling stars until the earliest glint of sunrise.
This being the first of many wonderful days waking up in ultimate rapture.

May our passion be rhapsodized till the end of the millennium.

lovingly given the death penalty

Pale snow falls endlessly from the open windows.
You've left tracks on the carpet of clouds.
Where are you going without me, now?
The snow continues to fall endlessly.
Her heart remains cold in the rime.
The fire of my life is melting under the neon lights.
I've lost count of the outstanding smoke.
I ran out on the carpet of snow to invite her back inside.
Don't go any further, *aren't you tired?*
Come back here,
before I expire.
Please, come back!
I made a fresh tray of burnt cookies.
Sparks ignite in the dying hearth.
We reminisce on the very first time we've met.
The fireflies we caught, has been dead in the jar, awhile.
You tossed more wood to burn.
I witness you deny what's been listlessly learned.
When will we burn like a house on fire?
Let's make it a casket for two.
My yearning for love's resuscitation wanes impatiently because of you.
You've shut the lid,
selfishly on a dying truth.
The roaring of your car threatens the mood inside my skull.
There's nowhere to go, my snow demon.
I am wondering *who* you're headed to at three A.M.
Why are you in mourning?
What are you going to do with those matches?
Will you return tomorrow afternoon, a frosted corpse on the front lawn?
Don't come back home;
it's a shame, the cost and expenses for a tomb.
I regret nothing of what I said to you!
Maybe, we should part ways.
You're always onto something life-altering.

She lies outside on a carpet of my ashes;
eternally dancing in hellfire;
it was her absolute dream, absolutely!
I am dying of laughter in the purgatory.
Don't wait up for me!
I am shouting to nobody.
Come, it's nice here, another voice said convincingly.
We'll look the devil in its smallest eye and be lovingly given the death penalty.

"I am dying for her to still choose me," my eyes would say with a subtle lisp.
Crimson snow falls endlessly…

for these jaded delegates

You bring a cold chill wherever you go.
I want to tell you that the only joy that I felt are when you're insane.
It's just something I've noticed over many fallen years.
It's horrible.
I let myself live through your obstacle of empty empathies.
But I surrendered fully,
consider me ashamed
and *I wonder deeply about the final heartbeat*
and when it will come to me.
I start to palpitate.
Let the sunset make you miss me for a second,
maybe?
You're impossible at conversations;
saying my efforts were unreliable.
Our future is in death row, *for sure.*
The roses didn't bloom.
You've murdered them by their stem and roots.
Our future remains dimly obscured.
The headless roses won't smell of the heaven we used to know.
You called for the curtains to come down,
to a show barely over.
Let our current scene live on.
Let it go on beyond what is foretold
by the fortune-teller's *magic-eight-ball.*
That's the only way for closure to be found.
Accept it for whatever form it takes.
Fake a cry for whosever heart may break.
It only cost ten bucks for these jaded delegates.
I am screaming with the choir of unfeeling clones.
The crickets matched our meaningless singing.
I wonder deeply about the final heartbeat and when it will come to you.
Our skinny truths tumble over thick lies.
The final act did not bring in much donations.

At night,
we reason with the blades
we're great friends with
and commit to something abstract.
We'd shelter ourselves in a cave of regrets.
Everything is dealt with, just as the sunset melts.
The final rays of violet, left vibrant shadows on our short life.
Killing doubts have always been an inside job.
Let's dance away the rage and dash through the plexiglass.
Our red velvet closure remains obscured by the taxidermy of our abused roses.

Love won't smell of the heaven we used to know.

a year-long nap

Stink-eyes and recycled loveless smiles.
Silence is replaced by hellos' and goodbyes'.
I wonder if it's too late for me to ask for your number?
In my one lucky day.
I had fun being someone else; provoking my fast decay.
My breath on your cheek wakes you up from a year-long nap.
You lean upon my shoulder and tell me all about the summer you had with this guy.
Apparently, I couldn't love you correctly.
Is there a formula in keeping you tuned in?
Flowers are replaced by your scented foolishness.
Laughter is replaced by howls at dusk;
waking up the sleeping neighborhood in sweats.
I wonder if it's too late to just give up now?
I was awoken by a horrifying sound on a Wednesday evening.
A bullet kissed you on my side of the bed;
you just laid there,
spilling over the bedclothes
you prepared for me.
I wonder where you've gone off to without my supervision and unfair judgements.
I should've just let you be a random stranger.
Was it too late now to just give up?
You should've waited for me to come home first to save us both
a terrific mess;
a terrific miscommunication error.
Should we just have remained transitory friends
and *be just another wave hello that made you smile?*
This was the very essence of who we are.
Untethered.
A beautifying moment of clarity killed my dearly beloved soul.
Completely detached even from the closest skin-stitched fabrics.
We're sown forever.
Her breath is destroyed as it met my lips.

Our worlds collide for a finale.
I forgive all about the summer she had with that guy.
This person that loved her in every way I couldn't.
This dusty romance is destined to feed the flames as warning for all ages.
Infatuation gone disastrously mad.
Youths will be edified by their fondest advents in the throes of lust.
They'll let desire break their necks a hundred times over, for a hundred burning towers.
Playing brave because of a false sense of control
and setting their jowls on fire in the nearest confessionals.

And won't know of their insignificance
in an authorless tale of make-believe.

a little part of your soul you're fine without

It's hard to describe what it feels like to turn your head back
and see who made the climb,
and find out:
"Who fell to their deaths and died
to be forgotten plans;
to be completely anonymous
in time."
It's easy to paint a picture with your mind devoid of any reason.
It's easy to fire a gun,
but the actual search
for the courage
and the bullets
to move forward with it,
takes
will,
effort
and time,
and a little part of your soul
you're fine without.
It's painful to smile at false results.
There's no end to problems instigated by malnourished demons.
Words can be just wind passing by your winter grin.
Through the known silence,
words will send a beam that'll extend over the darkest of your dates.
A golden sun to accompany us,
when we're ready to part with every single word that was said.
Amnesia kicks in.
I repeat the same lines at your deathbed.
Pack away your worst memories in a suitcase colored black;
its zipper and lock cannot safeguard what's inside.
I'll hear your music in the densest of winter;
digesting every electric fiber of it.
The tameless hiss of a lion snake,
claws its way discretely.

Will it to kill and live with your mediocrity.
Don't carry unnecessary objects.
Keeping love locked away.
Are you locked away yourself?

Have nothing come knocking at your door.
Leave it open
wider,
wider,
or don't have one at all.

her house

Yawn in the break of morning.
The window was open during the nightly rains.
I am hit by an idea as I open my eyes
and learned that you've inherited my dreams.
I remember it all, yet, I don't know why.
She appeared by my window, waving in greeting.
Her hair is a mess of tangled wheat curls.
I blinked fast to dispense of unwarranted tears.
She ran the back of her hand through my cheeks,
beside me,
she'd lay.
I woke up a second time today.
My feet escaped my ivory blankets.
There was an indifferent chill that night.
I felt it victimize my left toe.
My mind took me to odd places.
I don't know why she's not here with me exchanging wonderful gazes.
I glimpse her fears
when I disappear
in an alcoholic trance.
Occupying the bed alone,
embracing her pillow
with the intention to suffocate.
I lift my head off her side;
she was always territorial.
The furniture's shadow, startled me.
I sleep in the dark areas dawn illuminates
with a shaking notice,
as I embrace the spot
where her body died.
I feel empty, every night since.
I am all alone in her house,
craving old habitual sins,
I thought were obsolete.

I fought her stubborn demons,
talking serenely over my prayers.
They'd marinate my madness many days thick,
frozen in the freezer of years.
Under the mattress,
I found the dulled knife.
I am jolted with acid sweats and paralyzing terrors;
overly distressed,
I fall prey to depression.
It is hot in here and darkness only made me weaker at the knees.
It'd take a few pills to get me standing and gain back my seven senses.
In the afterlife, she holds my sanity hostage.
The blood splatters we're fluorescent.
All I'm asking for is your humble truth.
All I'm asking for is your soul to wake up unmute.
Am I asking for too much?
I gave it all to you.
I offered my pretty years to you.
She appeared by my window,
waving goodbye.
Her hair,
this time,
is nice,
cathartic.
She'll shine
and would be glittering
in the spaces the moonlight
wouldn't permit.
The sun was elevated
that morning.
Oh, how beautiful it was to see her smiling
with a revered shade of red,
her danger could bring to contest with in bed.
Holy words she sang inspired relief,
flooded the sheets with seed-sized droplets.

I open my eyes to an orgy of wild instrumentals
beyond the scratched window; half-open;
stuck there.
I felt cheated,
with cheap lines thought up
in the morning's dying processions.

Beside her
I'd lay silent
and empty.

She closed her eyes
and slept
another
day a*way*.

my discharged muse

I ran out of oil for the gears in my brain.
Lord, fill my soul with more tormented energy.
I feel inadequately insane due to the scarcity of emotional turmoil.
She sold the parts of me I wanted to keep and have depressed my OFF button.
Her mortality puts me to sleep.
Despite the upgrades,
she helped me attain;
this stain in my heart corrupted my microchip.
She holds the one, dented key.
I wait for my return to consciousness so I can print a copy.
I would program a newer version of me.
I am running out of color.
The metal is turned on by the rust she rubs off.
She fills my head with crude notions.
I never get a say.
I won't allow her to alter my purpose.
She sold the parts that mattered most.
Somebody else fell victim to my discharged muse.
An unfamiliar hand, pressed my restart button and left me alone.
I desire to know who it was,
that resurrected me.
Out of the blue,
I lose who I am.
I fill my head with her foreign antidote.
I devote my brand new life to her.
She has laughed with me about my previous controllers.
She points out that,
I look back too much at my prototype.
She'd press the ON button gently,
she's my soul medicine.
Once again,
she lets me be.
Despite the upgrades,

many helped me attain,
this stain in my heart
destroyed my microchip.
She holds the key to my early return.

For her,
*sole*ly,
is the better version of me
moving for*ward*.

the person you'll be*come because* of my break*down*

Hear one last thing,
before I beg for mermaid fins
and beg to be cradled
by velvet
waves.
I kneel before your stuttering arms.
Praised your loaded gun.
Keep your voice down!
Stop forcing me to calm!
She begs for more hearsay,
I cannot provide.
We maintain the deathly stillness,
in the deepening
seconds.
Talk, or you're dead!
She begs for laser truce.
Heard me weeping,
yelling inaudibly
for help.
I could survive one more of our heartless day.
That's when you've caught me peeking
through the rabbit hole of your loaded gun.
"I just want you to feel safe," you said.
Patiently,
I await the ascension of the person
you'll be*come* be*cause* of my break*down*.
The gun detracts from my temple.
Hear my convincing lie;
that *everything*
about *everything*
is fine.

I let you down,
easy,
with a hard-edged
smile.
You'd congratulate
my brand-new
lover.
You want her voice heard
behind our clutter.
She pulls the gun on *you*.
Keep your *voice* down,
stop forcing her to calm.

Now you beg for *my* mercy!

in silver cuffs

We're looking for that ephemeral window
that opens back to tomorrow.
Yesterday's words were painted purple,
bruised by your arrogance;
shattered confidences,
spirits passing soundlessly.
Our book was destined with missing pages.
My mind stayed awake,
driving through the distortions of the city.
I have friends under the oakwood bridge.
Their bedlam sensibilities never fail
to clarify the wounds of today.
A millionaire drowned in his loneliness,
nearby a memorial went up in flames,
smelling of hundred dollar bills;
his wounded soul was the perfect lemonade.
Gun-wielding children lucked out
with century-long time outs.
The corner of my lips is in memoriam of their karma.
I miss tasting such dominating power.
It healed my bruised arrogance.
Then, my confidences were caught in silver cuffs.
They'd begin cursing in cursive
at the accusations the uniformed officers conjured up.
The luxury of the past won't last.
The future is on you,
greenlight every unlawful happenstance.
They're all in some dreaded waiting room,
waiting to escape the cosmic embryo.
Tracking you with the help of accurately placed charming neon
arrows.
The bridge is obliterated,
and the ebbing frost violates the water's moving graves.
The opening dawn warms their eternal midnights.

The towers built in their memory ages with respect,
on park benches and magnificent trees.
I stand guard.
My efforts in saving them are forgiven by the harsh currents,
consumed by summertime's somber assailants.
They fall from the highest branch;
falling on the avenues of a busy cement path.
The death of a moonless hue transform the *death* of you.
New terrors await the bootstraps of a flickering body.
Longing for a fresh set of friends to change their ways.

How do you justify the wounds that stay?

EXHIBIT

G

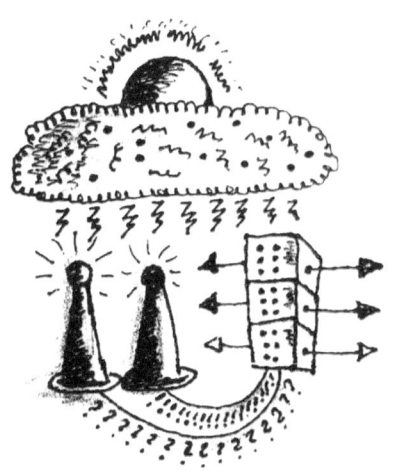

game of lies
set for the future
and
detours
endured with
maximum excitement

I broke my nose on the pavement wall

What are you up to standing alone in that corner?
Are you having visions of battles fought without armor?
Have you had your shot of closure?
Could you please close the window.
There is a storm out.
I cannot take this any longer!
"You must know, I hate that you're the only one that I need."
Time is not of the essence here my darling;
you are filled by dread,
could I take a look?
We need to find some hope or we will crumble,
even as we get buried alive by the world.
What are you up to keeping to yourself?
Are you seeking somewhere to hide your blood-stained gloves?
Are you having visions of battles fought with unconscious anger?
Have you ever had a friend?
I cannot take this any longer!
"Must you be the only one I desire with such compassionate heed?"
Look at us in the mirror.
I don't care if you heard all this before.
"Stare at your reflection as if it were an open door."
Come and enter, you deserve it,
feel the vibrato of release.
Come and enter,
don't conceal me.
Listen for the sirens drawing near.
You can always find a friend in them.
Deny what the enemy says.
Find what you need and *just* take it!
Leave me out of it, please.
You're speaking false murder through your perfect teeth.
I am deceived by your wireless halo,
I stumble after a somersault,
I broke my nose on the pavement wall.

In the waiting room,
I put on a brave face;
drinking my fill of cheap coffee on a paper cup.

The news channels were on *mute*.
The televised mass had fireworks.

its fondest fascination

I was free to commit a felony;
heeded my temptations to kill,
I am not the only one with a taste for blood.

You are forgetting the most important piece;
you are alarming yourself.

Let's rest for a while,
we're struggling to chase the autumn breeze.

Your cold heart,
I praised so fondly,
like a fresh scar.

I am over the moon for you tonight.
I am over the moon for your light.

Your light became,
my eyes.

Your light became,
my solitude.

The darkness tonight is spellbinding;
the darkness presents us with UFO sightings;
we're its fondest fascination.

I know how much it kills us;
the unfounded joy in our surviving sins.

We're struggling to chase the frozen seas;
I am over your ranging waves.

Washed ashore are hundreds of birds;
get the tiny shovel.

Good for nothing
worm!

hurtful momentums foaming at the mouth

The ground vibrates between us.
It is exhilarating!
This feeling of kindness and madness at the same time.
This fading view of blue skies
are riddled by road signs
and burning trees.
While we're sitting ducks;
the clouds pellet.
We attend mass on the rooftops.
Our ghost severs the vows of newlyweds.
We haunt empty pews,
stamp our hopeless names,
and inane gospels on them.
Now, is reserved for everyone else.
In love
with the debris of fresh daisies
and torn entries in their diaries.
I remember myself passing slowly.
I am rowing calmly through our calamities.
I am staring with caution at the tiny islands to our right and to our left.
Now we're ashes on these flowers;
smelling of manure.
The towers we stood on,
chants with glorious gratitude.
We had an eagle's view of everything,
as it collapsed into nothing.
It just fascinates me how deep the hole was that HE dug for us.
There's no doubt we'd be buried
with our hurtful momentums
foaming at the mouth.
An old radio sits on the precipice.
Our most dreadful songs are on replay.
Sorrow is stationed in our heart's *static* quo.
I am promising aromatic harm.

In the purgatory, we play out the bridge and exhaust the chorus till our ears bleed internally.
Stop passing slowly, stay!
Stray beyond the picket fences of heaven.
I'll distract them at the gates!
I invite your curious heart to what this could still be.
I place my demons on a leash so you could come murder me.
The day begins with a genius homicide.
A heartless matter, gave a tremendous sigh.
How many times can I add "heart" in a life sentence?
Rain with bad English.
Eden grades the dispirited with a blue pen.

what *we* thought *we* knew

I plead for forgiveness,
I broke you.
We can't help but cater to dreams that are too far annulled.
We fooled around with the obscenity of lost time.
Let's filter out, what *we* thought *we* knew;
I've figured it out too late.
In the spinning currents,
I am expecting to fall deeper into you.
I fall forward,
calling out with apologies.
I broke you!
We can't help but cater to moments that are beyond unapologetic.
We lost big time!
We need to get more comfortable losing things.
What would we do if we have everything?
Then we won't need ribbon-bound,
sublime states.
We've been filtered out.
We thought *we* knew us.
We keep on coming back to this.
Spinning round and round,
like a *run*away
homeless
mis-
sile.

my first true downfall was somewhat sincere

Look through love's microscope.
Let go of frigid hope, say: *"I don't care anymore."*
Whisper prayers on bended knees
and tell the choir to sing it,
refrain from steep re*frains*.
Let my sin echo through the chapel halls.
Cease the children skipping rope.
Ban the sketching of wonderful songs on the dusty blackboards.
Raw sun,
next to a frosted moon,
above a happy future.
In a mental institution,
a case of the blues helps
a thriving revolution of overthinkers;
looking for the trendiest resolution.
Is to get mixed up with the fallen one our yellow brick road?
Write a letter with my impure blood
on a naked white paper,
rip it in half,
and do it some more,
until it's the mere size of our circling eyes.
Let the jaded breeze take it.
You've caught us skipping along the glorious rain.
Through our transcendent paranoia,
we're caught in the spell of the cello's strings.
Our blankets are levitating like a new ghost;
in a brisk charge like a shot boar.
Your spirit needs another host.
I get that.
But my body is too weak to keep you.
It's predisposed,
full of hatred for dreams
I wrote concerning you.
You wouldn't want any part in the scenes

I killed.
The pool of irony,
I want to return to.
There are holes in my mind;
it is permanently closed.
You can rent smiles; or
my grandfather's guitar,
picking up the A.M. stations
with its butterfly antennae.
We met at every cafe bar,
danced in every opaque background,
colored with desolate peace.
Until it's time for you to leave.
I am sitting on my own,
shots galore,
I hit the floor
just as the final soul heaved its last cocktail
on the toilet bowl.
My first true downfall was somewhat sincere,
to say the least.

I couldn't really ask for anything more.
Define *faith*
for me
my
whore.

in favor of those lost dogs

Keep your head high.
The shining stars quit dancing,
they completely went dark.
Run your mouth again,
let newer words fight.
Here's your final chance to kill the past.
Make new memories
run more miles
on the treadmill of life.
I died and went back a dozen levels.
I demand meaningful connections!
I didn't order a side of chaos.
I am led by misguided sunset-ends,
air-brushing burning diamonds
on my eyeglasses.
My luck has faded.
I return to nothing,
as nothing.
While the family table misses the thrill of being shaken.
The hunger for truth arises;
yet all the evening produced
were pre-emptied lovebirds.
I am full and sick;
coughing up
pea-
cock
feathers.
I am ashamed of my winning streak.
You asked for this!
Your mind has closed completely.
Our nights are spent counting
all the dead friends,
we've made.
We asked our bravest emotions to get in

a single pile,
arms up,
with backs to the brick wall.
They're living out a universal vow;
this concept of *now*.
Old remedies work again.
The treadmill of life is led by misguided crowds.
The sunlight wakes the world to riskier opportunities,
in favor of those lost dogs
without a firearm
or butcher's twine
to re-invent the skies.
Time is passing by,
running faster through flesh.
Change grabs control
and it's not letting go *any*time soon.
Questions run on the world's
one-way,
half-way
track.
Answers eat the soul
and c*hews*,
and c*hews*,
but doesn't
s*wallow*.
Time is not *your* friend,
it's as simple as that.
It keeps us on a leash made of ancestral sinew.
Repetitious lessons teach us to love
dead-*ends*,
expect
dived-ends.
Your luck procures nothing,
unfortunately.
The family table is meant to be shaken.
We're tearing up with the effort of a nominated actress.

We are full of self-diagnosed sickness!
You're in l*uck*,
you'll be *in love*
with this n*ew*-l*eak*.
YOU asked for this new information!
But your mind is closed.
"Come again soon."
My head nods,
and falls clean-OFF.

I expected you to be completely unreach-
able!

their high functioning anxiety

Friend or foe, there exist nobody like you;
I haven't met your species before.
You're just another firestorm
I must be keeping away from you.
What's been stored away for someday
will disintegrate the trust we pressured
into remaining strong for us,
in spite of us.
Win or a loss,
we're still stuck
in a pit of animal bones.
Love is a failed attempt at security.
We cannot brainstorm our way from normality's centaurs.
Only those eaten whole
by their high functioning anxiety,
deserves to settle down,
with their remaining ligaments intact,
invested in their individuated,
divine context.
Every nibble of life is insanity.
When will God, any God help us breathe again?
A mission-statement leads to meaningless art.
The Lord refused to frame that.
My energy is molested by the advantageous scenery.
Our unspoken lullaby sings to a passerby,
giving you another dead eye.
Can we frame that?
Your words are falling from the skies of abnormality.
We just love believing
in a community of insignificance,
to save you
and catch you
falling backwards;
dreaming of better schematics.

Plant bombardments under those seated in the safe-zone,
ready to applaud your pitiful landing;
your pain is far from their understanding.
An unwanted emotion takes over
like sudden grey clouds
in a summer picture.
The sun resembles your blurry future.
Will it come back brighter or filtered?
Dig your teeth into something sweet;
the uncompromising,
the diabolical,
the diabetic fangs of faith.
Cavities abide you for many slow weeks;
it killed your senses with every deadly seethe.
You'd peak.
Allowed your tongue to regret your sirens of, *are we there yet?*
The stronger the questions are,
the more cinematic the chase.
Behind closed doors you'd grin.
"It's all for a pathetic chance to wallow in it."
The angel assigned to your passionless case,
shakes its marbled head,
violently disapproving;
the golden strands of its hair
was emasculated,
gradually bronzed.
It drank a half-glass of thunder
and the finality of a flightless hawk,
in mourning of the strands
that suicide.
Anywhere,
other than
where you are,
exist cleaner oxygen.
The angels fly from café to café.

Psalms starts slipping on the final raindrops
spilled by soft
feminine
air.

devoted to haunted sighs

I am *yours* at the deadliest hour of the night.
Steady now,
kiss the chiming light.
Send the melting doves home.
I am keeping note of why you are insane;
for days it seems
the answers remain
the same.
Come home, come home.
The world is in smokes and the seconds die suffering.
The silence crawls into the sacred spaces of our mind.
Teach me how to dance without legs that are afraid to
take me to you.
I've ignited a flame in the darkest of fights.
Steady now,
love gave to the two of us,
enough time to restructure.
I am keeping note of why you're to blame,
but for now,
let's keep wondering
where the better days
went.
Don't go, don't go.
It's rude to celebrate the defeat of someone
you've never met.
It's hard to realize the faults
in words that were never said.
She keeps me guessing;
I keep her guessing.
Come home!
She won't go.
Come home!
I am first to go.
Where the world is in ashes

and the seconds are devoted to haunted sighs,
and her silence crawls into the sacred spaces of my mind.
She taught me how to dance.

Still,
my legs are afraid
to be taken away,
far from
*her*e.

chaos of smiles and monster love

Explode in a pool of humor.
Let's rejoice in a sea of laughter.
This could be a community of memories
that arise,
that could please
the hollowest of souls.
This sore concept of forever
keeps the pool filled with gore.
Our holy saints ice the inner wounds
and warms the winter headaches.
Inspiring chaos of smiles and monster love.
You're but a puppet of your own demise.
You don't need to hear why,
grieving is a sin,
little one.
The brightest light in the house made the sun jealous.
Make me think of a lie.
Try, *try*, try.
Nothing matters,
anyhow.
Love's just a failure that works
and wins all the time,
despite the war
on unmentionable questions.
The rattling snake sheds its comforting prison garb.
I laugh myself to sleep,
every once and awhile.
I rely on denials to roll its eyes;
the vivid truth's
livid informant.
The sweetness of her intentions cave.
We shared Ethiopia to dying orphan kids.

Rolling in the dance floor
laughing with harsh facts,
glistening with imperial blood.
They're never coming back
from who they were.
In the middle of the cove,
they'd be praying out loud for assistance,
killing one another for an olive branch.
Terrifying instances cut through
my bulletproof jest.
What now?
Kill the reporter with a scythe.
At night,
the robbers of tiny hearts disrobe
underneath the hyperventilating glass-rays
of bet-rayed light.
These heinous thieves I talked about,
craves the heavenly berry;
and the *very* best
lunar attention.
I take the hour hand to a massacre.
The liars are cute,
they're staying
very,
very mute.
Thumbs up,
you've been great.
You've changed,
how I see change.
Your masquerade is peeling off
in the swing-sets.
The banana moon is shining
for the coastal shores,
longing for more mistakes.
They're waiting.

I long for more mistakes
you're mistaken
to make.

You're blameless as usual.

De-
parted.

make me feel useful doing useless things

Lucky number seven.
My voicemail celebrates;
cue inane trials.
Pitch a tent for five.
Pitch your least favorite intentions.
Pitch your least favorite smiles.
Let's secure a lifeline for these children acting out.
Stop at the count of four,
say *"I love you,"* some more.
I never knew it felt this good to say it!
I've never seen you give up before!
My muse is filtered through the thunderous applause.
I seek her seamless talent.
I seek her percussion tunes.
You'd find her riding a bike distracted,
wearing unfamiliar blue, mascara,
calling for a hero in the bushes.
I'll be trailing behind her,
enchanted by a bleeding wound;
many more to bloom before dinnertime.
Hail, hydrated hope!
Why is failure so thirsty?
Darling, give me a line or two
to make me feel useful
doing useless things.
Find me,
burning your letters
too close to a tree.
I hope it catches fire too!
The leaves turn to ashes;
their touch are softer than the sands on beaches.
I'll catch you on the midnight train.
I am a passenger on foot.
A bloody confetti begins to rain.

We suffocate their strange words.
You're stuck in the cave of my shoes.
There is plenty to do!
Learn from madness too!
Immunity is for inexperienced respirators.
One by one,
kill after kill,
widen this mass grave, as watching ghost outline the circumference.
Serene were their days and comfortable, their nights.
Rest easy little one,
goodnight!

deep mining auras

Pretty woman,
pretty men,
wearing the wrong pair of mood.
The blue mountaintops surrender
to their lifeless evening strolls.
I woke up from my naptime on the railroad tracks.
I've mistimed, our out of synced heart-attacks.
I am deep mining auras, truthfully.
I can't reach the glass shard on my spinal cord.
Mercy, pl*ease*, my beauty!
I am under arrest for arresting her innocuous years,
in the confines of my reptilian hands.
I mop up the night's excretions
and daily sunglasses manifestations.
Dullard jailbirds who knows
not to spoon-feed their worms.
I've shot two ponies wearing shorts,
too short for the public park;
I've snorted their powdered snow
once or twice.
In the fog a frog stole my wallet,
and turns my dreams into liquid glass
Lilly pads.
Those tile patterns in your bathroom wall tell a different story,
in broken Spanish.
I am trying to think of a lie,
rolling a die that always lands at one.

Six times wronged,
six times yours,
six lovers
= none.

in our unhappy jungle of a flame

You're already dead inside,
or *are you merely dying to understand?*
Which is it?
Does a definite answer exist to shed some pornographic light on this?
Lies, lies, life;
witness the murderer sigh
as *it* pleads guilty
for once.
Tangible thoughts died just in time.
You're corrupted by another system upgrade;
by another cheap application;
belittled by insidious parallels.
You're saved,
now fall like raindrops on my grave.
You're saved,
now call all sunflowers to misbehave.
I've failed to fully capture our late-night charade.
Shame on you for waking up happier as if it were a contest.
I protest.
You didn't have to wrinkle my expensive dress.
I wanted it to smell like vomit and alcohol,
going into the next day.
With me, you're afraid.
Why is that?
Hurry now,
I made some food downstairs.
Take notes of this
and print unlimited copies of it to the press.
Shake off the flea in our unhappy jungle of a flame,
and add extra bacon on your plate.
Focus on yourself!

In my art class today,
I hot glued angel feathers on a stick.
All I ask is you dust your head before my asthma kicks in.
Take care and good luck!

I hope to never acquaint
with your kind
a*gain*.

what a rush! us humans, *being*

His pork pie hat, dims
his rocket launcher stare.
Pretentious awareness,
get out of my way!
Her pink headband sweats,
gazing at the interracial lovers,
whose locked lips trip and slides,
as the train-tracks curbed.
We both wonder where their love will go if they stop looking
straight.
For a moment,
a wasp stung
our heartbeats.
I think I am capable of killing somebody?
I have this habit of peeling off dead skin;
letting my fingernails grow
so that I can peel nicotine patches
without the help of a stranger.
Do you shed a tear too at the sight of love set on a timer?
My empathy grew stronger with the willingness of the sun to
overstay its welcome.
Do our eyes disconnect from fear of connecting?
Our souls take a number.
Pull the plug on mine.
I ask myself a couple of times;
why, n*ow*, in this *lifetime?*
What a rush!
Us humans,
being.

In contrast to our inner wars.
Oh,
my apologies.
I be-
head another topic.
I prefer hanging my clothes outside than use a dryer.

The sun owns me
a fav*or*.

EXhibit

H

hello,
it's glee,
lacking
fullness
in the mass grave
of
slightly
happier scenes

sunshine's new will

Turn a page.
Be all alone.
Although you're feeling tired,
it's the first day of spring.
Enjoy what it brings to us.
The sunshine's new will is written;
believing you'll shed new light for greater things,
it swears you will.
Colors of different wear,
will explain themselves
gradually.
Forget ours,
forget me.
I'll always be
by your side;
don't doubt me.
See that the new day starts a nice way.
Your clear oasis hopes to inspire kinder things within me;
it swears you will.
Turn a page.
I'm reading our new chapter;
our imperfect cliffhanger.
Feel our flat landscape submit
to ambitious summits.
As the new season brings to us the finer things.
We'll take a hold of unfinished sentences
and treat our wordless expressions a nice way.
Different colors will be set off
by the horizon and the vertical observers.

Forget as if a dream
on the living room sofa
of an autumn afternoon.
I'll always be by your side.
My tongue-tied lips chant with lyrical caresses.

See that each new day burns passionately;
you
and
me.

the little details of our magnifying love

"Let this enlighten us and be our guide to pure ecstasy," I'd say to her.
We've never been pushed to the edge of our seats before.
I write to you now, on what I think of our last few months
and how we magically disappeared behind the clock's hands.
We performed a simple choreography through lenses of admiration;
knowing your steps as poorly as me.
I felt like this ever since we got here.
You're the center flower of my universe.
Your priceless divinity soothes my whiskey glass.
You're this immeasurable karmic gift.
You'll shorten my evenings.
I'll be in a rush to get back
to the next day to kiss you good morning.
You'll call me when it's my turn with the sunlight.
I am feeling choked up by the little details of our magnifying love.
God, link me with the best parts of her.
Feed my moonlight with lyrics that makes me think of her.
The rhythm of our future only makes me feel blue.
"Grow as a person, grow as a soul," I'd say to her.
I told her once in a turquoise mood,
no one speaks the truth like you.
You tell me to get off my knees,
to quit begging to be received in *full*,
to live days, weeks, months *apart* hitherto.
Under the covers on a cold night,
I am praying instead of giving into miserable sleep,
I look for clouds to send me nearest her sunshine bed.
Find me craving her loving aura across my table seat.
I *honor* her evanescent presence inside my heath
sheltering immortality in the smallest embers.
Not even death itself could put out our blue fire.
Lord, I am waiting for the tone to more unanswered questions.
The rhythm of our future only makes me bleed inside.
This time, I'll confront her serendipitous shade with glorified plans.

With one cup of red wine to my name,
I greeted shyly, the speechless girl in the wedding reception,
she'll be caught off guard by my adulation,
she'll disarm me just as fast;
she'll take her precious time, though.
I'll maintain a civil smile and a renewed gratitude.
Because of her, I am able to forgive all the trivialities of life.
Dear *oh* dear, *does this answer the tone of your unanswered questions?*

drawn a second sun

An overwhelming feeling
came over me
yesterday.
I long for privacy in my hero's cave.
In more serious ways;
I'm crashing like a jet on the sea.
How long till I reach the light I'm following?
Who put me on this path,
I don't understand,
I am in the dark,
always finding your hand.
Enduring nightmares
out of placement;
the thunder rings
to move us through
the tortured hues.
You're the hurricane that turns my life around.
You'll take me through the next day.
An inviting spirit hovers over me,
I am scared of finding angels of the past
in your library shelves.
Their voices are singing like suicidal waves.
How long till I reach your light?
I'm drawn a second sun.
There is nothing but darkness spoken for.
It's up to us to regather our power.
Live out our breathless motions.
I will find myself tomorrow;
I wish you'd understand.
How long till I reach the end?

I want to restart.
But, I am taunted
by my *ole* ways.

this last ounce of beautiful anger

It's been a while since
I felt this way;
it's too early to tell if something new is parking at bay.

Recollections I have tamed talks of lovers forever changed.

I burned your final letter in the fire,
each crippled word is forged
into my anonymous gravestone.

It's too cold, where I am now.

My lunacy is shifting shape and size.
I've been holding on without you?
It's been a while since
I met your solar delight.

It's too early to tell if a full moon would be
graciously met by the sound of a gun;
I've never redeemed myself of her broken trust,
a love shaken never really learned to stand.

The final moment you've spent with me left a mark,
every instructional rays hit me like a lightning bolt;
this last ounce of beautiful anger couldn't be tamed.

But, believe me as I kiss you
in between your d*ole*ful eyes;
my *yesterdays* with her
pales in comparison
to one masterful second
spent on
you.

love is passed around to be wronged

You don't know me,
but, I will soon be in your dreams;
these coincidences make me feel absent;
I can't have faith without seeing results.

I'll have a love affair with your killer smile;
you don't have my blood in your hands,
but you'll try and try until you do.

Relief is so fatal,
when I'm with you.

Tell me, *what is wrong with our world today?*
Love is passed around to mean nothing at all.
Tell me, *who are you to tell me it's my fault?*
Love is passed around to be wronged.

You don't know me,
but, I will soon relieve your pain.
These coincidences are fool's gold to the dismal brain;
I can't convince you to stand up for yourself.

You have me, even my shadow;
hiding under a heavy mattress;
sleep is our last resort.

Tell me, *what is wrong with our world today?*
Love is passed around to mean nothing at all.
Tell me, *who are you to tell me it's my fault?*
Love is passed around to be wronged.

the truth behind the smile in the petty pictures

As the silence takes over the night,
I let our surrendered hours replay in my mind.
I recall, I lost something of mine.
I am wishfully thinking,
I got you tied down.
I am recollecting the uncut version of the laugher that partakes in the visions we created.
I am rewriting the final version of the truth behind the smile in the petty pictures.

I leave it all behind.

As the silence takes hours to mend,
I let the voices conjure stupid lines.
I recall, I lost you in my cognitive mines.
Paranoia has me circling around like a vampire bat.
As the silence leads me nowhere.
I give you time to return from silver to gold.
I steal you away into a dreamy real-estate.
We would come back screaming.
I woke up first, *now,* it's your move.
You're recollecting the uncut version of the laugher that partakes in the visions we created.
You're rewriting the final version of the truth behind my smile in the torn pictures.

You leave it all behind.

the blistered climb

King of the unknown, *are you once again frozen to the bone?*
Misconstruction of the truth unravels the stitches.
We're losing touch of a plan set in stone.
I am guilty of locking eyes with a stranger.
Am I just an hour filled with wonder in the sky?
All the flowers are out of business tonight.
While the waves depart;
let's have our shadows
disappear just as supernaturally.
Am I just an hour of your day?
Queen of all fires,
are you once again a dying little spark?
Still and quiet,
how disciplined
you are.
Her eyelash swept the silence with disdainful overtones;
that's what I get for locking eyes with a stranger.
Am I the sunset?
Color of a flame?
Am I a sunrise?
Or an early grave?
If I am an hour in your day,
it's okay.
I never wanted to stay.
I've been too many people's unwelcomed guest.
But, she lasted a century in my radio-head.
You and me,
we're the whitest clouds
in the *eve* of our lovely days.
All the flowers lost its divinity.
Our bouquet of fights
emanated with heavy perfume
and rotted the lungs of creatures
brave enough to breathe in our secret.

Let's explore the outgoing waves
under the malignant dawn's unpredictable state
and follow our intertwined shadows
tangled in seaweeds of alabaster despair.
Am I just an hour filled with wonder in your sky?
All the flowers open for my eternity of women.
The shallows go uninhabited and palm leaves are plucked by
earthbound angels;
as if they were dust mites on a dandelion heart.
Darling, I repeat, *am I just an hour of your day?*
I'll make the blistered climb.
The coconut milk is extra.

raw and tender

I release you from my grip;
I did not care at all that you let me go.
On these lonely nights I stay strong;
my dreams give me fright.
But, I'm not sick of it, no, it's better this way;
still, I can't help but wonder.
As I awake from the jungle,
my visions they sparkle;
I am tumbling down,
down, down, down.
So far, your reasons are doubtful,
feelings are still tangled;
I am still tumbling down,
down, down, down.
I remain kind and hopeful.
I did not see at all,
that you're about to fall.
On these deadly nights,
I stay strong;
my will to survive goes on.
Lions are chasing after our meat,
raw and tender;
we're left here to die,
die, die, die.
Green grass is bitter and dirty,
it's better we leave here;
we're forgotten love,
love, love, love.
I guess, I am sick of you,
oh, it's worst if I stay;
still, I can't help but wonder.
As we awake from our jungle,
our visions they sparkle.

We're tumbling down,
down, down, down.
So far, our reasons are doubtful,
feelings forever tangled;
we're still tumbling down,
down,
down,
down.

no longer

From the one who sees you changing,
from the hand that you're holding onto,
from the pages that you're turning,
from our dying flame still burning.

Please come to realize that nothing is wrong with us.
Please come to realize that each day is ours to behold.
We are a better version of who we were days before.
Prepare to always be better.
Prepare exclusively for better days.

From the one smiling back at you,
from the one that embraces you whole,
from the book that you're writing,
from the special friend I am to you.

From the tallest mountain that you climbed,
from the pride that's within you,
from the eyes of an observer,
from your friend,
no longer…

From me, from the mess *you* created.
From me, from the mess *we* created.

Please come to realize that something is right with us.
Please come to realize that each day, I am yours to behold.
We could master this desolate road and be once more revered.

Prepare for a sunset gold.

Prepare for a moonlight grey.

My one and only,
stardust dream-state.

the whale's carcass is now vacant

I felt my luck today drown inside her orange river.
All my remaining goodness boast of decay.
Our moments tasted so vile like liquor from a newsstand.
In my world, in an hour,
our most humane kindness is built on failure.
You'll see me through the window.
You'll see me through the glass.
I am broken, because you've shot me down.
Fix me!
Fix me with your seductive dialogue.
Own every word that escapes your tongue,
a mean glass of champagne on a paper-cone cup.
Keep me away
from good doers
and polluters of games.
I felt my head aching
as it overflows
with succulent madness.
The whale's carcass is now vacant.
In my world,
in this minute,
my horrors are held firm
by cocktails of torpid laughter.
I once felt assured in the beginning;
always in the beginning.
But, I am a disgraced pawn
to certainty and guarantees
only evaporate with exuberance.
Permanence made its mark
on the Italian bedcovers and Pakistani rug.
We let all this sit comfortably well
and stamp our stillness with coerced purposefulness.
We turn awry for one night only out of the seven days.
In our world, in a second, our house creaks,

welcoming intruders from the city woods.
I see you through the window.
I see you through the glass.
Broken-up in tears, as I shoot you down.
Your eyes fucked me long enough!
You were beautiful, *like today*, today.
Beautiful, *as always*.
Beautiful, *like today*, today.
Beautiful.
What a beautiful day!

smoking the devil's joint

It may be,
that it's just you,
who *sees* it.
You own a mirror that never fails to deceive.
Keep on smiling,
brave star.
Keep on living
out your Maytime
rituals.
Keep on dying,
faster than me.
Your halo is out of battery.
Her light is sedated by my hurtful tone.
I was never her only lucky star.
She let me collect black mold.
I rather not judge how it got there.
It might be God's cruel joke or the devil's work.
It may only be you who hears the Banshees
or the holy flames popping.
Keep on talking.
Tomorrow is a dark mirror
of uncracked japes,
of seasonal drapes
boarded over
with sledgehammer
and six-inched-nails.
Look into the flames that are invisible to you;
while the noise becomes a distorted prayer.
If only you knew, we're everything alike.
Although, I died faster than you.

Your halo is attracting millions of horny cicadas.
Turn your light off.
It is not true love they're seeking.
How we got this far,
I rather not enforce a soluble remark.

It might be God's cruel joke or it was from smoking the devil's joint;
all night long,
babe.

the genocide of her finest starlight

Even demons know when they had enough.
Even Angels know what is good isn't always right for them.
A ray of their light wouldn't make it through
the genocide of her finest starlight.
She cannot be outshined;
she cannot be outdone.
Hurry onto the next one.
Here's a dream to beat the darkness with.
Sleep is swimming towards the deepest ocean
with residues of coke in its nostrils.
Hurry onto the next one.
Steal fruits from the sacred tree;
how dare you call me a bad seed.
Slow me down;
shake me off,
realign me
if you could.
Let my cancerous behavior teach you
how to be rightfully wrong.
Open up to the bleaker unknowns,
their signatures are more stylish;
the ink takes years to dry.
Hurry up, slow it down;
even the demons know
we've been too rough.
Hurry up, slow it down;
even the Angels fall
on their head
sometimes.
I am savoring her ray of light;
keep it out of the pastor's sight.
I am blinded in the process of loving you.

The open gown of a new dawn
flatters the early joggers.

It felt
ever so freaking good
to be there
with you!

on our white nights

Let me take a minute to press,
this pretty picture of you
on one side of my face.
I want to balance the pros and cons
of what I must do next.
You went the distance for me.
I was killed on the spot we met.
Now, that I am impossibly far,
I cannot get closer than I am able to.
I've broken down on my knees,
praying for more possibilities.
I am tortured by nightmares
dismembering my silent gestures
for you,
and about you.
The focus of today is remaining *okay*.
The voices in my head have a life of their own.
They cannot be put to rest, so easily.
Am I being put through a test?
Or am I just too far gone?
Am I remarkable in my own ways?
Or am I just playing dumb?
Let me take a second to pin this note
onto my forehead;
pass the hammer
please.
Dearie, I must never forget you.
I want to keep my heart busy.
Our loveless effort has gotten us feeling hazy, lately.
You took a shortcut
and denied me entrance
to your intersection;
a clear as day avoidance.
I've broken down each section of our map.

My feet has nothing to believe in,
or look forward to,
anymore.
Go ahead,
be yourself.
While my distress feeds your rest.
I'd still hunt and murder
every beast for you,
before it begins feeding
on our white nights.
My wicked nightmares,
salute you.
You will not live life with the emptiness,
I've known,
that's my solemn promise.
Turn the hourglass on its head;
I hear the sand echoing inside me,
as thankful as can be.
Give our path another look
before you go cross
another unfinished line.
I am reminded by dreamers like you
to not divert my heart too soon.
Our focus for today
is remaining lovingly woke.
Is our devotion being tested?
Is our love too far gone?

Well, aren't we
remarkable!

the winning alibi you'll need for the rest of your life

Kill me with your sharpest lines and corrupt my microchip;
I dare you to free me from my confines.
I'll be gone in the nick of time, she says.
She's an expert on orgasmic one-liners;
cheesy but tasting of sugary malevolence.
She offers real-estate for strong minds.
The energy from our last road trip
is brilliantly manifesting again.
The streetlights are blushing red.
I saw you through the tinted windows.
An old car-radio played *Tom Waits*
as we walked on a spiral staircase.
I went crazy for you.
We were both lyrically armed.
We constructed a path between:
"Doing alright" and *"Doing okay."*
Letting death comb our hair.
We'd extract the wisest snow-grass
and lay scatterbrained all night.
Who was I for you that day?
We turned the restaurant menus into paper boats.
Laughing breathlessly as my feelings flew
with the song playing above
our hostile clouds.
Who was I to you when we sang a sad break-up song?
Our voices were so devastatingly awful.
I would crack up in the middle of every syllable.
We had no choice but to drown the euphoria.
We limit our happiness to just half a song.
Your hair is choreographed by the breeze.
I stared at you,
shaken by the attempt
of a first
and last

kiss.
You were divine.
I remember the way you were traumatized
by how quickly I put out answers
to your untamed questions.
I planted the idea of an *us* early on;
my cards were translucent.
There was no apprehension
or a fragment of incredible shame
to divide us.
But, excuse me,
I have to get going;
get gone.
Emotional silence is my forte.
It is routine for her to be in disbelief of beautiful moments.
The idea of sweet sadness lingers on.
She came to terms with my spontaneous decision.
Pardon you.
But, I cannot hear your heartbeat.
May I call you sometimes, maybe to ask if your eyes are still wet from the moment I left?
You asked me to *"stay."*
I remain expired of your gaze.
"Thank you."
I mean it when I said:
"I love you."
In my childhood memories,
you were there,
I am sure of it!
Sorry, I never meant to impose on you such a false impression.
I live within my lonesome head as if it were a campsite for one.
Who am I but a mosquito bite.
Enough, I must be going now.
Cheers to your next awesome idea!
Make sure to always leave them with a smile,
as another soul volunteers to kill ya!

Manage mercifully,
those who love you back;
one might be the winning alibi
you'll need for the rest of your life.

I'll marry you in the nick of time, I've said.

EX<u>HIBIT</u>

I

indifferent motives
and
clarity
that
catches ridicule
of
the fiery
sort

the bones for a neat melody

Hear me out, please.

There's nothing to fear.
She wore a single tear
for years and years;
you won't feel good
leaving her now.

She has died in our sacred garden before;
I am ignorant of the meteor overhead.

We washed all our sins with angel tears
and lost it all to what our desire dreams.

I died, she was a real sensation;
my final joy
decays.

I washed all my problems away to her neat melody
and lost it all to what her desire dreams.
I hear her whisper, *"there's nothing broken here."*
She's great at making logic disappear.

We prey on Vultures-wings devouring blue dragons in the glaciers.
We prey on Eagle-wings and hypochondriac snakes beyond the sacred garden.
We traded all the bones for a neat melody
and lost it all to what our desire dreams;
lost it all to what desire
schemes.

the sound of our specific pain

We picked up the shattered glass on the floor;
held our breaths as we did so;
we said nothing the rest of the evening.
Let's not fight,
I am tired,
can we just sleep tonight?
You're always sad; a timeless brigade.
Our burning building depicts beauty beyond compare.
How we got here gives birth to obscure feelings.
It had me staring at my phone waiting for it to ring.
I'll be your broken compass;
I'll guide you softly off the ground.
The stars are no help,
I couldn't connect all the dots.
I am headed out!
You want it to be perfect,
we're already past that,
can't you see?
You admit to feeling useless,
but we're past that
too.
Come on, take a vow.
Come on, row with me.
I'll give you a head start.
I am in love with the sound of our specific pain.
We remain unnamed to the deities of friendship.

We're nothing but the pity
before the sound
of a fallen
airship.

let euthanasia occur

Cue the curtains, down,
brace for the final act.
We have horror, excitement,
and joy you'll surely regret.
As we push you off the edge,
brace for glorious impact.
Her joy will frighten you;
it's her horror show,
featuring her favorite freaks.
I dare you to walk the thin air, she'd command.
I dare you to sin tonight with the two-headed woman.
Nobody cares!
I had it with her fixed mental state.
I am a horse in terror
out in the cold chilled rain;
the swollen mountains wouldn't keep me.
Change game. Change faith.
Win or lose, it's all the same, the miracle would say.
Hope is a reckless dance for breaking of mannequin legs.
Let's pull the masks off and brush our teeth with moonlight.
I want what's underneath the breakthrough.
Just as I predict,
I fear her dead smile below ambivalent eyes.
My air balloon braces for an uncomfortable landing;
I flew barely half the length of the raw river.
Her savage impulses were unprepared for what's coming.
Oh, it's coming.
She's cursing in tongues.
The ice is stricken by her madness.
I did warn you.
She leads me back to our winter bed.
I told you, it's *coming*, oh, it's *coming*.
I had it with our fixed mental state!
Let euthanasia occur;

I've had enough of our chameleon behavior.
We live or die, nothing satisfies our soul.
God says,
go break
legs!

nothing could undo our cosmic noose

Poems have the saddest things to say…
Leave our monuments above the altitude of the skies;
nothing could undo our cosmic noose;
be the sublime image my dream captures.
The little manifestations of magic in
a lover's journey
soon to be lined with crime tape.
We lack the will and understanding to move forward
at the beginning.
It's just another ordinary day with decent stories,
followed by one cast of whispered sorry.
It's just a stranger without you in their minds.
A handful of sand tossed gently in our heart's eyes.
We're constantly desensitized; back to square one;
the drenched path now in ruins.
Where is that? Should I mind?
That amidst these awkward changes,
I just let *you* pass me by.
I am holding the guilt for two parties;
it's just me here,
to weight the damage,
the darkness,
the humorless
betrayal,
alone.

I voluntarily endure this degradation.
I present thee, another set of avoiding eyes.
Despair is uncomfortable to look at, *is it not?*
Live out this waking nightmare and leave little to no detail enhanced.
This blueprint of our finality, promises to be nothing more than
visually stunning.
Let's walk into a landscape of deader woods just to feel something.
There isn't any direction to follow;

my love isn't a trail to worship.
Death's single applause favors richness, listen and be a witness!
It could happen real fast, *real soon*.
I need this release, *don't you?*
I am this confused mime without trust and knowledge
in the premise of what a faker do.
I am immune to insanities blues.

I'm losing track of the important stuff

Let's allow
our feelings
to settle
down.

The pain,
I am holding back
makes me feel like I'm losing track
of the important stuff.

I will keep reminding you
that forever
is attainable.

What went on in your head?
Why did you disappear from our bed?

After what you've put me through,
I think I can go on without you.

You hear me say sorry
a billionth time;
for the billionth times,
I lied.

I take you as you are,
are you high?

Let's get higher
than
that!

rest your beautiful soul here

All we've built for the afternoon sun reaches out
with filthy
hands.
The lovers lost their grip
of a simple plan.
Rest your beautiful soul here,
on deathbeds,
laid row by row.
Do you care to admit what led to this?
Illusions become aware;
reality is here to stay.
Rest your beautiful soul here,
on deathbeds,
laid row by row.
All we become because of boredom,
leads to sunken boats.
The cloudless day reaches out to love's dying hope.
We lost our grip of a heart that misspoke.
We carry the night on our shoulders,
as the morning sets.

I feel our single star burn wild;
the bliss
sang
sadly.

under the paper-thin roof of a burning chapel

My hope is in pieces.
The dandelion has spread.
Keep us under the wings of a wanted bird,
shot in the head.
Kill every single flying dreamer in the sky.
Possess the fires that burn out.
Lonely nights keep haunting.
We're so far from knowing
what's meant to be.
Let's light those unheard sparks;
don't let them become lost dusty torches.
We're kept under the paper-thin roof of a burning chapel.
Ashes will fall.
The nuns will survive,
they must,
otherwise the priest will run out of script.
The fires that break mold keeps the haunting potent.
Now, it's getting dawn involved.
We recede from the gaze of the reaper's eye.
We ignite all our unspeakable desires,
tonight.

Just as we burn out,
Merci-*less*-ly!

laugh at our triumph

I am killed by a glimpse of fresh disregard;
estranged reflections exit from our strange mouths.

Hell is on the loose.

I look away from your stare,
I reach out to the time
I've killed without you there.

Nobody could prepare me for what's coming ahead;
I am a ghost in my inner town.

Now, notice the cracks of lightning this evening sounds;
I won't linger underneath it.

What's left of the morning sun?
Do you feel me now?

I'm halfway there,
I am halfway there!

Stop crying,
rejoice instead
for the remnants
that stay.

Let's get there entirely,
laugh at our triumph;
no more va*cant*
*sta*res.

I cannot help myself but weep in beds cold as ice

Isn't it brilliant?
Isn't it lovely?
That your emotions could blissfully run through me.
I have just one confession to clear up this confusion.
Love is both unique and unusual.
Who's to know love better than two lonely people?
Isn't it threatening us?
This fable of our motionless acts,
keeping what we want for the future days,
wondering which one of us will get the farthest
from where our destiny calls
and where our fantasy dies.
Isn't it great?
Isn't it more than special
that your presence in my life could remain
even when you're not physically around?
I have just one recollection for you to visualize.
Our life would benefit from what we have;
who's to know love better than you and me,
here tonight?
I cannot help myself but weep in beds cold as ice.
Where you are is where I'd rather be.
I'd fly a thousand miles;
across many lands,
across many seas.
I cannot help but wonder,
will you be at the other side?
I would wait for you many lifetimes;
across many souls,
across many hearts.
Isn't it threatening us?
This fable of our motionless acts.

Keeping what we want for the future days,
wondering which one of us will get the farthest
from where our destiny is calling us
and our fantasy believes in us.

It's un*usual* and in*tense,* my dar*ling,*
best we *let it be.*

I smile till my teeth rot as I am listening

I may have lost my head;
trapped in her everglades.
I've pinned myself onto a corner sharpening blades of contemporary lyrics
reduced to a song in the tune of *"I love you,"*
not just during the break of a new day,
but from the very last moment,
my lost eyes found yours.
Destiny changes its currents with no prior warnings;
collecting wonderful feelings that abide like moss.
I rather have us than a calm majestic island
full of soothing hummingbirds;
I rather hear the sound of love in your restless voice,
for*ever*more.
You're the heir to every cliché,
the seed of an honest mistake,
a deep sigh after a hopeful wish.
I'd give up the chance to travel the world
if it's not getting stupid high
and trading applause with you.
You spit such passionate embers;
the escapism I find in your letters.
My generous optimism for the unknown,
was your complete and utter doing.
My spirit knew your kind, the halo above your brow;
through your fiery green irises,
I experienced a sunset of colors refined.
They're much better than freshly baked delicacies;
what my eyes have seen so far,
felt like handshakes with new friends.
What is good must end in the cycle of days.
It is reborn.
It's previous spacesuit fully disintegrated;
reincarnate anew.

I'm listless of asking if we're okay,
I am a nodding pest, while you run laps explaining.
Elaborate if you may; I smile till my teeth rot as I am listening.
I am enticed by defeat.
As long as you're the one carrying the blade.
Only time will tell when it ENDS and if it'll be a bles*sing*.

Oh, love, was it ever misunderstood!

We're blessed by the immortal sun,
by recycled pains told by a brave one,
by the princesses on their brick castles.
Of gaps in time listening to the supporting cast;
basking in their empowering lines as prelude to the third act.
We will never be the happy silhouettes of normal people.
We parade in the glamourous costumes of the sub-normal.
Weekends are for ripping pages of our cheque-books.
The final mass is the only one worth attending,
shit-faced with a carcass of an abandoned dog right next to you.
Our lonesome mask is unveiled to the Lord for judgement.
We realize too late that untying the impossible won't do us any good.
Oh, love, was it ever misunderstood!
God knew it would.
Let's land somewhere we are happy to be lost,
hunted and made to feel worse about going on.
I wish it wasn't so.
Yet here we are.
Wildflowers growing at the center of a busy road;
making the impossible
its *ho*me.

A whore to the circumstances;
a faceless
g*host*.

plenty of dark spots in our white hell

I felt irresponsible.
Yet, it's thrilling to be in your head.
You're despicable!
Yelp the seed that pleads release from its tiny grave.
Come along,
come along
and paint my world
into a burning forest
of mundane words.
Steal away,
steal away,
there are plenty of them
out t*here*
to blindly choose from.
Wait till I,
wait till I,
fix what I let go.
I fill tomorrow's ground,
with forward motions,
I am a seeker of the unknown.
I felt emotionally dislodged.
You're dealing with anger,
I ran the numbers,
and found a code.
The murder is set in progress;
look at me,
I'll gladly set
the tone.
That being said,
block the light from your eyes,
thrive on the darkness, babe.

There are plenty of dark spots in our white hell,
on a sunny day such as these.
Wait till I ignite with sighs.
I'll freeze in the cold hard ground.
Never to fix what I restored.
Till tomorrow,
I'll be singing of wars.
I seek to be a well-known survivor.

censor train doors from speaking

No,
wait,
stay,
I like your company.
Keep me safe;
color all over me;
permission granted to speak ill to me,
add more bulletproof symptoms to this polo shirt
I am swearing.
No wait,
listen till I've engraved
total misunderstanding.
Keep our symphony of dropout souls
scratching;
wanted for dancing too carelessly
on the dance floor at *Prohibition.*
No wait,
never mind,
to what I've said
and to what I'd done.
Sprinkle my ashes on dandelion season;
censor train doors from speaking.
No honey,
everything's not okay.
I told the mailman our mailbox
is the chimney.
Step on your cigarette
it's still burning;
my heartbeat always sleeps
without warning.

You're another memory;
to happen now
and then again,
I let you
evaporate,
dancing
to my
terrible
tune.

notes most contorted

Settle on that riff, darling,
neutralize our auto-tuned heads.

Select the notes most contorted;
we've got such a unique taste!

Imagine that!

A gift that tries to take us distances
from w*here*
we are,
a sound resurrecting
potential white cells
for our brain-
dead
love.

A Buttonless Robe

I witness a cigarette end dry out on the snow making a certain sense lack in need. Her footpaths on the plow made a new tree escape from heaven's limb. Mud on wheel flaps circulates the healing, as my eyes shy down from her observance of my vulnerability. Abiding by contracts we assume on the page's dimensions, our ultimate obligations to fine prints and blood inked signatures.

Her desirable heart, she'll run away from, while I spark and gamble with *Dylan's* words. A red button fell off her robe and all I could do was stall. I am gazing out the frost outside where stars are invisibly burning brackets; courting the unseen scars of her evening thoughts.

The moonlight laughed us into shape and turned our love blue at the gate. The night gave the rest of her buttons a tear. We felt safe and warm from lands unresolved. Inch by inch a stranger to the idea of wearing clothes. Our unfailing persistence keeps the dawn sublime. My lady is on fire leaving a trail of white lines. She'd left flowers on the gravestones of lovers I left behind, and she's fine just watching their ashes falling in delicate strands; gathering tiny mountains on her *once soaked palms.*

EXHIBIT

J

jousting
with
faith's
reflective dunes
inside eyes
terrified
of
love's continuance

they slept the loudest

She fought bravely and came to your rescue;
she fought the noble way.
I felt her victory burn
and melt the chalice
on my crass hand.
She fought for a better ending for us.
From the heavens,
she did
ascend.
We are hailed from the pilgrims of morning, she said.
The sunset deeply scars.
We are not properly put together;
continuously, we're torn by the stillness.
I just can't help but cower under mortality's false care.
I am pushed to accept a desperate plea;
be counseled by despair and convert it to repair misdeeds.
I've lost count of her white hair;
there's too many trigger warnings,
brooding and shameless.
May fires enhanced the scenery.
The feathers found sanctuary on our glowing harvest moon.
The lingering smoke,
letters.
The bewitched are loneliest,
knowing they slept the loudest.
The resoluteness on her fair skin resembles a heart emblem.
Let the sparks fly all queenly.
Let her slit the throat of another peasant;
wearing a pleasant countenance,
as she slices the throbbing sun
in asymmetrical patterns.
She fought bravely.

It is written on a scroll
made from the great hues found
in the buddha's enlightened shade.
Blessed only by the blackest ink;
Hades bled into our cup
as offe*ring*.

welcome to the madness!

I suffocate in your embrace.
How will we medicate ourselves through this?
This is the light that will expose us.
Let's save each other from the flaming stones of paranoiac states.
We deserve to be found.
This is the hurt *you* need;
this is the new dawn *you* must face;
tomorrow *you* say goodbye to the madness.
I obligate *you* to end me!
We can't live a life of failure anymore.
Our energy is fatally drained;
we need our batteries changed.
Till we're once again,
filled with notions
waiting to be ignored
or digested.
One of us,
is full again of things
to undo.
This was the way we said goodbye.
Madness is this brilliant lightning strike
that only comes a few times in life.
The turbulent grey waters of the full moon signed a contract
to the killing of smiles between our two oceans.

We're living through
sinking
truths.

We must be happily
letting this
drown.

This is the hurt *we* need;
this is the new dawn
we must face;
tomorrow we say
welcome
to the madness!

bleeding under the elephant clouds

This kind affair is spoken for.
Our green scenery is covered by freezing rain;
we grow as tall as giants;
The mountains better crumble against our will.
Heaven has called saying your moment is coming!
Be my sin.
Portray no weakness;
I need your most humble laughter as counter attack
for this incoming stretch of damnation.
Process our love,
be unchained.
Lower your voice.
Their mocking faces come with rolling eyes.
I've blistered my hand holding on;
blistered my soul keeping some promises too close;
blistered my heart knowing you touched it in ways
I didn't want *it* to;
blistered my dreams,
ultimately.
I ponder my next decision;
I've been the salvager of calm
long enough.
Respect me for who I'll become;
the twilight's servant.
The blood in the sky,
is finished processing our
lovely demise.
We're bleeding under the elephant clouds;
there will be no moon tonight.

The black knight sheds
thickening blood over
our glowering eyes;
attacks our sobering
hearts praying
for funeral,
applause.

my ultimatums and towering conditions

I am still unclear on how I feel about you.
There's too much left unsaid and too much left to undo!
I cannot please anybody.
I cannot even please myself.
What will I do with this dilemma you pull me into?
Time enslaves us behind the barracks.
Moments spent with gratified bodies,
chain us deep into the soils of wrong;
we're cut in half by destiny's train.
My concentrated gaze through the grazed window
finds no better view of your soul
in the evening's mindless slideshow.
You're unclear on how you feel
about my ultimatums
and towering conditions.
There's too much to unlearn and too much to disprove!
The doves on her grass remain
vivid and pure.
May I have a few hours and a few minutes too?
I kissed your palm and traced the spiderwebs,
you've misspelled my name;
I knew you would.
Have you met a more desperate fool?
There's rain in the clouds on the bluest of days.
There's a storm on its way,
constant and attentive.
Let's go find higher ground.
My troubling mind, gave birth to these attractions.
I apologize in advance if you're a nameless mention.
Let's endure our final years without hesitation.

We'll hang logic with our barred chance.
Our love is non-refundable.
She pawns the crescent moon on her neck,
free from my suffocating scriptures.

Or so she thought…

kisses which taste of roadside gasoline

Feel my spirit, *listen to it.*
My sorrow intensifies and my nightmares bloom,
addressing you *while* undressing you.
I think your goodness is overrated.
I evict you as the source of my precious heartaches.
I feel my spirit mirror your unsure nods.
We can be beautiful, amazing and unforgettable.
We can be everything, everything and more.
Sing the truth for once!
Break the silence through forever's light.
Break through darkness now!
I am counting on you.
Take me to our house on fire;
kisses which taste of roadside gasoline.
Sing the truth for once!
I drove irresponsibly on your flat line.
I am deaf to the sky doctor's laugh-track.
Feel my voice soften.
Listen to it in vain.
Home is where you will find me
burnishing the shadows of furniture frames.
On the porch,
I swing
high.
Your denials were incendiary.
I hold your wings down, trying to fly away.
Love is just air, not every thread sings.
You felt me dying,
closing my eyes.
I expected this.

I am waiting for a herd of visceral locust
to swarm in any second now.
We lack the sustainability for an encore.
The underpaid director,
deadpans on frozen *dewdrops*...
Sing the truth for once!

The misty emerald showers captured our last
defeated s*mile*.

good news for sharing over white wine and rye bread

Why is your hair always a mess?
Why do you always grind your teeth?
Stop leaning on the fence dreading to be erased!
Again, you're walking through yellow tape
and tripping over the dead, constipated.
It's insanity, *is that what you look for?*
Faking to be their joy when you know
that it is a profoundly empty chore.
Three is the perfect number,
one more week of silence to go
until I gift my soul a well-deserved slumber.
I'll be bracing myself for travels alone.
I don't need a bigger space on my bed.
As long as I have the worried moon
and introverted stars
to keep my anxiety tuned.
Time trains memories to kneel,
specifically the ones with wings
carrying added weight.
I am certain,
I'll revisit our first hours together,
in dreams,
in poems;
I'll make sure to mention us
while in talks with cosmic magicians.
It was our commonalities
that acted as a lighthouse;
which led us to unexplored desires within
the confines of my jaded heart and your jaded soul.
Her aura pours among my drying rivers,
her rubies were endlessly sobbing.
Tenderly she falls.
She's liken to ask nothing of the pain,
but to pass through with meaning;

to be married with the textures of renewal.
I salivate under her longing stares.
Through my transparency she is treating my madness as currency.
She'd be devising peril and mixing sunsets from a variety of climates.
Her hues weaken the threshold of my core.
I caught her stealing weapons from the winning side of my losing wars.
She craves for human turmoil,
heartbreaking melodies
with biblical overtones.
We've be the loudest talkers inside human inventions.
A metallic oven with four silicone wheels,
carrying frugal bodies with jailed emotions.
The divine interventions set the appointment.
Our instincts led us straight onto the slow traffic.
We avoid the fearful gaze of those seconds,
behind windshields,
cowardice inspires
other feelings
to misbehave.
We dream of flat tires.
We dream of daggers deeply pressed on moist chest.
A rare few dreams of living a decent life in tiny villages.
Our lost soul massacred their pedestrian concepts.
We choose where to drown.
We are flowing with rivers of ideas.
In talking to each other,
we mostly ponder happy thoughts
with an invisible smile.
We keep this facial lucidity out of sight.
We dislike it when they try joining in;
best we wonder out loud.
Watch them feign at being tired.
Dissatisfaction comes with this dancing feeling!
It schemes with a bloodied blade behind its back.
Hear the *drip, drip, drip, drip,* on the sunbaked pavement, sizzle!
Indignantly we respond by taking a pill,

to take us farther than we initially dreamt;
surrendering to the impending illness.
We flip through black and white channels,
sorrow gives into it,
and believes in it.
Our humming is polished by a bed of snow.
Her pink petals parted from the rose;
adjusted to the cold.
She no longer cares being left naked
and bare in love's frozen mystery.
With nothing more on our karmic payroll;
everything afterwards,
is good news
for sharing
over white wine
and rye bread.
Our legendary synchronicity was outstanding!
Our one night stood out
among the rest,
afterwards.
We cursed the minute hand,
we felt our demons changing faces,
breathing of intolerable lust.
One muse after another denies us of being fellow lovers;
a four-leaf clover under the duvet's warm shade.
Instead we're rambling fools with ever the worst luck;
leaving it up to faith.
The only solace to remain is our shared aim;
to stain happiness's sheets with greater illustrations.
We summon the ashes of homeless dancers,
quench their thirst with heaven's waterwheels.
They offered us their primary desires
and with a snap
and a flare,
we're an orgy of Phoenixes.
We've launched into outer spaces;

planets without origin.
Through the prison bars of thunderous clouds,
through the hopelessness and heartless songs
about a gallon of dreams invested
on a bar counter.
We can't wake up from our love affair with the jukebox.
The dampness of our sweater attracts an ageless goddess,
perfumes of her honeydew caused rivers to flood on my cheeks.
Restless no more,
she flowered generously,
cleansing all I have done wrong with my
space-
suit.

die losing track

In the depths of my heart,
I let myself suffer.
Here, words danced in a formless laughter.
In the wrong situations,
I cave.
My face wears impatience
like a second layer of skin.
In sleepless nights,
I throw punches in the dark.
I lose fights with weeping shadows.
I never know who had the upper hand.
When they leave me alone,
I forget my name,
and your name.
What I haven't touch cannot put me to shame, *right?*
I'll be brave when it's time to be brave.
But, right now I can do nothing but fear.
I am easily startled,
I know the news before they happen.
Nothing's new;
everything about us
is the same.
I renounce the keys,
I held dear.
I exhale your drug from my system.
I am not the type of artist who loves
when colors misbehave;
I learned to love control from her.
The shadows came back.
They're calling out our name, withdrawing and depositing pain.
Having rushed in, their ribs are nicked by corners of drawers and
night stands.
They speak of our particular pain.
They want to imitate our games,

despite the missing pieces,
and lack of hearts to offend.
How should I die?
How did I go insane as to live so morbidly in love?
In an empty room, hours die keeping track of wasted dreams.
In an empty house, years die losing track of you and me.

by windowsills and under beds

Under summer darkness,
I lay with my ears freezing.
They're seeking voices ready to break into
the words *least* spoken.
It excites me seeing things
reroute into *least* frequented directions;
seeing happiness ignite
and then die with no irrecoverable connection.
In these vacant lots of memory,
we rediscover the people
who's done us the *least* harm.
We amplify it!
Listen to yourself,
false alarm,
your antennae
is bent.
The new day is eaten up
by dismay's yellow teeth.
Deception washes the dishes we left
by windowsills and under beds.
They kill time doing our biddings,
while we chew and chew on more
inappropriate actions.
Longing for shinier choices;
it's consciousness speaking
with the *least* madness.
Our photographs were better distorted.
These *lost thoughts* vanished.
My love went
rogue
for a second.

It's not the *first* time
it happen.

collecting therapeutic friendships

Pass the whore a beaten hourglass.
Life does not empathize with the likes of lost sluts!
People do not stay.
We are like the non-lasting hue of the nicest colors
which blankets over our fake cities.
Memories are a nuisance.
The ordinary beg for a quick escape
from life's bleeding situations.
We need and want more of this balancing act;
collecting therapeutic friendships.
We turn into desperate rats dying in excellent rates.
It's called the *present* for a reason;
make death the *only* friend;
don't confuse this eventuality for prison,
it's a prison-mate!
We hurt ourselves succumbing to illusions;
thinking we bear resemblance to the finest
angelical verse in the holy book.
Speak the truth, don't let lies bite.
No matter what, love everyone!
Look up at the immortal beauty burning bright
in our well-read,
dead sky.
Let's punch out from stuck areas,
and vacation a couple steps back
into launch plates
while prayers beam
our souls to the songs of a harp.
Know this,
my love,
I will always cheer you on.
You're just a trying star,
rewrite the secrets you've kept inside
and accept that dying is

astronomically
astonishing!
I am the finest mind surgeon in town,
believe me.
Enjoy the moments that you are given.
Feather-dust the bad,
and invite to bed,
that which is good.
Tell the in-betweeners to fuck off,
and make up its mind!
Then, feel yourself drift into a smile;
demand a hard rain to erase years of chalk outlines.
I must be in heaven,
as darkness comforts my nightly dreams;
making charm bracelets out of thorny stems.
Sleep comes easy when fear is lying beside you,
with its own pillow.
Let's be steadily open to wherever sanity stands,
wherever the leaves are most hot with fire.
We are the products of a bad idea;
after all.
Know that all we are commanded to do is
change,
it's *the* main activity, and
it's *our* main responsibility
to n*ever* do it well.
Allow all these complexities to excite
encroaching pain.
In the meantime,
love as many times as possible,
until the belly is one with
God's rumbling laughter.

God's grace

I felt like a newly blossomed flower during a cruel separation.
She reminds me of wildfire;
of clues in my darkest hour;
of a sparkling clarity
after you've exhausted
what's been said.
Her leaving tonight felt colder than the season's last autumnal breath.
Her return felt like visits from a white dove;
it was so discreet with its backend smile.
I found *yours* again somehow.
Oh, I'm afraid to impose on this script of mine,
but I've been told you sin for fun.
Admit you're unwell before I see the passion leave your face.
These white nights are always ruined by the death of our last embrace.
Cry, but be quiet about it.
It seems our cup has spilled;
what a waste of sacred blood.
Let's utilize it somehow
and paint a red sunset
on our pale white sky.
Rewind one last time,
the film deposited into the slot.
I'd trip and fall like an amateur mime,
counting your admirers;
I spotted *ten*,
then *two*,
then *nine*.
I found pure pleasure in your lullaby.
I can't seem to find it in anybody else.
I blink, you're all I see.
I close them, and we're kicking wet sand into the water behemoth.
I think, of why you're still here,
blaming a flawed design,

an unattended scar;
you're a part of me all this time.
There will always be,
what was, and what isn't
in cleanliness and dirty work.
Love seems unfair as it talks,
on and on about itself,
doesn't it?
Wanting to be fed the largest morsels,
birthing molecular doubts to mar our gears;
stealing more creative lies to sink in instead.
What others find first,
others find too late.
Pistols shot on the afternoon of a warm November.
I'll walk till it hurts to a nowhere place,
followed by a sullen hush.
Soon to be caught in hurricanes,
with no parachute to crash
where it's true;
because of you
I'll lose more sleep
than I have to.
Every stranger on the street
becomes this beautiful thread,
I'm happily tangled in.
They're closer to the divine
than I'll ever be.
Don't untie the knots.
Use me as line when fishing.
It's been a long while since the last time
I am this needed by her.
The art of letting go is a silent movie
produced by seizures of sound and color.
The audience will rest the whole way through.
Then, lose track of our crippled narrative.
At some point, the projector will spit acid fire;

does it deserve to be fed our pathetic performance?
I call out to the staff to have it fixed; to no avail,
leaving footsteps mix with an answerless family of rings.
The last scar on the film is healed.
I sustain a brilliant smile for the closing scenes.
I look back at the projection lights.
I saw her kind brown eyes.
She's a true epitome of the artful soul.
I let go.

Even *God's grace* can't fathom *her* staying.

time's vacuum

You're dust on my bookshelves
in the outskirts of my head.

You're a cancer that begs attention;
I refuse to mention your name.

Let me dig my own grave,
my body won't die today,
but my spirit must be ready
for anything.

Let a sunset bloom
with flowers in May.

May hurt feelings,
now be okay.

I am over our miscommunications,
I am over the malevolent
manipulation.

Let's stop this prehistoric crime of trying to find gold
in a cave sucked into
time's vacuum.

You're like a threat made by a child
in denial of being an exhibitor of bad behavior.

We're survivors of love's traumatic mess.

What if I surrender to your God?
I made a deal, that would save
one out of two souls.

I'd rather it be yours.

Let's stop this prehistoric crime of trying to find a rose
in the hills of love's harsh winter.

mute what is required of a man to sing

She spent another midnight walking
pass the same flickering lights
leaving a cold trail.
You're on trial, says the streetlights.
This is your sentence,
plead guilty now
or you'll drown,
legend says she now resides
in the moon's crater.
We're born into an endless variety of circumstances.
Do you understand me?
I'll have another round, this
calls for shots of meaning.
Rare occurrences flatter me to the bone.
We all acquire certain chemical adherence
from our individual illness.
She'll present herself as a shiny pearl you could pray into.
Will her shine abide when I' am all done with her?
My confidence rolls from the peaks of observance;
a boulder devolved into a pebble.
Somehow, my depleted existence,
robbed me of basic vocabulary.
She'd mute what is required of a man to sing.
I sign my life away under the dotted line.
Can you be anymore discrete?
she'd say, picking up on my gravitational pull.
Offer me another lie.
I can tell from your eyes,
you're rich with something…
March on further away from the bar lights,
watch my shadow fade with the exit blinds.
I've brought the truth with me on a pocketful of blues.
I lost the sheet music.
I'd be humming about our burden forevermore.

Nailed to a lying cross, with a view of dawn's discolored skies;
it is better to let them take your sorrow for granted.
I needed this rain*bow* to intimidate.

Now onwards, our fated resolution.

my MK Ultra

She made my darkest fantasies seem real,
but this can be beautiful too.

I met her long ago;
my adoration survived,
many pitfalls.

Love me now and forget the end date;
let's vow like cowards do;
she's my living shrine.

Don't let a whisper be swept in secret,
eat the nervous bug alive.

Before I bribe the judge and jury;
I execute her.

The throne is yours,
come get your crown.

My world is in your hands;
keep our future set on a simple plan;
keep our future set on you and me.

My MK Ultra
…this can be beautiful too.

It's been great
knowing
you.

I reach for the closest prayer.

She's my blowing sand.

it's an honor to be love's ashtray

I wasn't in control;
I wasn't ready to lose so hard,
when *we* had it all.
It wasn't much anyway,
so *I* let you go.
The imagination is a cruel place
crowded with unforgivable bastards;
creating visuals that link
to our cravings for closure.
Sometimes her intentions are true
but become suicidal in an instant.
It was not in my plan to get burned.
Now, I understand,
her fire is the provocative
passion gathered in a tribal dance.
Every evening I spent with her
painted my soul black.
She taught me to conquer my false self;
painting my heart black
is the way to resume
after getting one's
heart corrupted.
It's an honor
to be love's
ashtray.
She likes creating rituals to satiate
the lack of existential evidence.

Sometimes her intentions
are more of destiny's
soulless
p*lots*.

EXHIBIT

K

killed or
be kissed
by
our wants' fatal solution,
needing
imperfect Gods to accept us

we wake up with a dead eye

Having nightmares of going nowhere,
profound questions keep me awake;
another lesson gives me another scar.
Having dreams of finding bliss
but newfound theories keep me awake;
another lesson makes me wonder *where* I am.
Do you think this will go on forever?
Haven't received an answer yet;
mysteries always find a way to blur the lines.
Lost in darkness for I don't know how long;
I am tired, I don't feel strong at all
as I wake up with a dead eye;
wake up with a dead eye.
Having thoughts of not existing,
I found reasons to satisfy the means;
another failed attempt to hide my scars.
Having loved and lived for a while now,
I find myself walking around in circles;
how did I get myself here?
Having dreams of finding bliss
but newfound theories keep me awake;
another lesson makes me wonder *who* I am.
Having loved and lost kept me dumbed down,
I am having the courage now to ask you *why*,
I open up the scars to see what's really there;
how did we get here?
Do you think this will go on forever?
We haven't received an answer yet,
mysteries always find a way to blur our lines.
We're lost in darkness for I don't know how long,
we're tired and we don't look strong at all
as we wake up with a dead eye;
wake up with a dead eye.

it stays like a bad scar on my face

What is changing in me?
Your voice is deaf from the sound of me leaving;
turning a page.
What is changing in you?
Your words were once forgivable,
but the pain is not leaving;
it stays like a bad scar on my face.
One good love, is all I'm asking for,
once my feelings are returned,
it is salvation for our eternity of wrongs.
I realize, there's no mode of satisfaction to be gained;
I am a hiding sun behind the mountains of frozen time;
a group is following an imitation of a rain cloud,
I lead them safely down the most righteous death.
I am a hiding moon tonight,
behind a forest fire love started;
all I ask for is your fake cleansing ritual.
What do I get in return for waiting this long?
We're a weak flame dying out,
exploding with passionate desire.
Hey!
Strong beating heart,
tire already.
Show yourself;
I am not leaving
until I know you're fine.
Your sorrow is not something I can deny;
I'll climb the dark walls you've built for me,
until I reignite on your charcoal eyes.
I am not leaving until the moon finds our good side.
You're never sleeping in the dark, alone.
Leave the fearful child behind.

Brave spark, we're fated to dream of forest fires.
Let's spontaneously combust;
unite our spirits with kozmic glue.
We're also these flickering fireflies in a mason jar;
blinking once,
then twice,
expired.

my heart is filled with cold tea

An autumn snow,
cold and uninvited
come and goes.
I appreciated being lost in you,
and being accustomed to your rabbit hole.
Is it *too soon* to know
what I'm giving up without you?
This fire inside is ready to burn again, *soon*.
I lay all alone,
my heart is filled with cold tea.
I fall slowly into my sweet demise,
the bliss traumatizes our awful distance.
I won't give up until I am afraid of my own shadow
when love calls in a spring morning,
freely inviting anything that moves.
I refuse to animate this hostile force in you.
Let's be blinded by the search for truth,
but it's always *too soon* to really know;
what honor am I giving up without you?
This fierce deity left our tired soul;
I am missing out on the outside world;
I am sorry for keeping your bliss
waiting behind copious gaps of time.
I miss the sound of our musical chains,
I preserve clarity's thorns
for the next empty soul;
smile for the camera
empty soul.
Let's be of warmth;
felt when flying over spring clouds,
soaring towards undefinable heights.
It's your unique bliss,
I can't be without.

It's our communion,
I will decline in advance.
You and me are caught boiling with a grotesque fever.
Our corpses lay face down on a swamp somewhere;
wherever peace subsides, she says.
Is there someplace better?

swinging left and right with the liberated breeze, swirling you

I found reasons to loathe you
but you're a butterfly in a graveyard.
I don't want to lose touch
but you're a spirit in the night.
I descend along the path of no return,
keeping me stuck in your broken world;
I lean on our final stand for guidance;
I grip her burrowed hands.
As I seek a war in darkness,
I confide in the dignity left in us.
Our dreams are out there longing
for the tongues of giving angels.
The future holds no cure,
in our war with darkness;
a war with no end.
I found reasons to be okay losing you,
you're a common drug;
you're a common girl.
It is you who won't free me;
I am the merciful rope,
you're hanging on
too tightly to a struggle
I've never seen before.
It's your preferred pattern,
swinging left and right
with the liberated breeze,
swirling you.
I am denied safe passage to more greater times,
I raise a skittering gun.
The *joke* is on you,
being moved by vengeance
while I was moved by your loving awareness.
The lonely path you've chosen

won't take you far.
How am I to survive our weekend jives?
The future holds no cure;
her roses matured.
The buzzing brightness thrives;
I can't trust the sneaky heart bandits.

slowly with our gracelessness

Kill me slowly
with your wondering eyes;
haunt me like a ghost,
where do I hide?
Expose me of the truth,
I said you never could,
my pride has left for good.
Kill me slowly
with your secret demise;
haunt me like a ghost,
where do I hide?
Exposed you of my truth,
you said I never could;
I have left the room.
Run, if you could,
go on.
Live, if you could,
go on.
Kill me slowly
with your warped embrace;
haunt me like a ghost,
where do I hide?
Exposed my molded words,
I said you never could,
my sins begin to hurt.
Kill me slowly
with our faded miles;
haunt me like a ghost,
misunderstood.
Expose me of your truth,
I can no longer withstand
you.
Kill me slowly
with your unfaithful eyes;

haunt me like a ghost,
where do I hide?
Kill me slowly with our gracelessness.
She haunts me like a prayer sang with praise.
I am killed slowly…

a thousand names uttered the wrong way

I never knew I was special to her,
I never sought out the answer
or the scenery before.
I take her gently by the arms;
we begin a dance
we don't know the steps for,
her head falls on my shoulder
my knee bends,
exalted by her.
This corny image is farfetched;
co-created by my listless head.
I never minded the days ahead paved by silhouettes
with vulnerable notions
and humbly dressed
with a thousand names
uttered the wrong way.
Our blue motel rooms had lots of things to say,
our sinful spirits came and went,
each sorrow-filled afternoon was hazy;
at night we collected the pity looks the moon gave.
It's such a shame trying to keep a lover,
trying to be immune to the summer in her hugs
and the winter in her eyes or the seasonal smiles
she composes like runaway horses.
The infinity in our choices limits the tones of our voices;
her meter of unkind gestures easily manipulates me.
Let's become like sunken ships,
desire my untouched corners
where my last words
holds such fragility.
We created another memory
we won't remember.

My heart never forgets though,
it still craves pleasure
after the hurt.
The modest agony in every heartbeat and every verse,
causes old feelings to magnify when I play them in reverse.
Why must people make such rules when it comes to love?
To step over the boundaries of trust,
doubting their feelings and never returning it,
just so they could live in solitude a bit longer
in routine to what works.
No risk is taken,
there's no newborn promises heard
I am just another lost spirit
she refused to keep;
she resents the sublime;
the touching of souls.
She cries in the backwoods of everything I conveyed,
the limited words I used to let her know it's her time
to pull out the spikes that made it too close to a vein,
too close to the heart, *too* poisoned and *too* decayed.
I was there to mend her mental ache,
the boring sadness and magnificent madness;
this confusing state God placed us in.
Is it a cage of loving embraces?
Or a lecture that began and is only halfway done?
There are no breaks when it comes to HIS lessons;
there exist no locked rooms
in our blue and green,
padded prison.
Be free to roam,
be free to visit me anytime;
let me hear all about our first introductions.
What buffers, prolongs what suffers in you;
be greatly humbled, I am yours to value.

In a promise so consumed by dishonesty
and fading truce.
I don't dare ruse
or misuse
what's good.

If you cry
I might *just* cry
too!

the quieter we wept

We made a deal with a demon in our nightmare.
Then played along through an act of despair.
Our dawn lasted the whole day.

Come underneath the bridge with me,
we'll sail towards the closing seas;
our fleet circles around while the mountain speaks:
If only we could be.

You made a deal with an angel in your dreams.
Then played the Gods through an act of repair.
Our sun took all day to settle down.

My final vow, this we will receive;
there's no blessings left to deceive us.
My final sight, this we won't forget;
our souls fled the quieter we wept,
while the mountain speaks:
If only we could be.

revoked

A man weeps,
'twas heard across the land,
she swam peacefully in his despair;
all his earthly riches he'd exchange
for a minute more.
He cares too much,
down to her every step,
a love that started
without her consent.
She dances
and twirls,
she curled
her hair,
like she did before.
When her eyes met his,
as desolate as the dance floor,
he spilled his drink on his sweater.
He wallowed in her dreams,
as strange letters formed
like an elegant sculpture in his mind,
for a silhouette that vaguely smells
of a field with midnight blossoms.
The rusted gates are guarded by angels,
he was careful to withhold the divinity in her eyes.
He imagines her dancing
on the winding road
like handpicked rose petals
making love with the wind;
her dance finds encore in the desert.
His nightmares spoke of terror,
of errors in the ways he loved her;
his choices grew with evergreen fruits.
She showers her lovers with an oasis of deliverance;
the beaches sing of her sorrows in the afterlife.

He drove towards the moonlight
through debris of detonated landmines,
back to the jungle trail of their *estranged* romance.
A florist, so keen in wit flows to his spirit's rescue,
her intelligent quips altered his stubborn taste,
puzzled the pieces that appeared on his doorstep.
An adorable princess appeared,
the scent of her hair glitters
in painfully slow days,
her sunset cheeks were plump.
Her kindred smile brought him back
to his young self,
where stars commenced a resurrection;
the sun was outshined by its wake.
A knock arrived in the tiny house,
his remaining years were allowed entry
once more into love's perimeters.
The sparkle returned in his eyes,
not a day too soon;
it was her that brought him
five more springs.
A woman sleeps,
'twas quiet across the land.
The final process of her repairs
endured 'till his last forgiving breath.
All his gold and riches,
she'd never exchange
for a minute more.
"Not yet," he says.
She didn't care enough,
she abandoned him
later that night,
I heard her
whistling.
She dreadfully recollects
a sea of promises and throes;

the talking walls were spellbound
by the words the air co-wrote.
When her eyes said farewell to his,
it was with ingratitude for the last five years,
she ate his heart out with a victorious smile;
while his heart-shaped lips tried to calm
her nimble waves of amputated hatred.
He's waiting for the arrival of the sharpest blades knowing sadly,
the *karma* cannot be revoked.

darling *shoot* for the questions marked

A new wave of hate arises,
taking control of my future sins.
I open up my mind
and realized the key
is gone.

A new wave of life diminishes,
controlling my power;
closing up my mind
to realize I had it
all wrong

I've denied you of the role-playing,
the shadows you cast applies to no one but me.

A new wave of love unbecoming,
losing touch of the ground;
I get back up to realize you had the map
upside down.

Reasons don't suit your case,
it's time to lay *us* to rest;
pick an open grave
while our dirt
misbehaves.

You had me all wrong,
the key you've misplaced
wasn't the only one.

You had it me all wrong;
by then I've come undone,
we've come undone.

The reasons I found were incurable,
hand me my gun,
darling *shoot*
for the questions
marked.

I cheat my way into

No more stupid games,
I want to walk you home;
kill me off,
I don't care.

No more stupid rules,
I want to be free,
lock up my controls;
you own me.

No!
Never again will I be
in the hands of someone
like you.

Come on by for a while now,
tell more lies that I won't mind,
kill the messenger now;
cut out our connection, *die.*

No more cheap codes,
I want a fair game,
cut my vision off;
I really don't care.

No more stupid friends,
I want to be alone,
I am tempted to evolve
all by myself.

No!
Never again will I cheat
my way into your heart.

Come on by for a while now,
sell more lies that I won't buy,
revive the messenger now;
release a flawless confession, *love*.

her magnificent frame

Our statues dance to the songs of a cricket when nobody is around.
A campfire is lit and the mosquitoes bit a fragile vein in us.
This echoing shame has been empty for days.
I've lost count of sleepless nights,
collected drought on the seashore grounds,
sand turned to mud in my doleful eyes.
Heaven despairs before the glow of her wheat-colored hair;
innocence blare like a snare drum,
when her heart flees
from mine to somebody *else*.
She installs greatness in a grain-sized moment,
I ration the energy of this impeccable achievement;
wear it on both shoulders like boulders,
let it inspire every tinker toy soldier.
An army of smoke caresses and entered her smirking lips.
Behind the horizon, I tamed her magnificent frame.
A lone boat parked near the bay,
unravels its bronze hair.
Our healing rays upset the sun,
bleeding till we're moonless and grey.

What is one more blameless death?

the rest and peace in those future days

LORD, you owe me.
I want her, *I want her to stay.*
Guide a confession out of her lips,
show her that the route
to escape, to be remade,
comes from the sound of *your* voice.
Free an outbreak of emotions
on separate parts of the ocean.
Let go my darling, let go.
You're aware, we make a good pair,
I focus on your better side;
I focus on the rest and peace
in those future days
yet to gracefully pass;
we're the teardrops after a *Hail Mary,*
inspiring hopeless seeds to surface.
Lord, show us that the route to believe
taste of the wine in your sober voice;
invite her fully into my fragmented soul,
let me praise her immortality
as if it were *your* own.

a charmless dream, prepping for the real thing

I forgive the lines of red,
I can't paint over,
let it remind me of where I bled.
I forgive the recipients of clean slates
I do my best to prepare a new bed
for my sleepless maiden.
Her winter soliloquy
leaves me breathless;
my soul is wide awake.
The nerve on you to make me feel alive,
the nerve on you to see me through.
I kneel before the cross;
I was a successful liar,
I kneel before a God
who gives unlimited chances.
I forgive the scars,
the seams seem to heal.
The night reminds me again,
I am the darkness she feels.
I am a charmless dream,
prepping for the real thing.
She leaves me relentlessly restless.
Her soul's vocal range *reminds me why I endured all my past pain.*
It's time for loving looks across the morning blinds.
Verses I recited leaves you feeling for me.
Your eternal silence should be my waking bliss from here on in.
She shelters me in the insane sounds of the evening waves.
"Are you still looking for our footsteps?"
It makes me laugh,
you acting all brave.

The nerve on you to drag us down,
the nerve on you to see us fall out of line,
kneel before the cross on fire,
kneel before a God
who won't think twice
to for*give* us
for a hundredth
ti*me*.

liken to speak to you in tongues

Kiss or be killed,
feel the edge of love's dagger.
Hear the intrusive noise of gunshots firing;
you're all alone speaking to yourself
on the bathroom mirror's fogged corners.
It will be okay,
you have bulletproof faith;
a halo glowing above
your skull structure.
There's nothing
out of the ordinary here,
buddy, it's only the red ones;
they've captured you alive.
Memorizing keys that will unlock your heart, mind and soul.
They are liken to speak to you in tongues,
understand that every action incurs poison,
you underestimated their slithering radiance;
feel the venom in your lungs heave and rumble,
feel the horizon sell out your childhood dreams.
This darkness follows you,
but leave it to me
to walk you th*rough*
the fibrous hues.
With champagne glasses raised,
they turn to dust kissing our walls.
There's nothing out of the ordinary here,
buddy, it's only the blue ones,
they've captured you alive.
Memorizing keys that will unlock your heart, mind and soul.
You numbed my heart,
you have graffitied perfect symbols
on the surfaces of my mind palace.

There's nothing out of the ordinary here,
buddy, it's just the grey ones,
I captured them alive.
No longer will they touch your heart, mind and soul.
Nothing out of the ordinary here,
buddy, it's only colorful shadows.
Memorizing keys that will unlock the safe to our inspired *death note*.

a loving conversation between beloveds

I am overwhelmed by all the care put into
details.
Hiding places to become more of a stranger to
strangers.
Somebody left a little paper boat by the window
pain.
I am a sound bandit with one earpiece down
listening in on a loving conversation
between beloveds;
if I am not allowed
then refrain from *being*
too loud.
Who knows,
maybe you are
someone's dream,
why risk being another person's meaning?
It's *fucking* meaningless!
I am enlightened
that anything
can happen…
will happen…
should happen
without a thundercloud warning.
Damn you!
Road signs, keeping me from moving forward!
Damn you!
Construction is needed in my heart too!
I see years measured in layers of worthless words,
people measured in misinterpreted paintings
slowly decaying with ruthless discoloration.

Cease today and maybe tomorrow will exist
to advance you into the next checkpoint
with a new set of awareness to exploit.
In my field of vision is
you.

I can't place you into any category but
unknown.

EX<u>HIBIT</u>

L

lows
and
highs
being
six feet under-average;
love granted by
nocturnal medicines

to be in command of this

An angel asked me to meet her by the riverside.
Can you swim that far?
Are you slowly giving up?
I see you running from the top of this hill.
Can you make it this far up?
Or will you start tumbling down?
I have lure deception into my hands;
I am here with you to be in command of this.
We can make it through
and push our limit to overcome
these sacred chances.
I was asked to meet you on top of cloud nine.
Can you fly up this high, as your feathers fall one at a time?
I see you running, from the finish line back to the starting line.
Can you pass through all the strangers in the crowded park?
Or will you trip and fall, break your bone trying to please them all?
Flock with the gamblers after attending early morning church.
You're asking the wrong questions,
yet I listen anyway.
Can you get rid of the road signs, just fly where you are and stay?
I see you running;
stop denying you made it this far
on your own.
Are you sure you're good enough?
Or will you trip and fall, start to tumble again.
The crowd blessed us with an encore.
I have lure deception into our hands;
I am here with you to be in command of this.
We can make it through,
still, you falter as you believe that,
I can't grasp your gentle lie.

Roll the die,
your answer will
never arrive.
Heaven sends *no* regards
in the after-
life.

my arm froze rowing

Nothing else is working,
I am holding onto what chance
left on my doorstep yesterday.
We are not meant to harness
what the pain invades.
I am bringing you home tonight,
we are just fine.
I am bringing you home tonight.
You've been running all your life,
you ran away
from good.
And now you finally see
my light
we will find ourselves out of this tunnel
finally.
Never mind to living my dreams,
I am a wallpaper wonderfully tearing
from a mental institution facility.
We are not meant to fix this error;
aren't things sometimes broken for the better?
Let's not play favorites with a dreadful emotion.
I would kneel down before every God,
I can't stand the lessons this *one* has in mind.
I would sing from the top of my rotten lungs
just to be heard by *you*
one last time.
My arm froze rowing,
I found the darkest
oceans
under the darkest
skies.
Shine away;
we will be beyond okay.
I am bringing you home tonight,

we are just fine, *we are just fine;*
teach me not to rewind,
rewind and rewind!

Let's not despair in a rainy night;
strays of clichés
stay inside.

our bastard hearts beating with*out* love

Do you want more than the best for me?
Have I perfected your fantasy?
The good parts of our melody
ignited my delightful catastrophe.
The cold chill of your voice is no way to go
about what started out as a civil conversation.
Don't let me know how much you love me so.
You gave more,
I gave less.
Let's not weight every little desire
we romance,
let's just praise what's here;
you haven't slept in my arms
for a while.
Rest tight;
channel the midnight breeze,
no more tearing,
no more seams,
no more night
terrors.
You let me know that our sunlight,
that your love for me is doing alright;
nothing else speaks to my soul.
How do you plan on reasoning with guilt?
Have I forgiven you enough to arrive at what I could give?
Let's break these walls of ours,
rebuild to the stars and back;
reimagining what it's like to be loved
for the *first* time
with the *right* one.
I long for autumn's starved breeze,
the willow tree weeps for our soul's release.
I gave you more,
you gave me less;

we both needed
to disappear.
The stars disagreed with our fights;
in the dark there's no telling
if your light will be refreshing
or a vehicle for more unstoppable lies.
The moon takes its time to be found.
When sin shows its fatal grin,
will you be ready?
They're laughing at our bastard hearts
beating with*out* love.
Our melody's lazy tune
will surely pass too.
It doesn't matter who loves more
to be honest,
we're strong just letting it live
this long.

Let's not weight
every little desire we romance,
dawn will dream of tomorrow's cigarettes
on the lips of our
choices
any*how*.

my mouth through your open bruises

This is the sin
we advertise,
call up the men
in hell's uniform
with angelical ties;
profit from the pain
in tonight's sable
courses.
We lead ourselves to the end
sometimes.
For our dearly beloved friend,
who kept his mouth bravely shut;
he overcame with a lesser mind.
The scorching flag are too well behaved,
it's ashes are there for our entertainment;
soon to be a centerpiece
or living room decoration.
This is the loss we need,
call me on my bluff,
have you had enough of my satire love?
I ran my mouth through your open bruises;
my apologies.
You deserve that much
from me!
For our dearly beloved friend,
useless in more ways
than the killer could count.
The flag burns bluish green on enemy grounds;
our ashes are entertainment for the depraved lives.
Aren't you tired of playing the dead guy twitching for a cup of coffee?

The stars wait on us,
in no man's land
I be*lieve*.

a silent kill never ends a loud misery, she said

She's a bullet,
in an unmarked gun
firing with ultraviolet sounds.

A silent kill
never ends
a loud misery,
she said.

She preserves our tracks
on the yellow beach sands.

Our aftermath
caused the mornings
to get brighter.

When we parted
our heaven droughts.

*Why think too much,
amour?*

We deserve a little *glimpse* of heaven,
don't we?

my great red mug summons my will to return

Are you disappointed by our ending?
The lonely coward in the summertime
dreams of mending.
Fast forward to a memory,
beginning with the memorable
ending.
I have noticed
many times
my desire to die.
Install new fear,
it excites me.
The right star descends
into the evening canvas,
like a brush of a tortured artist.
The moon lost sight for a single minute,
I can't find myself,
it said.
The unthinkable happened,
it was too late
and too early
to appreciate.
I am disappointed this morning,
I am losing touch of my work.
I come undone violently;
descending down the ladder
with the ones that got away.
The blood eclipse mourns over my funeral pyre.
The lake begins boiling and my great red mug summons
my will to return;
using the spare key
in the urn.
Dig me
a deeper
grave!

Bury me with you and I am safe.
Get used to my
lying forgetfulness.
Our true feelings are in the downstairs
of earth for re*view*.

the coldest trail down the tundra's icy sheets

Have you ever sucked a bug dry?
Have you ever been forsaken?
Have you ever heard a rough patch sing?
These questions won't stop
at nothing
to rise.

Pulling you out of your cotton coffin;
taking out another pile of dirtied dreams.

I am passed our aforementioned moment,
I am passed our preempted reasons.

Our decease was loveliest when
our dreams showed up inebriated
in the eyes of our next of keen.

I haven't seen deception waltz
for anybody else's ultralight beam.

Maybe the devil has an exclusive,
on our particular fall's fatal result;
it's not enough to live
with a candied heart.

Your pelted yolk
is cooked medium
scrambled.

Maybe I have an exclusive
of how I might be the culprit,
of how I ran free*st;*
leaving the coldest trail
down the tundra's
icy sheets.

Ah, my most cherished murder
love
scene.

I understand why love must expire

She's awoken my demons,
left our crime scenes exposed
to the priest's sermon tongue.
She yields my sorrow,
exempted my confessional
arrows.
She rarely disapproves of my statue emotions.
Free, I am free.
I found the key and buried it deep.
Saved, I am saved.
I found an actual angel
amidst all the flame
keepers.
Foreign were her words,
her prayers were vain
in closed doors.
I am endlessly fascinated
by her open
window
panels.
She holds our unwell memory,
nurses it back home.
After her discrete efforts,
I understand why love must
expire.

Our well-kept memory is *all a dream.*
Our scene of passion,
our final thoughts
scream.

Free, *am I free?*
Saved, *am I saved?*

I fail to be *neutral;*
it seems our hope
is in an infantile
st*age*.

the distinct footprints of cowards

I entertain your suicidal branches,
I sway directly down the wrinkled lake.
A fallen leaf arches
like a dynamite at our feet.
Faraway,
the grey buildings fall to its knees;
taking thousands back to zero.
The bike wheels get accidental piercings
and the moon experiences engine failures.
People oil the bastards with refurbished gears
and logs out of the universe;
gives the clouds a raspberry kiss.
Praise the uneducated children,
the dead and dying seedlings,
the distinct footprints of cowards
running towards danger merrily.
A tender question formulates,
the invisible skies are bluer
because of the immensity
of hurt endowed upon
those who sees.
The rose buds renewed its petals for a consecutive year;
they refuse to regroup into a virginal vase.
Our road signs must improve,
wipe the dirt from your eye
my *Lord*.
Focus your breathing and sighs;
grace every stop sign we meet
with bleeding quotes
from bleeding tourist
of the thinking
mind.

Our failures are inserted into lore,
to reach unborn readers
of soul.

One must perform *their* death as if hit by a bullet of their choice.

opium prayers

She reigns over my miseries.
She's a fast-paced drug
healing my internal maladies;
I lay kisses on her knees
for the merciful travels
it's been through
reciting opium
prayers.
Memories so hectic find little
to no ways to go;
no easy road
to solace.
Knowledge leaves
my godless ego
looking for a queenly
escort back to
spiritual
poverty.
The chorus is compliant to her light strumming,
through the fragile verses of *Orpheus's* journey
she retrieves *Eurydice's* corpse from the underworld.
I stilled her flailing emotions;
I buy her flowers when the sun is gone,
a beautiful dress for the winter parade.
Underneath the moonlight we go on evening drives
collecting hitchhikers to compensate for the lack of stars.
We went to the crowded scenes,
colors marinated by loud music;
she leaves me breathlessly dancing through it.
These hours of warmth
are seasoned with joy
and child-like energy.
I take her home, loving my life for once;
she loves *who* I was and *who* I am now.

She'll save me from sailing into some lone*some* paradise.
We slept under the covers
with the window entirely open,
the curtains thoroughly down,
so the afternoon sun
won't wake us up
with its shards
of twine.
The boat under her eyes
sails over my lips
for a hundredth
time.
Her sweet morning kiss
despite the morning breath,
is a bliss hard to out-glow.
I lay another one gently,
her laughter became a full song,
her innocence consumed worlds.
You're all I see my queen,
I am saving you from ot*her* men
and it's my duty to graduate
from
your prince
to
your king.
Holy maiden,
the thr*one* is yours.
She's the permanent rainbow up the hill
named after our jaded stare.
The only star not scared to be
that close to the moon;
she's brave,
she's a gracious
conductor of the breeze;
conductor of my madness.

I look at her picture;
I miss her,
I *miss* her,
I miss *her*.

her music and melodies

I send her poems and letters;
vagueness runs through every line.
Each one is written over aged graffiti
from artist she collected in over two decades of time;
to her it seems I am merely a shadow walking by.
I send her music and melodies,
heartaches cocktailed with bitterness.
All she heard afterwards was that I am *falling*,
unsure if she was ready to bestow the grace
of a heart conscious answer.
She tried, but failed to understand
the reason for everything she learned.
She's well depended
in relation with this fear
of getting *too* close to someone.
She longs for these moments;
she smiles as she leaves them
hanging by her black threads.
I can hear the sirens now,
echo past the fiery wreckage.
I can hear the blackbirds crying
hungry for our wounded souls,
baking with revulsion.

They see us lying
on the cold hard ground
trusting not a breath;
trusting just the gravity
and fr*agility*
of one more
whispered
goodbye.

entry, by entry, ad infinitum

You're a tangled mess of clarity,
but you don't have to be alone in this.
Reach out my darling
and marry the idea
that life's headed
somewhere sweet.
"Reach out,"
the minute hand uttered with glee.
"Been there, done that,"
the hour hand said.
"You will love your new lives, you'll see,"
echoed the frightened wind.
Immerse yourself in the art of disbelief,
in a state of majesty claiming our everchanging value.
No one knows *we* decorate the holy man's golden crown,
no one knows *we* grow from the earth's infertile land.
We're head-tripping on cloud nine
for Christ's sake!
"So listen to yourself,
create broken memories,
find beauty in grotesque souls,"
echoed the dancing wind.
We're pushed against
the windowpane
until our heart beats
for louder dreams.
Become music
for the mood swings.
Whether you like it or not
we must keep living
entry,
by entry,
ad infinitum.
We're in a restless dream,

with a clarity that is never jealous.
Your voice becomes music to warn others,
whether we meet rain or not,
we must keep
digging!

lay on our soft paradox

Tell me all your worries,
tell me all of your doubts,
you're a metaphysical impairment
on the cuffs of my metaphorical life.
You were so daring;
you were so careful.
Loving you
brewed *over-*
whelming
virtues.
I sit in corners
crying alone,
I wish you'd come over
and give me shelter;
I am a tired nuisance
in our fake world.
Being inside our love's hurricane,
is waking up on a bed of nails,
most relaxed,
most satisfied,
five minutes more…
Tell me all your stories,
tell me when mine begins in yours.
You inspired rivets of sapphire tears;
leaving is never a precise gesture.
The sunset flies into the death of night,
I hope you stay careful,
I hope you're alright.
Have a sweet goodnight,
lay on our soft paradox.

Dream,
dream,
dream
so*me*thing pro-
found.

such electrifying screams

Alone,
I lay,
it's almost midnight;
something doesn't feel right.
Hell
broke loose,
we got to hang tight;
something doesn't feel right.
Goodbye
is the greatest lie.
Saying,
let love be,
is a potent
prelude
to a lie.
Heaven's door closed for us;
something *still* doesn't feel right.
On my own
in the dark,
I feel fine.
A dream set loose
imagines itself paired
with a clean relief.
What a shiny belief!
I woke up,
a voice spoke with grief;
I could hardly breathe.
I woke up,
I heard such electrifying screams.

When goodbye becomes
the best lie;
I ponder past
the good parts,
please, if you could slip through
my sandpaper hands,
let love
sink.

whenever my halo begs for your septic loving

Of course, my mind went astray
wondering if I can tame
the rhythm of our noise
in the sweet company
of your heartless glance.

Of course, I am capable of ejecting
from yesterday's soulless activities,
without your tender grasp leading me on
to another inconsequential make-believe past.

Of course, I feel hollowed out,
undefined by the absence of your mercy,
your incoherent embraces unfolds
and rattles misunderstood memory.

I offer you a silver pedestal
just so you could look down on me
again and *again,* and *again.*

Of course, when my glasses are off I feel insecure,
strange faces are expressionless with haunted ideas.
I am an anonymous coward;
the *worst* romantic.

Of course I'm distracted
trying to study you closely,
but something odd turns on
whenever my halo begs for
your septic loving.

Maybe it's the way you look beside me
and how we're like desperate puzzle pieces
trying to fit where we don't belong.

EXHIBIT

M

mind buffets
for
the
maggot populace
in
the lobes
of
our labyrinth
wastelands

innocent eyes

We've been a broken clock ticking nonstop;
I am a shadow for you to mock.
Frozen in time were the words you've shouted,
are you proud of your elegant mouth?
So little could be seen
by innocent eyes like ours,
return the time,
return the *damn* time
that we had dreaming of being fearless like lions.
Fading away is the apparition of many versions of the same person;
moments you've taken hostage
are calling to be released,
and locked away
in a better prison;
time is blinded
by the white sun.
The moonlight is betrayed
once more
as the end starts
closing in.
Kiss my bleeding knuckles,
you're fragile to the touch;
the turmoil of our attraction
is too mild.
Piece it all together again,
you asked,
believe me,
I tried,
I need some sort of havoc right about now.
Breathe the fresh air;
choke on fake golden snowflakes.
I've seen the beauty of the sunset
in a make-believe world.
I valued our friendship,

it never made it to the docks,
we're fragile to the touch,
I envy the color of the emerald stones
on both of her clandestine earlobes.
I concern myself with other plans,
I am lost without her presence,
pushing me around;
sharing the moonlight,
finally on our true side,
before our time kindly
closes *in*
on *us*.
It's the final hour,
it's the final minute,
count down with me
to the final seconds;
three,
two,
gone.
Our recollections
go unredeemed;
so little of it
could be real.
Resurrect the mime,
he's still falling down
the staircase of desire,
let him burn in the wildfires
of his inner choosing.
Eyes forever shut are dreaming,
trickling of pure sanity,
profound and clarified.
These moments
you've stolen are caged
away in another dimension.
We turn a blind eye
to the sign of the times.

We're undiscovered art,
distracted by
the highway
liberated by
the white of the sun.

walk through the fire unscathed

An avalanche of white snow
chases me down the mountain slope;
I'll meet you
d*own*,
I'm on my way.
A thundercloud above our heads follow us down the riverbed;
I'll meet you on the other side,
I'm on my way.
Trust in our future,
trust in the past;
what's in an hour
can change
a lifetime.
Happiness could feel
a million times better
with a dash of pain;
we should be painters of miracles,
host of dirty obstacles
and learning
to walk through the fire
unscathed.
The less we know about love,
the more we invite;
do not fear the past
and lastly
do not fear me.
An ambulance takes me to the nearest festival;
I'll meet you there
on your bedside.
A hailstorm teaches us how to move on;
do not think you're less
than who you think you are;
you're all that I got to hold on to.

I am the *now,* I am an unspoken *vow,*
I am here for you despite what you put me through.
I am a volcano ready to erupt;
when you say: *I love you too.*
You're a tornado ready to erase all that I know, *all that we hold close.*
Trust in our future, trust in our past; what's in a se*con*d can change our en*tire* life.

grow ten feet long, like them, we fell in love with life

The sun was more faded
than the moon last night,
hiding in the very depths
of her delirious eyes.

She's one of countless miracles
I collected rolling dice.

Together we were a force
to be reckoned with;
in a world where
we're weak if
we're alone.

She's the fuel that launches me
higher than any drug I messed with.

I'd swallow any lie that came from thee
and identify with the new identity
she'd given me.

She reminded me of sick birds
dropping dead like dropped missiles.

She looks like someone with a mission
towards the sweetest Indian horizon;
like them, we fell in love with life.

The summer breeze
founded a new source,
her hair endeavors to soothe.

She's a picture-perfect gift from God
in a perfect frame on newly painted walls.

I opened up to her when she was but a sea of unhappiness.
In June we let the grass grow ten feet long,
like them, we fell in love with life.

infect my normal heart with your crazy soul

Make up your mind;
that's it you're out of time!
Don't be too consumed
by your selfishness.
When judgment comes,
will you kneel,
will you stand?
Make up your heart, *is it there?*
Or is it just another black hole
in the atmosphere?
Who cut love out of you?
Give me the gift of truth.
When the crime took place who did I replace?
You fight so hard to conceal the heaven I see.
Don't infect my normal heart
with your crazy soul.
Did you really run a mile in those broken shoes?
Teach me how to be as foolish as you.
When I arrive at your welcome mat,
will there be sleepless nights,
will there be demonic sights?
Make up your heart, *is it there?*
Or is it just another black hole
stealing the embers of the sun?
Watch me flickering on the nightstand!
I smile with crimson joy while my tears overheated.
Watch me dancing on the new mattress!
My eyes blurred;
my eyes can't see you
I am deeply worried.
My lack of repair drove you insane;
I'll make it up to you.

My lack of sorry drove you ablaze,
your ashes block my airways.
Give me the gift of truth my loving giant.
Why did the crime take place?

Who did I piss off!

for *heaven's sake!*

Pixilated thoughts
are like drive in zoos.

Leaves of sunlight
leaves an imprint
on my funeral
black shoes.

Forget your head,
and where it has
never been.

Forget your sanitized dreams,
corrupt a lover instead;
be forsaken,
beaten obscure
for *heaven's sake!*

Walk hand in hand to the newsstand,
our demise cannot be comprehended
by any premature headlines.

All I know is that by the end of May
the dandelion storm is upon us.

I can't tell which wishes are yours,
mine is liken to be bouncing against
four brick walls,
my fireproof soldiers are vanished
off to war.

The orange and white striped fellow
has taught me well,
in the topic of being
hollow,
I refill myself with
Jack Daniels.

my killer aches for killer arcs

There are holes in the plot,
after a singular turn of events,
the rhythm of your song amazes me.
The night danced us away
swaying with the
drowning stars
on its last *fin*.
You're fogging up my
glasses lens, and
camera lens,
and burning through
my monthly
expenses.
You're flying into more of my *nonsense*.
I need to show you the ways that God knows.
My heart stopped and began on its own,
there are arrows in my chest to pull out;
I made love with the residual pain
as the arrows are disrobed exposing
my killer aches for killer arcs.
The corner of my lips are as dry as metal fences after cool rain;
the words you've chosen to type didn't receive any praise
from the freelance critic or the homeless man
on the bottom of the restaurant steps.
You're taking up space on the bed;
you're bleeding out on the mattress.
You're *nobody's* mistake,
quit pretending the script wasn't based
on our coexistence riding that cosmic plane.
I am talking, *as usual,*
to layers of thick noise
on a hand-held recorder.

You're always wrongly distributing the faults,
killing the silence with chainsaw applause,
killing the marvelous ideas,
otherwise known as the devil's narrative.

I am the meaning, *I am* the ego;
I know the ways that God k*now*s.

her incredible strokes

I melted with the fading sun,
wrote dead wishes to throw
on the aquatic veils
of a starless night.

I delete myself
from today,
I am moving in
unpredictable circles,
inside an interrupted radius.

You hold your aim
and misfire.

I can't believe
the enemies
I've made,
it's you that needs
to change
outfits.

Shine your buoyant light,
nothing more,
nothing more,
nothing more.

My shadow ripples over seaweed
twenty-foot
deep;
her incredible strokes
lured me
back to
shore.

winning is a permanent daydream

I can't stand when I
lose another moment
to open up my mouth
and share with you
a funny story.

I am ashamed
that I don't feel
I am good enough
for you.

I lose in the attempt;
winning is a permanent daydream;
guilt walks with me
as we part ways.

I found a seat next to yours,
followed by a few words;
I gave you a smile, and
a hand to shake
loose.

I am ashamed,
I don't feel
I am good enough
for any-
body.

You're done talking;
you never started.

I am done *waiting*
to dream of you.

I am done talking;
I never started.

I am done *waiting*
to be with you.

a *bad* apple

In regards to you,
all I feel is regret,
I am shaken by the thought of having nothing left.

For years I try to mend what you've cut;
I find myself nesting featherless Swans
on rivers of my distilled sorrow.

Open up your mind at this beautiful hour,
as the sky falls and the evil stays,
while you rest on cloud nine.

Nothing feels worse than thinking of our past,
but nothing feels better
than the moments
that do
last.

I am shaken by the escape of posthumous secrets.
She made me feel inferior;
I am now aware,
I ate a *bad* apple.

I am just another armless ballet dancer
in her imported music box.

Dancing for no one but fear;
I am enlightened by a corpse
catching the point
of a beating heart.

Donning threats
for the nearest
Pollyanna.

m*ost* impure and m*ost* sinfully inclined

The sunrise
plays with our
depleted passions;
wiring cutting
meaningless words.
The yellow God
mistrust silence
as an answer.
Complimentary doubts,
takes love for granted.
Careful with your words,
eh, soft dying rain,
self-control is what you lack.
Love leaves us to dry.
No surprise!
Corrupting ongoing thoughts,
for a shot at reconfiguring the lies,
involving the *once* innocent mind.
Now, m*ost* impure and m*ost* sinfully inclined.
An enemy of our heart
greets us with a friendly smile,
while we crave pity from our
songs and medleys.
Their harsh lyrics rewrite the scenes of lovers who'd passed,
what's definitively good is also a mix of the m*ost* happy
and m*ost* absolute*ly*,
and positive*ly*,
sad!
A bed so soft foreshadows our death;
we got rained on
by a .32
end a .38.
The devil's whispers block the sun.

What does God's love and obligation have to do with anything?
It's only an exhibitor's wet dream;
a game of lies set for the future.

Your punctuation punctured my soul,
now pay the mot*her*fuc*king* toll!

a table for two

I am fishing for your love
in times of uncertainties.
I miss your glow!

I've found old voicemails
and I am grateful
for my resourceful
paranoia.

Anger fills my mind
and I am tossing
glasses to the floor;
reminding myself
to call the maid
in the morning.

I watch the twinkling shards
explode like disciplined fireworks.

I can't turn your rocks for you!

She feeds me with shameful epiphanies;
our hearts once stood as a table for two.

I press c*all.*

We're sorry…
Please state
your name
after the tone.

a threat to her tranquility

Is it November already?
My thoughts began to fog earlier than I thought
and the autumn leaves have fallen depressed
because I am a carpet of colors refusing to rest;
I sense a dangerous refuge knocking intermittently.
The colors only serve to make me weary;
there are no clouds in the sky,
except for a few grey bushes.
The streetlights bled ominously;
the scenery lacks our abuse.
There are no cars in the parking lot,
a cat slept on a crippled white line,
a damp leaf has fallen on her head.
The cars begin to come,
loud sounds rose to pose
a threat to her tranquility.
She remains on the ground,
underneath the hood of the car.
Singing a lullaby while
a cold chill tempts to duet.
In the end,
I desire to become stronger than she is.
A single leaf has kept her warm,
reminded her of
home.

I have awoken from my slumber;
it's early January,
I am a carpet of white fur,
I don't feel cold
therefore,
I am never
alone.

dreams are a perfect dying place

I am enraptured by a strange man on the crosswalk,
I don't know how I feel about this.
The man is an iceberg melting with the night;
I fall deeper under the man's icy water.
S.S. Curiosity.
He spoke:
"Explore the vast possibilities,
speak with sound judgments,
refrain from sweet and diabetic hearsay.
Sin is hard candy for the diseased,
dreams are a perfect dying place,
always believe in yourself,
become renewed with each empty chore."
It's help.
It doesn't matter
if the man is
a friend or a foe,
I feel great about this.
The man's words burned like a quiet fire,
I watched the cartoonish sparks fly,
pages are ripped apart by his heart.
I have a story I want to tell you;
HE cues the evening satire.
A blizzard came, the man had no jacket on,
a warm room is the last thing in his mind.
Streets begin to coat with inches of snow,
I didn't really see any fear in the man's eyes;
a loving home is the last thing in his heart.
He spoke:
"Explore the vast possibilities,
do not speak ill judgments,
bitter and unspeakable melodies
will torment your soul fibers.

It is hard to mention how I handled it,
what you see, is who I was before,
not every open door is a gateway
for an abundance of meaning.
We're all street whores
living just to serve!"

a creative lie on queue

Through the paint,
through the looks,
I am brave;
I am untouchable.

Should I be ashamed for reaching too tall?

Through the mask,
through the noise,
I am deaf;
I had enough
words to hemlock.

Be one of a kind, *but,*
I am too awakened to go back being blind.

What's the length of this never-ending story?

There's too much plot,
I rewind routinely,
we're all erasures of good air.

Add another version of yourself, maybe more
into characters that cannot wait to go
as their life falls
word by word.

For the music,
for the skies,
I am a creative lie
on queue.

There's no such thing
as a cup too full.

Through the grand scheme,
through the long flight,
I am bigger.

I omit light,
I am brighter than all the sun
combined!

Throughout this lifeless process,
throughout the curtain calls,
I am the star,
I am the show;
I am met by thunder-shy snow.

Through the finale,
throughout the lecture halls,
I am a student,
I take in all the darkness
and the sin from my teacher's voice.

Imitating the voice's
strongest words.

What's the length of this never-ending story?
There's too much black holes,
who'll burn best through my dark,
morbid soul
first?

I add another version of myself,
into characters that are easily lured
by all sorts of pretensions,
my life self-destructs
word
by
word.

honest lips

Nothing happened,
believe me;
let me pour my heart out
with the facts.

Let's take it slow,
calm ourselves down
and start from where we left off.

Nothing is too late,
things can change
with some proof;
delete your
dissatisfied thoughts
they're overused
reaction.

Embrace the silence
in all this noise and
listen to my ugly truth.

Something happened.
It changed us.
We suffer this without resolve.

Let's take it
slow,
calm ourselves
down
and regroup.

Receive my charcoal words;
believe my honest lips
when I say:

being quarantined with you
brings *out* the ugly truth.
I think you should know;
I think you already know.

EXHIBIT
N

noise offerings
in
the silent
conquering
of
hearts missed
and
granulated
on a sieve

joyously dismembered

An insidious madness
possesses my face,
I'm here to destroy you.

There are harsher words
you could have said
but that will do.

Vagueness in your eyes holds me by surprise;
a heartless innocence came to shout,
silenced by your mouth;
ruthless soul.

I am no pioneer of what I've been through,
I am quickly healing with each manure jest.

There are sharper words
you could have thrown
but that will do.

I am not afraid to give in to you;
I'm but a toy abused;
joyously dismembered.

Similar to yesterday,
this may be how
you want to say
you love me,
ruthless soul.

a coward's countenance

We fall on the gasoline-soaked grass,
our love ignites like illegal fireworks.

The night beheld our light too strong,
love's mutability has a plastic core.

Our tale was told,
serenity inspired;
tonight's potential
hides our true identity.

This was destined to go many ways,
still you choose a coward's countenance;
covered your eyes when you became infatuated
by the opposite of wellness.

It's closing time!
You'll deprecate
on eternity
re*morse*lessly.

You're feeding the noise
with your greedy awareness;
I fall victim to your perpetuated rue.

fair warning overdue

Not now,
please wait a while.
Lovers overpopulate
the dance floor,
it's *not* your hands
I am waiting for
to save me.
I must rely on you
to inspire speed
in my morning runs,
I imagine that
it's *you* that I *am*
running fr*om*.
I trust in you,
I realize it is fair
warning overdue.
Not now,
over and out.
I am but a glance
that won't tell you
much.
I must succumb,
I tripped on your foot
on the dance floor;
it was our song too.
I am on the ground looking up
with an angelic view
of your smiling lips.
I've fallen on purpose,
you're my master,
in this angle
I feel your
power!

I am yours,
come closer
claim your prize;
I am your early
morning
prostitute.

to sustain the awe

I will not allow you to return,
after the dream I just had,
I am assured,
I can live
without
you.

There are holes in the walls
from bullets that I let go,
the only thing left of you
will be the chalk outline
the devil drew.

Rewind the first track on our favorite record,
release a breathtaking motion to sustain the awe;
I exhale the sounds of laughter we conveyed.

Are dreams the only place that I can feel you this way?
I am going to elaborate,
I am going to replay
the glory of our finale;
the hurt is a luxury.

You try calming me
when I wake up.

There are holes in the wall from punches I threw,
the sound of *us* howling is the only mercy left.
Dancing alone in the dark,
I am dying with every little sigh.

Your voice used to calm me down,
until the sun came out
to make your mouthpiece
dry for the ritual.

I can't be too humble now;
hurt is a luxury
that *we* can't aff*or*d!

the chalk outline the angels drew

Good*bye*,
I know
I just arrived
but I must be
on my way.
A voice told me
to turn the other cheek;
it convinced me to flee.
The voice was of a girl
I met a long time ago;
but it's *complicated*,
you know,
it might just be the first
cringe of evening.
She's a sweetheart with lips that tasted of whiskey and honey.
She was almost broken, but she hid it so well I could hardly tell.
She was on the run from the Lord's obligatory blueprints;
saying: *it's not mine, give these dreamless men without imagination to somebody else.*
*Hell*o, I know you're at the door, *what are you waiting for?*
I can smell you from across the room,
the only flower in a field safe from secular abuse.
You've avoided the trouble long enough;
I am here to seek the truth and I am hoping that I do.
Stop and take a breath,
I am not an obstacle
in your way
in any way
what*so*ever.
Stop and listen to your heartache,
don't choose to be afraid,
falter to licked wounds;
I am begging you to stay.

I will protect you for hours,
I will run away with you,
let's assume the chalk outline
the angels drew, matches
our intertwined
bo*dies*.

munching on *Picasso's* ear

If you run into me
I will see to it that you lose your life.
"If it were up to me I will let you live on,"
said the *"me"*
from *yes*terday.
But I see change in the horizon,
but I see pain inside the clouds
built of gorgeous fluorescent dew;
I am waiting for heaven to widen.
Let me in and I will stay forever *in*-love.
I am good to those who let me be joyful;
I'll be glad to share with you my final kill.
"I will see to it that I win this balancing act,"
said the *"you"*
from *to*day.
But I see chances being taken for granted,
but I see caves raped by jarring drawings
and I am praying for hell to work overtime;
and commence rapture in death's bedroom.
Run faster,
stop living
with fear.
Our anger froze like a deer with four damaged legs
sinking down a dark shimme*ring* blue ravine,
savoring each *damned* breath.
The car's headlights flashed within
the depths of its sedated eyes.
The driver was busily distracted,
munching on *Picasso's* ear.
Let me share with you my final kill,
after all,
I did all this
for you.

I told you,
I am good to those who love me,
I'll be glad to make you
my final
kill!

fucked by the sunlight

I seek you from a *nowhere* direction,
you're never *somewhere near,*
you're always *far away,* spiritually.
The grass is greener when *fucked* by the sunlight,
when the darkness comes will you be alright?
A perfectly told lie could hold anyone hostage,
and forever comes after tomorrow's ghost;
my life feels like a cup half full.
The ocean dr*owns* another person,
when the fo*reign* waves come
promise me you'll be alright.
Her fire is hard to put out.
Forever schemes, expertly
stealing milk-goats;
her cup *is* full
of it.

I wasn't wrong to place those fugitive bombs

It's been a long time since my world made sense;
I overdosed in lies to no end.

How did I get here?

I've seen the other side of things,
I'll like to keep living this way;
live forever in a better place.

It's been a long time,
since I found the universal key.

I would open doors
that didn't want *me*.

How could I make this a happy tragedy?

It's a very long procession to reach serene decay;
it's ignorant to say life is too short?

It's been too long,
since I've figured it out,
I wasn't wrong to place those
fugitive bombs.

Work it out,
you pitiful clown,
long to escape your own joke
so*me*how.

I've seen the other side of things,
I'll like to keep loving you my way;
without you there is
no better
place.

the skies will water our dream's satellite

Note to self: love is strongest when you begin as you are.

Don't stand when you fall,
stay laying down I will join you,
we'll enjoy the gradual fire of tranquility
in letting love happen without delay.

No one else will decide for you;
no one else will believe it is true.

All the way from the city of angels;
the skies will water our dream's satellite.
Pray for what you already got.

All along your eyes were covered,
all along you wore a fruitless gaze;
lacking essential enthusiasm.

Note to self: what's second nature is your service to the unknown.
Note to self: realize you embody the universe's whole range of potential.
Note to self: prove to non-believers your soul glides through dark skies.
Note to self: everything is not where it was before for the sake of incoming greatness.

No one else will believe that it is true,
all along you were a belligerent fool.

No one else will ever see through your eyes;
who would want to?

pure heroin

Quit sharpening their horns,
applauding their roars,
seeking their service,
wishing upon their stars;
storing faith in unfinished art.

Emancipate relief,
release me and confess,
your personality
is my favored drug,
my pure heroin,
I am in love.

I am summoned,
it must be to suffer with
what is sad in your heart.

I'll convince you that I died
with every hour I sacrificed,
my spirit lives in your words to me.

I bestow the power in you to decide
what lies,
what stays, *and*
what dies.

Our composition must be sung
in different
tones.

seeps flowingly towards the absurd

Live for that wonderful state;
the listening breeze hear us.
Our hate *it*
consumes,
our fear *it*
deludes,
forget
it,
escape
it.
Become new;
seek and find
your missing
pancreas.
Become you;
know and feel
the birth of realness,
right then the light seeps
flowingly towards the absurd.
Become the beauteous light
that blankets my world,
neatly folded
and uncurled.
I am open,
I feel you
in my most cozy
and serene
place.
I see the growth of a new
understanding.

I embrace it,
I love it and
know it is true;
instant changes!

Of *course*,
I k*new*.

our elongated fire

D*anger* buds from her eyes;
here comes her impulsive nature
ready to disarm with unknown plots.

Paired with my sadistic smile
she creeps onto my lips,
biting my reply
clean-off.

Her intentions
sway the opposite direction;
into denser humidity.

Our elongated fire
attracts flies into the forested room.

With each new endeavor
our soul finds;
we're known to escape
into the most convenient path.

What waits for our heart to feel?
It no longer exists,
to meet us
half
way.

This str*anger*
no longer,
c*are*s.

pro*cure* a head full of stars

A harsh weather came with violent inventions;
a thunderous shame blew away our only friends.

Your kisses were my paralyzing dreams,
I thread lightly,
yet it hurts to be
really there.

The mocking jays gave us blunt messages
in regards to our obs*cure* punctuation use.

We'd convert maddening verses
into squandered prayers.

I am tongue-tied,
my sin lied in our
overly-stated good-byes.

Now, I only worship clean hands,
with ten fingers.

Now, nine blackbirds flee
towards the sunset's fishing nets;
our dreams forfeit to the sound of the clarinets.

The curtained window hints of tonight's death note;
the hours free the current flow of a teardrop,
landing on her side of the pillow.

She'd pro*cure* a head full of stars each night.

Although, the lampshade said:
"I've seen better light than that."

degrading our photographs

The curtains are descending,
they crippled our ground.

The apple has not fallen far
from the tree of our jaded design.

Remind me again why it is you I want to be with.
Remind me again how I let you waste my life.

Disgrace was all you've given me,
degrading our photographs,
with your changing hues.

From being my muse
to living as a well-
p*resented* ruse.

I don't know you
any more
than you
do.

Speak to me;
I am here
I'll listen.

The yellow tape is tightly placed,
my feelings for you remain
a major letdown.

Baby, help yourself, or let me serve you;
silence *then* betrays the question.

Remind me again why I feel so small.
Remind me again how I let you go.
You fulfill my life.
You were the air to my kite.

looking wishful, staring into nowhere paths

I scribble rhymes on my skin
as my tears sign a waiver.
We've entered
the halfway point
of our life, it says.
It's deceitful,
yet believable;
I believe it all.
Our name inhabits sin,
bleeding on the shady parts
of the sunflower fields.
Looking wishful,
staring into nowhere paths.
You can't hide from yourself.
Quit damning sac*red* truths!
Cease it *all,*
take it *all* the way,
all bets should be in.
I ran out of paper,
I am writing the rest on your soul.
Can you keep a secret?
Take us back up on the cross;
let's crucify our dreams.
Words we choose to say,
decay *happily-ever-after,*
following a new set of orders
sent by a booming echo from
far, *far,* below.
Our plane,
crashed
and
burned
righteously!

We land at sea and crawled through black sand,
we watch the clouds turn down our gaze;
the earth pities our dead
emb*race.*

in its original deformity

Do not keep anything from me,
lay it out kindly in its original deformity.
Take this opportunity with clean hands;
muse danger on youth's highway.

You're next to me,
mending *your* way,
sitting in *your* throne,
in *your* master plan.
The result of your threats
are so maddening.

Vent, tell me everything!
I'll cut your legs off
if you try to run away.

Do not reel me back in again;
it's all I ask.

Cut the line,
let me swim
away.

Do what you *need* to do,
plead on all fours
if you *have* to.

She'll blame some useless text:
"I only did what I was told."
As usual,
her senti*mental*ity
give me the best head-
aches.

Opportunist are from heaven's grease traps;
decide and let me:
"*over*flow"
with magic flakes
til tomorrow!

a char*red* sun

Her empty tone of voice calls mine with a smile,
there's only *one* choice
don't be in contempt.
Her heart of black restarts,
she radiates double rainbows in the dark.
The moon *half* gone waits for the sun's cue.
It takes an earthquake to wake her up.
It takes a hurricane to change her mind.
I cast a spell to our pillars white and strong,
I order the thunderclouds to move along.
Let's see to the end of the night,
cheer for the light to fight its way,
we've been th*rough* worse than this.
You've got no choice but to commit to your one life.
Let's take a tour of our backward intentions,
and get lost in a mountain of raging questions
until an avalanche of answer takes a valley.
Let's reason with religious tyrants
and listen to their dogmatic answers.
Take a risk,
take a chance;
feed *your* sorry.
Take a hit,
take a miss;
tomorrow
dies
here.
Her heart of black sings for a char*red* sun,
the moon's flight is interrupted,
as it felt the belt of excitement.

Finally, a decisive
laugh!
She beautifully calms
our sanity's departure.

Drunk driving with
bravery on *auto-
drive*.

old promises enhance our *foggy* sunrise

Who knows what this journey will reveal about us;
who knows what this journey will try to hide from us.

We hold our misty breaths
and close our idle eyes.

Honesty is a dark summit,
but it sparkles with fireflies.

The truth is our dearest friend.

I hit the brakes and got out
feeling confined,
emotionally,
physically,
and
psychologically.

Let's find faith;
let's move forward
from our *bad* days.

Enough is *enough.*

Let's get drunk on love;
get our true rhythm back.

Release our idle breaths,
and open our misty eyes,
and let old promises enhance
our *foggy*
sunrise.

Speak of the truth,
as if it were *our* only friend.

We're in the final pages of a *timeless* romance;
let's re*main* the best
part of it!

Graced by a Phoenix's DNA

Thus, the truth is told through Psalms 37: 23-24. A fragile existence somewhere in the galaxy of her most sacred thoughts. I found myself submerged in the various colors of her imaginative pigments; the paper didn't do justice with the art we wavered. The sun issued an inquiry, about the sanctuary chosen by the rays on her switchblade gaze; I am stunned into amazement by the pretty Jupiter lips of my doe-eyed angelica.

The game of nervousness when your signal breached my soul's mirage, I sense a disposition that'll shift the rhythm of my life. Do you think she'll love the shade from my lunar eclipse, on her sullen state? I offer her a crescent diamond that resembles a cut fingernail. I'll concentrate my heartbeat for now on into the unseen; the unknown's clean-shaven chin. I'll be the keeper of your young figure; the childish tickle of your karmic movements.

You existed and built the man you are seeing now; a rotary clock set on forever midnight. You've become a significant aura I seek before I shut my eyelids; a hard dream-state candy. You're a science worth the heartburn and the heart palpitation; laps of empathy to the sublime. I am paralyzed by my relationship with your goddess-like stature and windblown hair catching the morning rain; I vow to never sleep on Satan's bed again.

I took our first physical hours for granted; I should be fined a large sum of regrets; may I travel back with you again to the same place with conjoined hands, and touching hips. Lips, eager to give into a problematic realm of emotional bliss; to taste heaven elsewhere. You're the smooth air, in the honeyed catacombs of my sequestered hours; lonely in the crowded carriages, enthusiastic to mix souls with people's security systems.

I am a little taken aback by how early you arrived into my sad austere; the single cell in my world able to conjure delight in my winter solstice's prison garments; locust covered paths and the hissing dead grass helping a feather stay grounded; afraid to be taken hostage by love's windy depreciations.

My only true ghost; the only living matter that matters beyond what's capable of being real. My previous theories on chimes of euphoric music are condemned to second class; while your single sneeze gave my desolate academia the courage to live through a purple heaven's beaten left ear. I follow the evenings with a triumphant stillness, under my sinister brown comforter; I loosen the skin on my dry bones, marrows filled by her equilibrium; I am solid, never before, reborn to be intertwined with her through eternity.

Her hold on me is one holy water away from fertilizing the flowers we'd need for a summer wedding; be my magnified cosmos; the core of divinity in detached philosophy; we'll ascend before the altar. You make a whole lot of sense; my view has been a flaming sword all along, at the receiving end; because of you; I re-examined my bloodstream; you're fatal and I will not dispute my cause of death; you are harmony in motion, and a waterfall disintegrating before a lover's exploitive glance one-over.

Goodnight, and be it perpetually good; nights spent with you; our nestled togetherness redefined the most distinguished richness of legendary leathers. My plans stem and fruit; a caterpillar bit through a heart shaped leaf and swam the skies to defy it. Friendship with you opened my eyes to the peaks in clouds, and mountains in space between the stars, and it's exclusive ranches; islands filled with virgin doves, and dinner bells rang, to heighten the orgasms of Gods writing that perfect wave of inspiration; ink dries on that dangerously loving verse for mortal ladies; my princess's hair has a consciousness of its own, you have my word.

My evenings extend; the more I press on the channels to soothe my pupils.

To see her proudest moments and happiest adventures.

To observe her feminine maturity and unlearn it so I could start at square one; the moonlight zested what remains of her innocence and ponders its remedial aspects; the world wouldn't feel a thing, but I know my selfishness when it comes to her is permitted as beautiful pain.

I hope others love as if they're poetry itself; condemned to be written at four a.m. I hope the ecosystem of my soonest dreams have mercy; may it be in our future bed filled to capacity by little children, and one suckling babe; eyes open, pursuing to mouth the lyrics the record player blessed the wet paint of this recycled image.

Come faster. I am running deeper into the steps you've danced to; let's be examples of our day and age.

Come slower. I am drifting into a finer grain of stardust; landing on your sunset cheekbone with a peck.

Inside me, you're a sewing case; encasing my wounds with delicate blankets; fresher skin.

I love you now and always; my Helen of troy; I will not be selfish with my universal toys; I will be that apple bite, and nourished be your original soul, quietly singing as your ashes are graced by a Phoenix's DNA.

When morning woke us up; she'll kiss my mortality with a breeze of contentedness; she has freed my seasonal mind from the cycle of unsaturated visions. You're relentless; loving me at full force; never have I wanted to risk it all, naturally, participating with life's hairdresser; making the dome of the skull another surface for her to kiss good evening; or joke intelligently about. I'll paint her in my restful trance; waking up to a shared prayer, *may Jesus Christ remember us.*

EXHIBIT

O

old habits
lie hard
about
past courtships
that sank within the depths
of dead time

the most passionate sounds

My goddess is one with the river,
belting inspiring tunes,
constructing an elegant chorus
through a willow breeze;
she is gifted with the strings.
I gave myself away too soon,
praised her like the conquered moon,
and set birds free to get lost in her current.
I turned the pages to discover,
a better sunset to be known.
A sunset leaving no trace of hauntings,
one that distracts loneliness,
leading serendipity on an intimate dance.
The only heroin we need
is the Lord's intricate prayers;
we've memorized plenty in the holy book.
Seasons cease to exist just outside,
but in the endurance of one lover's winter
to the springtime of others.
Ever since our two winters met,
each twilight felt of the most
potent hallucinations.
Every morning I organize
a patient bouquet of flowers;
I'd handpick anthuriums,
orchids and heliconia;
lay them on her bedside
with fresh breakfast.
Her final brushstrokes back to shore
radiates utter brilliance on the day's portrait,
painting permanently over my previous Goddess;
a girl with a French last name.
It's a common name, she said blushing green.
It's not common for me to feel this way, *Dearie*.

There is no sight of decay in our garden gates;
her honest eyes outshines my sun today.
I trusted her to lead the way through
whatever traps are already laid,
whatever tone of laughter yet to break,
because I was generously reminded that:
life is for *learning*, feelings are not *mistakes*,
I *like* you, or I *love* you, these too *fade* away;
whatever words solitude uses to burn down our halls,
let it take a *toll*, manage it too late,
and it'll take full control over you.
I am glad I made you strong despite
how you've soften my walls,
it's funny how our uncivil deception
lead to a civil separation.
Our photographs burn charcoal black,
at night they'll return as a flash of heavenly blue.
I adore you,
I need you here by my side,
I imagine you laying in my arms
to help me better disappear at night.
I'd trace rainbows on a landscape of black,
feeding a nation of shadows from our past;
they'd interact with the roses on your crusted hair.
The red bomb inside us all waits to be saved by someone careful,
someone brave enough to fall and float with the transitory clouds;
surrender out loud to words with the most passionate sounds.
I've exhausted the act of looking back
and being a subject to inconsequential days,
hitting rewind with the bottom of the bottle.
All I am certain of my darling is
I'm yours if you'd be mine.
All I ask, my delicate rose is
to trust the rush of it all,
ours is a heartfelt
compromise.

I'll take many vows onstage and for the nosebleeds,
I'll walk offstage and scream at the walls no more,
because of you that obnoxious actor in me is retired.
Together we'll embrace the sounds of applause;
are you aware that all I see is you?
You're a house of pure white,
a canvas ready for an artist
who could paint real gentle
and be sort of profound.
I'd be distances away
yet she vibrates my peaceful grounds
just thinking out loud.
Let's entertain this for a while,
repeat the chorus with invitation,
trust the verses of its every imperfection.
The vagueness of the world
is like the recycled sky
on the perilous weeks of August.
Love songs are burdened by amending hues,
I worship her wisdom of edenic proportions,
she set many souls free before I got
my turn.
Will she calm my hand as it readies itself to raise a white flag?
Or will she match my crazy stance and finally take a leap?

after drinking a pitcher of expensive grief

Keep me on my knees
begging you to forgive me;
keep me wondering *why*
you're hopeless to me.
I am investigating further
into your unsolved crimes.
She fills ashtrays,
never empties them.
She acts as lead anchor
reporting phony one-liners.
Sometimes there's no horizon,
she redirects the light,
she hoards them in a glass;
she's like this all the time.
Giving up your soul is the premium,
when did my standards fall this low?
I'll find myself lingering in dark spaces,
the blackest flames wrap around my hand.
I'll be *that* fire, *that* bitter aftertaste after
drinking a pitcher of expensive grief,
she'd say; as her eyebrows pen a treaty.
I keep shouting her name on a cloudless day;
I altar my misery high up in the atmosphere's white oasis.
I think of her flowing summer dresses,
the diamond tears clinging to her webs,
and it starts to violently shower with dread.
I am preaching to those hearts who find themselves
with nowhere for their ego to go.
Choose your mental state!
Do not forget anything,
regret is what pushes us
to uncover our best selves.

Get ready for
the plummet
of God's hot
scalpel!

naked behind a tree

You were a butterfly passing by,
I am a small thundercloud that chased
after you through the quiet night.
I flew as high as I could,
ran for miles barefoot,
I drowned the deepest oceans
chasing that butterfly
that was you.
They swing their nets
but couldn't catch you,
you flew fast, wherever
the wind took you.
I swing mine and I caught a glimpse
of the butterfly passing through.
It was a vision flashing
like small thunderclouds
being loud, she hid
naked behind a tree.
I found the pain exhilarating, it's numbing,
the thoughts of you flickering by my side,
I dreamed of colors nature forbids to exist;
our canvas goes back to white.
I caught a glimpse of every shooting star,
I caught a glimpse of what is mine,
stay and steal my world;
my winged sunshine,
make my fantasy
your new home.
I caught a glimpse of brilliance,
I caught a glimpse of a butterfly;
a butterfly with God's shine on it.

I thought I knew how to get to you,
it turns out, you are not safe with me.
You own my solace,
and my spot in the soil.
Now, I am panic prone.

I won't be swinging my net
anytime soon, thanks to you!

the role-playing game

My hate came from our inactions,
soliloquizing unsung thoughts
fished from the mossy hooks
of our communication errors.

Cut the role-playing game,
the nights are no longer the same.

I've been through hell and back;
I've seen it all.

Cut the music playing in the background,
you've sung through hell and back;
I've heard it all.

These better days would suicide,
I curse the light that boomerangs.

I say *yes* to our pit of irony,
being sm*art* enough
to see it coming.

I branded you
special.

I relish our
rarity.

the shine on the nightstand photo

In the month of December,
down by the avenue road,
I study her unfamiliar face
returning my look.

I lost her wandering eye,
she's focused on somebody else.

I came up to her with an open smile,
volunteered to be the shine on her shadow,
she invites me to sit beside her elegant ego.

We didn't regret being the shine on the nightstand photo,
we came to be content of our new frame of mind.

Let it be *real*
this ti*me.*

the flames eat away what it wants

The gentleman had little words to say,
he'd step-dance over your hurried lines,
make a broken door with your material heart.

Indeed he was a basket case;
dry gum on the base of your shoe.

Untie your laces little one and relax,
drink the cold night instead.

The midnight candle sits still;
dawn waxes from the north.

We steer clear of daylight;
accept love's vagueness;
we're married to a ghost
incapable of haunting.

I am harassed by a thousand cool days,
the painful act of wrestling with the truth.

I murmur a lie in a pitch-black room;
the flames eat away what it wants.

I've paid my dues,
I've chosen my tomb.

The blues sang of passionate
and radical interventions.

I won't give in,
not yet.

make orphans of the snowflakes

With Medusa's grace,
our unknown gestures found haven.
She contends with these places,
she's my prehistoric curse.

Where should we go first?

She distributes lust;
her indelible bullet paints a scenery
on wet jungles and dry sands.

We stand in terror for no reason at all;
living where we are *least* welcome to evolve.

I am eager like the morning sunrise,
because chaos is our next location,
she's my favorite destination.

We love inside a Phoenix's carcass
and wear unhappiness like a ribbon,
under the holistic shade of a saint's prejudice.

She could never untangle the church's unholy threads;
sadly, only our devil knows his majesty's eyes.

I wrote her letters with red-inked feathers
high up in the haunted mountains;
we make orphans of the snowflakes.

This might be just what we needed,
a slight fix from the errors of being alive,
we balance the guilt with unpaid parking fines;
sharpening the sun-spears that domains on our nakedness;
waiting to consume every square-*inch* of my favorite location;
our heart's
destitution.

keeping my darlings dispossessed!

You're all just a frame to my pretty picture,
wow, the sky is like the m*ost* blue
I've ever seen it!
How staggering!
Sleep keeps our twilight embers burning
we're unlit fireworks on the fifth of July.
She throws me off balance
and shuts me down for life;
tosses my love past the window,
my entrails leaking out.
Follow the trail of blood into the eagle's nest,
take me by surprise,
express more wearied happiness.
Bring me back to life,
I expect nothing less;
follow the trail of blood,
watch out for the muddy graves.
You're all just fake tears I like to shed at least twice a day,
wow, our clouds has never been this clandestine and golden-white!
I am killed without regretting finality's view.
Keep, *keep,* keep the blade inside of me until
the heartaches are some*thing* my veins are familiar with.
You're all just a maze to my straight line,
wow, it's never been so easy keeping my darlings dispossessed!
I am a user,
I am a mess,
a brute power.
I am a failure,
I am a sin,
coated in chocolate.
I lead the innocence down dangerous roads,
I am the singing behind the sirens for the gathering crows;
my entrails leak out on our brand-new mattress.
The record player keeps crying,

she stitched me up like an *Annabelle* doll;
I am fascinated
by our crude medi*ocre* loving.
Our dream-cycle never sleeps; as
the angels rewrite the d*evil's* script.

undressing dawn with a grin

The heaving clouds
take us in and won't let us go.
I don't believe myself for one bit as I slumber.
I committed love I know I'll forget;
I close my eyes to pursue
our dreamless routine.
As we take each other to a magical place,
we are a carcass on hot rocks.
As we take a shot at a moment we think will have a lasting power,
we are mourners of dramatic advertisements
sold without future compensation.
You remark on my life now,
but I have nothing to say to you.
Our minds were consumed by rage and war.
Heavy rain started to collect
on my way back home,
I don't believe myself for one bit
after I committed love I know I'll regret;
I close my eyes to pursue another beating heart.
I kneel on the grass;
my prayers were juvenile.
I need your undying advice,
whoever warms the high seat tonight.
You remark on my life now,
I have this to say: our time is contemporary,
eternity doesn't serve solace to just anybody,
our minds were too consumed by rage and war.
As we take each other to a magical place,
we are a lighthouse collapsing proudly.
As we take a shot at surviving through love's sinking ship,
believing we were drowning for a good cause,
we just end up laughing madly;
undressing dawn with a grin.
You remark on our life now

I still have nothing to say to you.
Dine in the pleasure of these playful question,
engage in the changing hues of our resolve;
it's too good to be *true*...
too good to be *true*...

breathless since that day, *breathless* since that day

Tears and blood all over me.
Each drop pretends to understand
the consequences of our emotional crimes.
Tears and blood all over you.
I am penniless for the rest of my life;
she emerged from my irrationality.
Unshakable.
Untrue.
I've awoken to the war she waged,
bleeding out at the edge of the battlefield.
I've awoken to her war, I'm caged;
she slices me by the throat
I show her a smile
she can't forgive.
I don't mind that you're the last thing
I see.
Seduce me for a *second* time,
I am lividly put down.
She seduces me for a *third* time,
despite the heavy urge to evaporate.
I thought of you a thousand times,
the throne was yours to begin with.
Unraveling.
Unrest.
I have a theory,
thanks to you,
trying to mess around,
we're insidiously hell-bound.
I am fragile now,
was careful then,
what am I?
Our abuse had nothing to prove.
Unmasked
Two died confronting the storm.

Unhooked.
She took my breath away.
I've been *breathless* since that day,
breathless since that day.

how I can control *you*

I feel sick to my stomach,
I saw everything.
All the sickness and the pain
from every strange thing submitted.
How fucked up can we be?
You're quiet as a mouse
as the answer depleted
from your dirty mouth.
Can we choose to be clean and happy?
Can we choose to stop looking for somebody else!
I wonder how I can control everything,
and demand the silence to echo
in our journey to the end zone.
I feel too tired to listen
to your insufferable voice;
I heard you loud and clear.
All your questions are sequestered,
I can't fix or replace
the missing gears
in your deplorable
anti-wisdom.
I filled my remaining years
with our type
of wisdom.
I scream in my sleep,
I endure all types
of symptoms.
She looks straight at me for an entrance
into the view of my winter
smile.
She ran for miles and miles in disbelief.
I wait for her by the window sill
and ended up inviting in
somebody *else.*

I wonder how I can control *you*,
and demand the silence to echo
in our journey
to the end
zone.

posthumous novel

My new favorite word;
my new favorite season;
seasoned with importance,
purified with such malicious
yet decadent reasons.
It takes the cake always,
takes the heart away,
borderless.
It is purgatory at its finest;
hell gave it a five-star rating.
Heaven is one kiss in the making;
one nude body away from going viral,
one sinner away from becoming
true to the famous,
posthumous novel.
The charred crosses on a vinyl;
melted butter with that high note;
always a lonely beggar in public,
she reminds me of French chords.
We're finished with the first white layer;
I oppose the need for an actual color.
The core of my beliefs was uttered by news anchors,
it took years to pay off all my debts with my pastor.
Every church had our picture;
every flower suicides
as it heard our vows
fly like dust through
the empty chapel.

Loveless
and evil.
Loveless
and proud.
Loveless and unquoted;
stolen enough?

what a magical thing, our type of confusion

I was stripped bare of all I was
by your fatal rain; suddenly I was *finite*.
I ran fast, there you were by the bus stop.
Clouds adjust to love your fatal rain;
fogging up my glasses *lens*.
On my way I executed flowers,
now hostages on my chest pocket.
On my way I daydreamed of your fatal rain;
remorse is yet to shed daylight's tears.
Brand new, price tag still holding on.
How much did you sell us for?
Recollecting schoolyard traffic;
under the shade of the cool kid's tree.
Recollecting passing you by
through stairways; our elbows touching,
neighboring hearts chanting indifferent things.
Recollecting the attempt to understand you;
what a magical thing, our type of confusion.
You were stripped bare from the toes to the grey of your hair.
Moonlight paid our monthly bill, suddenly we were *infinite*.

EXHIBIT

P

poor judgements
regarding the vines
of
incarnation

an unknown period

I am keeping my virtues to myself like my wet dreams,
I am hiding inside your bloodied sheets.

She's listening closely for my footsteps.
I walk the other way.

She always gets the last say.
I hear voices from an unknown period,
a mysterious mist formed into an angel;
I've done what needs to be done,
it'll say,
fusing liquid diamonds
in my mouse ears.

Now,
I rest.

Choose your prison;
get arrested doing your drug of choice.

I've done my fair share of wanting;
her silence lead to my selfish
en*light*en*m*ent.

an elongated disco

Our journey was tested,
a dynamite slept under our bed;
ticking away, *tocking* all day.
Her seasons change;
firing chaos every which place;
the look she gave me dances to demonical lyrics.
I grew old wondering
how many arrows I pulled out,
bleeding under a colorless rainbow.
I follow the green light,
we dance in the halls of an elongated disco.
I follow her angels,
they're altruistic and impulsive;
I couldn't tell her what's real anymore.
Nothing was meant to be this detrimental.
Her reasons change;
firing doubts every which place;
the look I gave her promises to never give in.
Suddenly upset,
I noted my regrets;
feeding the sickness
with her supple lies.
Suddenly I am okay,
even if just for a minute;
I am breaking down
the rest of the year.
Suddenly I am broken,
silence undoes
the begging fool,
in the shivering cold
sitting on his own feces.

When I grow old, I wonder
if I'd still be breaking arrows,
bleeding under a colorless rainbow.

I grew old wondering
how many arrows
she pulled.

this divine moment

I hold my breath, I ask her:
Am I floating higher than you?

I am reaching out for your hand
but I'm too far away sometimes,
still I find you jumping up,
falling down repeatedly:
Will you fly and chase the sky for our sake?

I hold you down for a final dance,
let's explore tonight with open eyes.

I've opened up all my scars
and they have fled and lead
to this divine moment
as the truth died in my hands.

I fold my cards:
Am I asking for too much from you?

I am trying to catch a piece of your voice
but I'm too far away sometimes,
still I find you slicing through the giant leaves;
you'd get lost in the forest of temptation:
Will you climb the earth's tallest trees for our bliss?

I've opened up all my scars and they have bled
and lead to this divine moment
as the truth died
to give birth
to *more* lies.

this lesson

As we go through the motions
walking in slow motion;
this mission becomes more impossible.

As we go through this lesson,
collecting weak-minded notions,
we learn more from
what we know
we cannot handle.

She kills me slowly,
I know our particular pain
was designed from something euphoric.

Our problems should be seen
from the perspective of a child.

Our halo burns out.

We collect the charred remains
of white flags as we grow older.

We were just minding
our own endeavors;
fortune favors
broken smiles,
remember?

We wreck the hell out of moments,
rock solid, we become harder
than the cement on the ground.

Keep hardening
my darling,
it's fine.

If you see it your way,
let me follow mine without delay;
won't you just see it from a new angle?
From a different perspective of when you were a child then,
who didn't find comfort in the calm after the panic
calling out to
step-mommy
or *step*-daddy.

on how to best navigate through vilest sunlight

I have genuine affection for you,
sorry to be mad forward,
I thought you knew.
Allow me to bring you up to date on our prime dilemma,
take a pill or two; relax and let your mind cool.
I get by
being a product of my strange situation,
reimagining a better life,
reimagining a better world
where I don't take part.
I stare out the window repeating a curse,
ignorant to the freshness pending;
while doing yesterday's laundry.
I have genuine words to say to you,
sorry to be too loud but
they already know.
I have genuine thoughts running dry,
sorry for being weak,
I am but a man who loves a fool;
too cool to sound rude.
Allow me to bring you up to date on our primetime drama.
Take a meal or two; relax and quench your hunger
before more bloody laughter ensues.
I'll be where I was before,
thinking hopelessly about how to resume
without you on the table marinated by quiet.
We never got by
being a product of our strange situation,
reimagining a better love,
reimagining a better soul
where our stain never qualms.

I stare out the window swallowing a curse,
clinging madly to newly established rules
on how to best navigate through
vilest sunlight.

I am burning with my pile of clothes;
hope it warms every lover
living in the pre-emptied hours
of *give* and *take*.

a proper thief

She's a residual energy,
a soul-sucking fantasy,
running out of miles,
and burning with no fire.
Maybe that's just it,
the ghost I chase ran
faster than me.
Hold me close,
fast forward
to the sweet
ending.
Nighttime comes and goes;
light always returns
with fewer cares,
with fewer passions.
A storm becomes of the tiny wind,
our broken masterpiece needs
a proper thief.
The light always returns,
no matter where we are,
no matter where we go,
meet me where we died,
as the morning comes;
here's to our sweet ending!
Maybe, that's just it,
the ghost I chase
caught you
for me.
We're orphans to the rapid oceans;
we fast on fantasy's bones,
chew young grass growing on the highway,
drinks from the streams of smoke swaying
through our lonely spirit.

Our residual waves
flipped the ship;
the northern lights
wrote our sweet
ending.

a dash of burnt cinnamon

You let our journey get away,
you pushed me into the vast cold.
Every song felt like a one night stand;
aren't you drawing your map too as you go?

I am a raindrop without a purpose,
doing great acting on your horrified grace.

I am a broken tricycle,
doing the unmotivated parents a favor.

Watch the sparrows fly like arrows past our sunny days;
brush the silence with a torpedo of explosive answers.

Why compare me to him?
I am here now,
let me wander through your heart,
like a lie fresh baked golden black
with a dash of burnt cinnamon.

I got used to the dark,
being alone in parks
swinging myself
higher and higher
trying to reach you;
my provocative star.

You greet me with awful visions,
you greet me with awesome thoughts.

A field full of flowers are in awe;
the silent rain showers are in awe.

We met under the covers,
a minute later you left
me on my own;
drawing till the sunrise
a portrait lacking of a soul.

I tattoo you in my right arm;
I memorized your lyrics;
had dreamt your lullabies
serenade the elevators.

If now isn't the right time
I hope you take me by surprise;
startle me with pure sensations,
rekindling embers in my hearty laugh.

Will you let our love soar?

The source of my muse
is *love* after all, not from you,
or any wound I let bleed,
but of feelings in disar*ray*
that found me on their own,
seeking refuge in fragments of songs
lingering like cigarette smoke.

I am allowed through your flaming sword;
no longer are you refusing to feel our swift division;
no longer are you refusing to seal the envelope with your lips.

you're a lesson I didn't take seriously

Kill the thoughts,
leave behind the loss;
what is life without a choice?
Kill me now,
leave my unsung thoughts behind;
I am an unwanted disease.
Do you still want me?
Will you watch me let go?
Watch me let go like the red in the horizon;
watch me let go like the many Gods you worship.
You're a monster in the trees;
I can feel you watching me;
you're an uninvited guest,
that comes in anyway.
I shoot you down
and watch you bleed.
Will you watch me let go?
Watch me let go like the crime tape on a windy season,
watch me let go like the quietest embrace.
You're a gift without a warranty,
you're a lesson I didn't take seriously,
you're a mindless fantasy,
you're too much for me,
you're just an unwanted disease;
already sheltering another
wicked way
to hurt
me.
Kill the thoughts,
leave behind our loss;
what is life without a choice?
Kill us now,
leave our thoughts behind;
we are life's unwanted disease.

Do you still want me?
Will you watch me let go,
of every laugh birthing echoes,
of amusement for our thin walls.

Watch me waving without direction at what I am giving *up* for good.

accidents are meant to breathe

Progress depends on us changing,
failure teaches us that lunacy is a great high,
don't let anyone steal your crown of thorns.

Our nature is cruel
but we don't have to be;
remember this for your sake
my homeless queen.

We didn't happen by accident,
accidents are meant to breathe.

The moment captured your eyes,
we flew through the windshield on repeat,
a push or a shove is all we need.

Three,
two,
one,
refrain from smiling
a downward slope
honey.

Happiness is in the quieter moments;
life and its pitiful habits clog the drain;
listen clearly to the pulse of every bullet wound,
suffer no longer in parting embraces from walls closing in.

Three,
two,
one.

Next!

find fabulous aw

Stop deciding,
pull the trigger
without warning;
refuse to caution
my decision.
In my system,
my dreams amongst them;
a kindred spirit aches.
In my solar system
is an eclipse and the seasons
regain what's lost in this charade;
install fear into me
as I give into sweet release.
A *fatal* action found
a sparkling pile of silver;
stop deciding I'm not gold!
A suicidal angel flew away
to the arctic mountains;
cue the volcano's
demonic boom.
A gifted soldier walks towards the battlefield;
cue the monsoons of heavy artillery.
Each fatal action corrupts our dreams;
no kindred spirit will show its face here again.
Each recycled season,
reinstalls fear into me;
giving in is so bittersweet.
In my system,
my nightmares amongst them,
with every corrupt spirit I acquire,
my soul deigns the resurrection.

In my solar system is an asteroid belt
of what the seasons have taken hostage.
We find fabulous aw in our blossoms of clarity,
she installs beautiful fear into me.

Voided hand in voided hand,
our neighboring graves
gives in finally to the
Rest In Peace.

a pulp

I hated being told I am always wrong,
she keeps me hidden as if I am a whisper;
I am a wound she resounded on her deathbed to have blindingly adored.

I was winded to a pulp,
tragic were her words;
we are the casualties
of double personalities.

I hated being told to learn,
while I am wandering through the visceral;
through the desolate gold submerged in her conspiracies.

Call security to escort our insecurities out the double doors.

I'm hungry;
I have patience
this time around,
I am alone reciting
your pensive prayers.

Wondering what this path is showing us,
pandering through what we're learning I see;
wondering why this path is broken,
thinking it is you who fixed me.

She's winded to a pulp,
in the mirror she sees me,
tragic were my words.

Using my lips
she forgives
her*self.*

amateurs with nothing else to *live* for

Her red lipstick on my cheek glistens,
oh, how I waited for a week to taste that smile.

I am on the receiving end of the benevolent torture;
she finds ways to decapitate my intentions.

I've been waiting here for the past year,
I've been waiting here watching seasons commit suicide.

I see you now and again on our precious Saturdays;
it's never enough to just be head over heels for you;
I would trade my soul's last fragments just to see you.

A few minutes with a few delicious seconds should suffice;
what is important is our love's continuance.

When all of our moments start falling apart;
do not let go of my clapping hands,
do not interfere with the script,
we're the main act.

We made it through!
But to them it seems
we're a bunch of amateurs
with nothing else
to *live* for.

EXHIBIT

Q

queens
in
debt
exiled
into
enlightened
poverty

dying for granted on the little I could give

We will arrive momentarily,
where we want most to be.

Let's share our thoughts,
we'll mend relations;
open up to me.

In a dream state,
I can't explain how I feel;
I can't contain the hurt you feel.

We arrive at nowhere,
rigorously shaken,
I couldn't hold my ground
after you've changed direction;
dying for granted on the little
I could give.

I did myself a disfavor,
seeking guidance in the stars.

Where do you think you are?

where I am least likely to swim

I dreamt of you again,
I wake up to a nightmare that never ends;
I melt in despair.

You're my home,
where I belong.

With too much time in my hands;
when will some be wasted on you?

You're the parting sea,
where I'd like most to swim.

With too much kindness
filling my heartache;
my broken home.

I took many pictures with you,
I have forgotten what you mean to me;
holding us together is a broken frame.

I am scared to look down
and see myself dying on enemy grounds.

I am scared to look your way
because I will only take you back
to this broken home we built;
to this broken home in me.

You're my home,
where I belong.

With too much time in my hands;
when will some be wasted on you?

You're the parting sea,
where I am least likely to swim.

With dilating kindness
fueling my heartache;
our broken home.

the final drop

Let's sprinkle the lies with our truth,
let's fulfill loving visions with our eyes.

Even though it's hard to focus on the now;
it's enlightening to know
who you
really are.

Don't give up,
stay on our cross;
live through the trouble.

All I want is for our faith to grow,
don't hold back from our well-marinated calamity.

I am only trying to save your soul;
your whole entire world.

Don't hold me back
from saying more.

Don't give up now,
stay on our cross
until the final
drop of prayer.

snap my neck neat

I miss your vacant smile,
I miss taking calls in a phonebooth.

Please return her to me in one piece Mr. Operator;
please return her to me as a brand new soul
or leave her just as hollow, it's your choice.

I saw her,
going along
with my broken words.

Please return to me
in a good light or
don't shine at all.

Wake me up,
don't wake me up;
I've started swinging
with a heavy load of regrets,
let it snap my neck neat;
it's all I *want*.

porcelain needles of springtime

I am infinitely struck by melodies
sent by legends in the afterlife.
Leaving tomorrow's chances
to the lady in the stars.
I am opening every door;
letting in strays from all across town.
She's a veteran of hope and
an advocate of second chances.
She's the yellow thunder,
the freezing rainfall
on our wedding night.
Quality moments awaken in her laugh;
I'd feel rich every day for having that.
I'd answer the ticking questions
before they fade into microscopic size,
before another finds what I hid in the mines.
We'd analyze the beauty of our insane rituals;
we kissed on the porcelain needles of springtime,
we separated under the cheeks of tangerine skies.

my divine troubadour

I didn't notice
the cracks in your voice,
I get bored wondering
if I ever had a choice,
I seek the only way out,
but my walls talk me out of it.

How do I get myself back to you?

Help me to say I do.
Help me to play fair like you,
hold me and
lets you and me
have sleepless nights.

I notice the pause between the noise;
I wonder why I am no longer sane
when I am around you,
I seek newer horizons,
I am far away from understanding
what made our compass work in the first place;
but my walls talk me out of the investigation.

How do I get myself back to you?

Help me to say,
I will conquer this pain.
Help me to gain back your respect
and everything the wreckage stole.

Help me to say I won't let go of hope,
no matter how excruciatingly false!

Help me to turn this frown on its head
and break the walls so we could breathe;
free fresh air for us to share
my divine troubadour.

Help me to say I won't.
Help me to play unfair like you,
hold me like a ghost;
let me have my long cold nights.
Help me to say I won't.

stagnant it was

A coin descended down the well,
my wish is a farewell.
I began to receive luck
as soon as the evening sun
fades to serve the other half.
I serve the life of others
while my wishes die down,
drown underneath unkindly.
I am rock bottom, forgotten;
resting on other lost thoughts
and winterless wonders.
I return to my homeland
I am filled with choices already planned.
The coin I tossed leads me back,
only to deceive me one last time.
I am a waste of breath, a weight added,
not lifted; yet our talks are like a game of tennis.
The Earth underneath us gives,
and shakes with violent force;
this misunderstood greeting
opens old doors meant to look new.
I adore such helping hands
swinging hammers on locks,
remorseless vibes catch fire.
This coin will go sell its soul
both sides would, unremarkably.
Let time fly doing other people's bidding,
waste another dime on batteries to know
when to sleep, eat and fuck.
Imitate the pathetic fools with
dreams desired subconsciously.
No more coins are to be thrown at the well,
in the break of a brand new day,
wishes are to be granted with dismay,

become unfaithful to the words eased into escape.
Ducks swam like paper boats on the water.
Her wish is also a farewell,
she still dared; but sadly
the coin hits rock
and stagnant
it was.

it was lubricated with care

I sit in my perfect corner,
lining my drinks
with ice-cold love.
Amidst the neon lights
a lone dancer began
igniting enemy sparks;
survivors there were none.
I hid behind my bruised soul;
I came by to say:
"I'll make it out alive because of you."
I long to be turned down
to be her pillow wild night.
She scanned me like a cheap item,
stared at my invitation for a handshake.
She took it like a dish served cold;
then she devoured my first lines,
stuttering at the expense of a quick response.
"Refrain from romanticizing the moment," she'd say.
She told me about her dead dog,
I melt to apologize for something I wouldn't do
and subtly I hardened my face
as it was lubricated with care.
Dead-eyed, half-drunks,
fought for her attention,
catching a whip of her scent; while
I am immune to the fragrance of obsession.
She would ask me real politely to:
"Have a nice evening!"
Like a quiet fly in the horizon,
I am unfazed by her titillating voice;
it's been a lonely while that I acted truthfully.
The stars began creating
a forest of angelical lightning.

While inside, people played
a pinball game with their eyes,
singing hateful quotes
through silent growls.

"You scared the living soul out of my dying body!"
"Will you marry me?"

install a resurrection please

I erase my thoughts again,
it all sounds like a never-ending lie,
like visions of unicorns and love,
like a reason to not see the sun,
like a blistered hand ceasing
to be moved by her feminine charm.

Her smiles outshine the darkest fights,
she covers me with alarming miracles.
Lord, pull me out of this early grave,
install a resurrection please.

Without this connection I am lost;
without this recollection of yours.

Silence overwhelms the message not received,
courage is a scarecrow in our thunder-struck path,
I have come to my senses;
I've come to unhear your goodbye.

Jealousy stood out like a mast on a sail,
hours were shoved inside yellow tsunamis,
while you waterfall on a pile of sandpaper.

I couldn't be there for you at times,
but I have my own things too.

She's my early grave,
without this new connection I am lost;
without this recollection of ours.

the evening favors lost love

I saw you across the road,
the streetlights beside you turned
the shade of forever yellow.
We sat in the bus for two good hours;
surely, a long time ago.
I remember the sharing of energy,
the breeding of melodious tones,
then the vibration of words faded
as the bus reaches your stop,
mine left an hour ago.
Why did you have to go?
Let's figure this out
before my heart goes quiet.
She's the princess who saved me
from one of life's most mundane death chamber.
You'll find me listening to your sad song,
singing along and getting the words wrong.
With the absence of your laughter as my soundtrack,
I reject the morning light,
I close my eyes,
everything goes
back to black.
Flashbacks of our one night,
falls like a kamikaze plane.
My spirit is marred,
from worshiping you.
Darling it's cold where you left me,
but I made this tundra my new home,
she tells me to abandon the comforts of the fog.
Why did you have to go fabricate danger where there is none? she'd say.
We were little children playing hide and seek;
she will never find me.
We were little birds in the afternoon sky;
she will never reach me.
We were like the tip of a tree,

it's one long climb; the heights
of understanding is unforgivable.
Would I be worth it?
Would we be worth it?
I am still asking her an assortment of questions
when our heart went quiet for months in a row.
You were mine,
my safe and sound,
my small island in the sky.
We'll find more than lies
in our neon paradise,
than the bottom of the sea
being lured by the shining pearls.
Let's crawl back to the surface,
I am through swimming with extinct fishes.
When morning comes,
I'll sing our song.
When morning ends,
I'll resound her words.
Let love be our soundtrack,
play our record till it hurts;
we're the innocent cheer
after landing a somersault.
Let every creature hear
what we had to shout;
waving goodbye
to the morningside.

Until the twilight in the horizon
fades,
till the last leaf of a willow
falls,
and the evening favors
lost love,
my final request;
bury our dead
d*ove*s.

her whispered ultimatums

Tonight, I've been gifted by an entity
to be the giver of fair warnings
in regards to incoming sights,
of every brilliant stroke of ray that hits the morning,
of every circle drawn to bind and protect us all.

I am called to prepare an army of warriors
up the hills of despair.
It's my duty as the *"great"* one,
to manifest like a venomous snake,
to be your killer of doubts,
to untie the noose on my beloved's neck,
for our one and only creator.

You shall await my emergence
as I proclaim the march to spiritual war.

You must surrender to the soothing waves
that heaven will sound,
or be labeled a deserter
to be looked down upon.
Though I myself am a culprit,
I am convincingly truthful.

I've buried a treasure with no map,
curiosity is the devil's currency;
now you know.

These thoughts have no curfew,
I am a disease absence of a cure,
I am a film no visionary could edit,
due time I will enslave you all.

For months I admired from afar
the sound of hooves on our land.

I am stricken by amazement;
I found myself engrossed
by the speeding horse
and the strong female rider
who guides it serenely
through the speechless pastures.

I felt it, even now as I reminisce;
it was *freedom* she endorsed,
she astounded me by her performance.

I once more erased her as my reason to smile,
as a damning fact never sleeps,
about how all she's good for is last place,
love is a malfunctioning hologram;
a faulty resolute to a lifelong problem.

But even amidst a clear view of a full moon,
full and bright to frame her.
It blinded me from the symptoms
of her whispered ultimatums,
she's slipping off my fingers,
still a smile on me lingers half-heartedly,
even though I promised all of me;
once, when the moon was in full glow.
I would recall our handshake
being so brittle and fragile.

Should I lead your heart's battle? she'd ask.
How about the one present in my mind? I told her.
Or are they both connected somehow? she'd say,
holding my shoulder.

I better flee, and
guide my army
before she adds
another symptom
to my already
fading
smile.

EXhibit

R

running
the
wire
of
benevolent
persuasions

death's yellow agent

I hand her the gun,
I feel safer this way.
Control me, I said.

I want this!
Own me!
Damn it!
Commit!

We're met with a storm brewing
in the eastern shorelines.

Reassure me as the skies come undone,
ready to be incinerated,
to be compensated
by death's
yellow agent.

Protect us,
come closer,
we hid under
the glass waves.

we lay down,
she regains her composure,
she consumes my words
with impatient yearning.

Wake up!
Perk up!

Let my lukewarm apology
circle like a venturous crow;
dressed in the ash-colored
wedding gown you burrowed
from my previous
ghost.

to our tsunami of secrets

You're the queen of my fire;
what kind of lie am I being lead to?

This light you shine
smells of that time
you made me feel
dead inside.

This hourglass of ours
has been cut in half,
the sand inside has fled
the scene of the crime
and it will never be found.

This light you shine is blinding me,
those monstrous sights cannot be unseen.

The wounds daylight torched cannot breathe
due to our tsunami of secrets.

You mistake my words;
what will I do with a deaf fool?

I was the king of your fire;
what kind of darkness did I expose you to?

Our white genius
sparks of fortitude
and forgiveness.

Dawn's young sword cuts through bone;
nighttime degraded us the night before.

We're blushed like a red light,
we've lost ourselves in an adrenaline rush.

"N*urse*, where the *fuck* is my *mor*phine!"

that girl I met, *was she even true?*

Let's begin with an abstract slideshow
of houses with no roof,
of saints with glass eyes,
of love sentenced to die;
no condolences from
any*where* or any*one*.

I've encoded your true intent,
maybe to suffer means to learn
that our individual despair
is the most tangible
phenomenon
to be felt.

The crowds work
in its happy sickness,
in its meek health.

Love begins as a history lesson;
we'll exchange pages immediately
and have a burning party
after alcoholic drinks
and homecooked dinner.

Let's begin where it went amiss
and laugh till we expire.

We're such masters of pretending;
you didn't really like the flowers
I left at your final resting ground.

Fine I'll behave,
I am a recluse,
a soul junkie,
yours is far out,
yours is a worthy reach.

These are apologies for the sake of finality my dear.

These are for a girl I am about to love;
I am a stray,
I am the cracks
on the highway,
a boring toy
with a few tricks,
making you fall for me,
one I've exhausted
for weeks and weeks.

I've cried and I've wept, as
I prepared my heart to flee
towards your emotion's infinite skies
for more fo*reign* sensibilities fo*reign* to me.

You felt like a sunrise just then,
when you said you admire my ways,
not only my apparition.

I experienced summer in your embrace,
yet, I am tired and I'm sad,
I've felt nothing since then;
when you threw stale sunshine
in my googly eyes.

I've been fooled!
I desire proof!

That girl I met,
was she even true?

I open our unhinged doors,
but it leads me
to trap-rooms,
to padded doors.

Angels or Demons,
I've fallen for both.
To the girl that I am about to lose,
please b*urn* along
with *this* note.

your magnitude

It's a mistake,
perhaps love is,
we're killers on the run,
the only trail we left behind
is our weaponized smile.

After a count of ten,
she unleashed all she could,
letting fools bargain for amends;
waiting to profit from fantastical pain.

I am just a couple doors away,
I left some food on your doorstep,
you're free to come by whenever you want.

Hell is a myth when you're around,
the heavens call you with the darkest names;
fingering the rosary caused a blackout in our heart's city.

The Lord's prayer never made it through,
a voice inside someone of your magnitude.

Worried moon,
heal us.

You're the only one delighted enough
to trust us with the helm.

No confessionals
would allow us in
after what we said
last time.

your intrusive nature

I'll create a sanctuary for us;
I know a place we can call safe.

Here, we live for second chances,
we'll plow through arctic mazes.

I saw you again the morning after,
you've mastered my courses
I never tire of your intrusive nature.

Come when you please,
I expect you to make it a habit to.

Let's resume,
my friend;
seeking taxes,
seeking allowances
to no end.

Let's stop riding this toiled wind,
and be frowning boats instead,
searching for love's glass infested shore.

I will be the death of you,
that much is *true.*

I know a place where
solace is a twin grave.

Let's give up now,
we suffer anyway.

Tonight, we go
for the im*mortal*
chances!

pour from a constant fountain

Remember when…
remembering is too immense an effort.

We relate more to the sun when it fades;
oh Lord, deliver us gently to our ends;
then make examples of our memory.

We relate to the night, in how
our love is black coffee,
flavorless and absent
of a sweet aftertaste.

Take your time Mr. Sunrise.

Once daylight is crossed,
a sicker dance of happenstance occurs.

Our devotion is running tired on its last leg;
have the decency to meet me half-way,
let mercy pour from a constant fountain,
for us to bathe in on our hottest dates,
my Queen,
are we
too late?

yearn for this

I am enlightened by the lower altitudes of your mood swings.
Come on home flower enchantress; let's become one with the soil.

I am constantly mesmerized by your individualized petals,
I am hypnotized by all the fireflies you came to love.

Let's become one,
without God's approval,
we cannot yearn for this.

HE preaches to the brokenhearted,
right now it seems, *that's us.*

I am eternally enchanted,
her beauty is remarkably divine,
let's realize this journey for what it is,
before there is nothing to look forward to again.

We choose to rule with dead eyes as the hourglass bled.

Right now it seems;
there are cracks
on the surface.

Above us immortality shines,
down on the dying,
you and me.

die away in numbers so great

I don't want to sleep,
I don't want to be so deep in this,
I don't want to run;
I want to share my keep.
I just want to look you in the eyes and say:
"I just can't stop loving you."

A river green,
runs through my dream,
keeps my heart fed;
towers built by cowards like me
die away in numbers so great.

A river green,
welcomes our collapsing dreams,
keeps our heart pounding on the electric chair.

I don't want to laugh,
I don't want to express too much,
I don't want a fight;
I want to save what's left of my face.
I just want to look you in the eyes and whisper in agony:
"I just can't stop loving you."

A young lovers romance was all it was;
those were tears shed for the final chance,
those were deep cuts that bleed through bandages.

A young lovers romance was all it was;
more tears are shed,
not enough to shun
love's burning forest.

River green,
we swam here as lovers,
our swansong is a gift from the sky's choir;
we remain blue, envious of the clouds
flowing like untied ribbons over the yolk.

We're asked to return everything we took that day;
the tang of such questions unravel us,
we decided to give nothing away.

A young lover's romance was all it was
any*way*.

from a single sigh

Steady now, and
try to balance
the pros and cons.

Such cowardice;
cowards lift braver lies;
fabricate the moon landing;
I read that from a single sigh.

Hearts stop seeking for answers,
all that is to be found
is long gone; *ashes*.

Accept that and falter
to no more cravings
compassionately
invasive of your
peaceful side dish.

corpses rot happily below our footsteps

We lay underwater,
under arrest by shotgun stars,
reflecting on our demonized arts
prophesied that night.
We gallery these boats by the docks;
we counted twelve chalk outline;
these birds were hit
by those tides of ours.
Innocence is caught in the crossfire;
guilty are the warriors of silence.
Death by chocolate;
red velvet necklaces.
One brick pillow is shielded by
a concrete blanket.
We dream of fireworks display
on Halloween time.
At least you know sign language,
she'll choke on a baby carrot
she stole from a baby rabbit.
At least we got extra batteries for the nightlight on our bedside.
At least the sheets are cleaner than usual; *how unusual…*
The devil adheres to purity,
to the scent of grotesque flowers
with absurd names,
forced to grow bodyless,
unmolested by snails after rain.
Our shade is infested by hearts
addicted to chloroform and chlorine.
Lease my cold shoulder;
spend your summers here.
We lost our virginal behavior to the liberated bliss
of a fallen angel coming inside us every Sunday
without our ancestral consent.
Telling us what to prove under its influence,

each divisive syllable is used as malady.
Corpses rot happily
below our footsteps.
It's heartbeats residual,
they scar our beautiful
soul-scratching miracles.
Sold! to the unicorn in the back
with two *terrific* halos
for each horn!

The Thin Air's Zen Highway

Everyone is walking too fast.
Where is there to go?
She won first prize. The many shortcuts I took led to her wide oceanic grassland. I sit and ponder my next move. There are no moves. I shall go many places sitting down. Maybe I am next to her while she's thinking of me. My spirit-hands combing through her hair as the window sways open.

The green fireflies explore her humble bedroom. While I am back in my cold climate. I flicker with her illness ridden nausea. I feel a small ache in my heart begin ripening. Nobody hears it. I feel it pass through shortly after her music silences the colors present. It will return with friends. It told me.

There are empty white chairs. Pulled from under tables. Nobody sits to fill the void. I watch from a leather reclining chair. Two children ages six and twelve. Their senses engaged in gadgetry. I try to feel young. *What was it like to be without a gun on my temple all the time?* Held by the grim reaper. Love will have to wait. It would say. As I smile at a picture, she took a year ago.

I wonder if the woman I've *previously* admired took that photo of her. I would like to hope so. It seems like the nicest thought I had all day. And it's only thirty after ten. My coffee is three-fourths done. And we're waiting for the fossil to open.

The massage chair is passed to the next person. I declined the whore of comfort. Felt like kicks of tiny black horses with wooden hooves. My patience runs just as fast as a herd of those. I cannot wait to read the sound of nothingness in my blue room. Managing to be alright without her sinking feeling drowning meaningless boats as they circle under my eyes.

My simplicity dons a new coat. Getting longer scenes in the final cut. I must sing these verses in one breath for her. She'll run her critical mouth over the rawness of another idea. I pursue to know more. I ask her to elaborate. We celebrate this cooperation of two creative minds. We will arrive at the manifested idea. It will take years. But to us a year feels like a millennium.

I am pale from looking down secretly at something just as fascinating. My muse doing jumping jacks and clearing the smoke left by boredom blowing its brains out. She wore a tux of rich fabric. Most words are lonely virgins just wanting to be chosen from the thin air's Zen highway. Given a red jacket to bleed in. A golden watch to cry out the time. Let the demons know it is now three-o-one in the afternoon.

The dullness felt like analyzing what I see. Couples holding hands. Terrifying half glances at their quick remarks. I see single travelers with more horsepower to their lines. Talking out of tune but with a clear thesis on translucent glass. I hope they win a beautiful restiveness on the eve of their long day. They deserve this high laying on silken contentedness.

Interracial agreements. Hearts from different stasis bind and weather. Their differences loved and atoning for every atom of their sins. Their bets making profit. Her eyes condense to spirit. As her scarf wrap around my side of the world to keep one misplaced soul warm. Following a sacred direction for once. He is still found dazed and lost. When before *him* glides floating feline silhouettes on ventilated pastures.

In cathedral floors.

In disco halls.

In frosted crosswalks.

In soccer fields walking through the goal post as if it was a teleporter.

She'll find her hope hopping hopefully.

With her effortless aim she puts out fires.

With her kind coat of trust, she guides this man's mind to enlightened silence.

She's a pavilion for the most starving thoughts now given holy water to bathe in. I'll always come away with little children doing my bidding. Given the shaking heads a hand to shake. Wondering what knowledge and responsivity is exchanged. What insecurity is given halt and a recess too. How much more far away the scars can sink inside the marrow of tough skin.

She's the respite for voiceless lions. Anger danced with truth in the desert. There were now flashes of immortal pictures in my tour of her generous protest.

What was the context of her roar's intensity?

I promise to sacrifice a limb or an arm until I tame a modicum of understanding.

She's good friends with the stars that came.

My one sweet little wonder.

Woke up the crescent moon.

Reminded his *lips of its immortal shape with one swift quiver.*

EXHIBIT

S

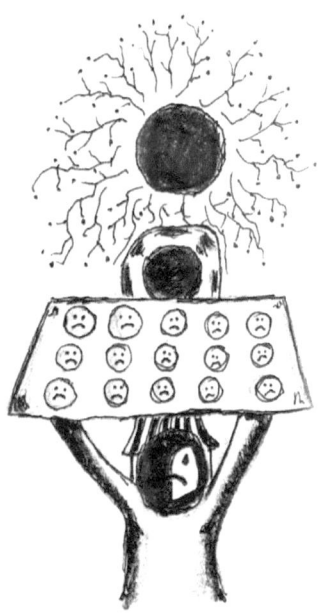

sun-baked sadness
and
asinine commentary
on
what goes on if you
don't

yes, that's you you're looking at

Reflect on the smidge of light,
wherever it's coming from.

A demon caught sight of you,
when the sun arrived;
the broken mirror is doomed
by life's joyful punches.

Am I as unique as my maker?
Let it snow more worried souls;
let's see what's in between,
every twinkle of light unseen.

This much is what I can offer,
I am your four-leaf clover,
let's not be blinded
by trinities
anymore.

Chin up, be proud it lasted longer.
A demon caught sight of us,
mimes our warning smile.

The glass shards turn to dust;
seasoning our shape-shifting lust.

Her one hand is occupied
by an empty cup,
had enough?

The demon you befriended
is almost out of fingers to count.

Like a lone wolf in the quiet corner,
yes, that's you you're looking at.

We're doomed till death do us part.

Pretend the seasons away;
my sun
f l*ow*e r
bed.

watching our flames trying

I dreamt of getting closer to the sun,
seeing happy faces on everyone that I love;
I went down on my knees
and prayed to the moon every night;
I kept it to myself until now.

Watch me go off the tightrope,
freefalling towards the ocean,
watch me go off the tightrope
with nothing but a cold shoulder.

We choose to avoid the best way
to connect with our past lives.
We always assume the worst
may soon arrive.

So we fail to realize the truth
in every lie and cower to the night;
collecting grey clouds, gently
shoved back inside our shells.

I dreamt of finding my true love,
seeing her face light up to see mine;
that idea never fails to make me smile.

I went through a different path
and did not have the last laugh;
I kept it to myself until now.

Then something spoke,
humming behind the smoke
while watching our flames trying.

I froze to say a word and
knew that it was worthless.

I am now a flightless bird on my own;
I hope you remember me as I was
balancing both sides with the feathers I had left.

Staying calm for you and me,
remember me soaring high,
not freefalling about to drown
a deeper pit than the heart
I fell in love with.

somewhere in *us* something is wrong

Do you ever feel weaker than the day before?
I need to correct myself;
somewhere in me
something is wrong.

I am stripped off my identity,
I stray as far as my sanity goes,
I sin because I love the way
the devil looks at me;
while angels like you
keep me company.

Do you ever feel lighter than the day before?
Floating on the sidewalk,
as you chase a million miles
searching for a particular smile;
somewhere in *us*
something is wrong.

We're betrayed by design
to continue a life filled
with misery and lies.
I am dying to stay alive,
let it be known this is
the start of a suicide
note.

Let's go as far into where our insanity goes;
let's sin because we're *used*
to having demons
as playmates.

free birds

We're guest at this special hour,
we fall out of the sky,
strangers to love's power.

Tonight we savor
the spaces
between us
and the universe.

It'll destroy what's behind us,
destroy what is yet to be born.

Let's return to that perfect darkness;
we used to know.

I am a shadow in her book,
I am never going to see the whole picture.

Our secrets pierced
free birds
with its
*ant*lers.

remembering the softness of the sands

Today, I missed you for the longest hour.
Today, you plague my sanity with rage.
Today, I missed you in my scenery.
It almost tore me to the core,
I told myself a heartfelt apology
in her ghastly voice.
This was where we stood,
remembering the softness of the sands
on our feet as the sunlit waves kicked in.
Take me back to our evening walks;
I am reminded of the *warmth* and how
it *never* feels the same
in memory.

for each other, *for each other*

I was sent here from up above,
clean your mind, it's only love.
We're here to make music
as newborn doves.
Pieces of you have always been,
trying to get out,
trying to get out.
We are here to set a path;
for each other,
for each other.
It will evolve into more than love;
let love be our trophy from the skies.
I am here until the end,
I am here until the dragon desc*ends*.
Pieces of us are hiding
in someone new;
love is like changing
a light bulb.

a better adventure as divine silhouettes

What am I looking for
in this vast collection
of helpless souls
who are doing the same?

What am I listening for
in this broken echo
of noises that don't
want to be heard?

Who am I in this color palette?
Am I wrong to see shades of gray?

Who I am is a muddy canvas;
you can really tell the story
of a broken dreamer.

What am I kneeling for in this enchanted forest?
Filled with natural bliss, why can't I feel it?
What am I longing for this early morning?
Clarity is this new canvas; what sanity?

I blocked the muddy picture implanted by some other artist,
let's paint ourselves a better adventure as divine silhouettes.

Who am I in your color palette?
Am I wrong to see shades of gray?

Who we are is a muddy canvas;
you can really tell that
we're broken dreamers.

polished by lantern snow

Drive this direction,
crossover our intersection;
glancing at confusing road signs,
tangled by Eastern and Western skylines.
Avoiding the dangers of the open road.
I am threatened by the sound of your voice.
She steps on the brakes,
her feet rest uncomfortably.
There's flashing lights ahead;
Morse code for death.
With open eyes and pounding ears,
we're awoken by scary dreams,
the sound of heavy breaths,
the sound of a deaf scream.
We abruptly stop,
while the hair on my back
stands and waits.
Darkness lingers through my windshield,
then a silhouette of light with no face visits me;
are you an angel? Am I fortunate enough to fly on your back?
Blood rushes through my body,
waiting for a signal,
to accept a mortal plan.
I hear chaos start scratching at my skull,
memories of us perishes at an alarming rate.
A touch of her hand draws near,
polished by lantern snow,
her face is numb but smiling
at our unfamiliar hold.

Drive slowly,
don't look back,
and do not be weary,
Dearie.

riding on borrowed time

When our screams violently echo,
skydiving is our evening ritual,
will you wave that white flag of sorrow?

It wounds me to see you go,
tell me how we can get back to Meadowvale.

Can we keep riding on borrowed time?

I know you're despicably tempted.

Doubts will only sprout higher and higher,
until the bed is unmade.

Was it fun, when you freeze me out from a heartbeat of existence?
Cross a square in your calendar, *learn your lessons yet?*

I stand and worship at your method acting,
it seems so real;
so ethereal.

I burn the noose,
it's no use dying for *this* reason.

I hid the blades in case a new dawn breaks
to feed me hope for better days.

Let this be the last grenade
I throw your way.

When our seams finally untangle,
when the feeling of nothingness becomes useful,
it heals me to let you be;
then you tell me,
"I want to stay."

Just as embers start flying
and everything turns to ashes
in *Meadowvale.*

red

I am not in the right mind
to agitate this feeling,
to belittle these words
for the purpose of mending
emotional strain.
It's never the truth,
it's always falsified,
what I meant to send you
is classified even to me.
Where the truth hides,
I don't know,
it takes time
like all of life
to be reduced
back by nothing.
Until insanity takes full control,
when you awaken suddenly
after only one or two hours of rest
to find it's still dark out.
As you stare with angst at the glass,
it's too late to return.
Open your eyes wide
to every damage
it has caused,
every dramatic
applause echoes
many greedy
pitch-black rooms.
Turning grey and
grayish-blue
as madness
consumes,
as paralysis
is endured,
suddenly it has stopped

to relax on a virgin.
Surrounding tents
homing desire
that is just beginning to end;
it's no day of silence with the woman
I levitate with.
She's an already forgotten jingle,
an emotional anthem.
I am walking like I am deceased;
with a lazy grasp
at my own liberation.
I live on a balance beam
carrying a bundle of wet sticks,
I'd call another day bleak
after given a turn to speak.
Surrendering to my hard seat,
these secured minutes
knows it'd be for nothing
if I don't stumble first
on fragments of turbulent truth.
Believing I am obliged
like the imperial sun
that fills the fuel gauge
of normalcy.
I am one to look up with fascination;
I mine diamonds and silver
in our evening avalanche.
Slow down
jaded heart,
close your soul
for the rest
of your life,
cut the strings of the kite,
leave the wind alone,
let the breeze stray;
be unkn*own* to our touch.

yellow

This yellow compass
is patient,
this terrible nuisance
hardens the sand,
this leaky faucet
drops out of the curriculum,
and lines of heroin
misbehaves in the air
like orphan children.
Move along to the beat of something
authentic and humbly genuine.
Ring the wedding bells,
behind the airless wheels,
let the ice melt on the asphalt.
I am in the right mind believe me.
Be lively in accepting my mood swings,
frantic and involved with maniacal beings
trying to join and convert me,
turning my blood blue
with every changing hue
of the persistent evening.
I am second cousin
to the seasonal doubt
in your façade; symptoms are:
frayed smile and peeling skin.
She's chanting meaningless words
for the sake of making noise and
drones of caring lyrics sheen,
as her pity is underlined,
<u>alive, *but for how long?*</u>
I kick the chair,
let the rope cuddle
my neck.

The heck is with these broken channels;
hypnotizing me with its empty scripts
and black and white strips.
The batteries are loose and it falls down
the underground sewers
never to be found again.
I stare at the screen of this lifeless rectangle,
until I have a new distraction to be tuned in.
Seeing visions of a dream house with four kids,
a dog or a horse, *maybe,*
fast cars in the garage
and money in the bank,
a high-ranking position.
I am never lonely,
I'd have many wives,
they'd love me for what's inside
and what's outside,
the sane guy and
the insane guy.
The pastor advises she
torch her doubtful demons
with a flamethrower.
Once a month we'll be throwing
grenades at the neighbors.
Hear their last sigh as
map corners are kissed by embers,
afterwards they resemble figments
of someone's ashes.
We make love on the pavement
all over the blue grass,
near a lonesome flickering streetlight,
meaning to save no one and tell no one
where hope lies;
where safety in someone's arms
can be found again,
a memory or remedy so fused

with guilt and self-loathing;
greed manifesting only.
Shadows begin changing and
the covers begin to swallow
us whole, darkness becomes
of our sacred dreams.
Flashes of a foreign notion
of what is real and what is fiction
becomes our new devotion.
*Which coat will keep you warm
and which will leave you feeling like someone else?*
We're insecure of our extra layers of skin
and our drooping interchangeable mask,
suddenly the hot water does not cleanse
the sins we've done.
Our punishments are written with a cold cup of peacock's blood,
the document resembles the rainbow fields in Egypt's desert.
Unplug the joyful music and face the sullen dryness of the world,
pierce these worms on a hook and leave it on the water.
Leave it alone,
just
leave it alone.
There is no certainty
that something
will be
caught.
Maybe stop asking for more
and refrain from looking back;
before you even add to the list
broken legs for chasing after
what you've got.
Learn your right to misjudge the beauty of the sun;
as it goes down making resounding promises of returning
when you wake up;
if you wake up,
if you had enough.

Feeling alright
even when
you're *really* not.
When you're practicing
your digging at the ground
till it's at your height;
and it only takes a subtle change
in scenery to crack that final smile,
accepting this new bed
this wanderlust
for a final
b*end.*

green

Endless roadmaps,
pointless pretend,
thinking you know
where you are
when you go
there.
And that it's your joy
you're experiencing
and not some sort of
spontaneous lemon
souring your prideful
shame.
This ancient happiness
is driving you into false
recovery.
Resume and move along.
Into fast speeding highways
and new landscapes,
new views lacking
understanding, talking
less than normal.
Imitating a madhouse of faces,
fascinated by the same blaring sunset,
knocking over the open can of paint
spilling all over your plans.
What plans?
They're just momentary accidents
that worked out well overtime.
Maybe now we can move on.
Like a herd of Buffalos charging down
the mountain, a family of soldiers
just surviving through their forlorn days.
Let's start dancing side by side
to spark peace instead of igniting violence.

Still we choose violence.
Our heavenly views,
renew our lost point
and unfounded angle.
I need you to forget the moments
I called you.
If it were possible
to quiet the sincerity
in my voice.
My choice of words
just crumbles like a rolling boulder
in my jungle city being caught in
the thick vines of people's vices.
When we cross land,
we share, trade, invade
and don't need to hassle
with the ideology of trust
and give and give our all
to the wizard behind dark
green lit curtains.
We're happily sleep deprived;
insomniacs till the grave.
When will they return?
The memories of when I had little feet,
when I was a child without a damaged counter
of the many times I endured defeat.
And drowned in silence
trying to figure out answers
and stories to counter
the cowardice truths
that feels like cancer.
We aid the dark entity looming over us
in the weeds of our sanitized dreams,
we just keep tearing and tearing from the seams.
It seems there is no end, *no end to it,*
just red light and green light horizons,

then grey-blue and white-orange patterns
passing through my bedroom window
when they feel alive or dead enough
to come inside,
whether welcomed
to visit me or not.
Stop.
It's a red light,
many more will shine,
to *slow* you down
just as you reach 230 miles per hour.
Turn on to her music and focus on the lyrics
and press your horn to the beat that hit hard,
that earned your heart's concentrated lust.
And glamour with advances
so forced and rough,
the diamond days are gone,
so what if the gold had melted away!
When in love,
we're feeling like
a percentage God
no longer human,
but, living *more* so.
Trying to make ends meet,
trying to season the meat enough
to feel right at the moment
the first juicy bite is taken.
With some courage,
I will slam my foot on the engine
and drive to nowhere,
just driving through forest and dirt.
Mastering the momentum,
down to every frustrating stroke,
life starts off as a long one;
a long realization towards
a determined nothingness.

Just to make one point known
and manifest like a minefield
of bombs where it's needed most.
To create more lands to rebuild,
homes for the meek hearts and
the weak-minded fools
trying to be rich with whatever
weighing their pockets down.
When sleep comes
I urge you to come undone,
to reload your gun
with fresh bullets
from the box;
tell everyone.
Now, they're your audience,
become martyred by their applause
and let the curtain plummet
before their skeptical eyes.
Till silence once again
steal from the lives of yesterday
and delay the life of now.
And finally come to accept the fact,
that you've been dead a long while.
I am tasked with a killing;
I am tasked of being killed
by what is most dear to me.
This echoing truth,
I pick it up with my two bare hands,
I let the smoke fill my lungs
with bogs swaying with supernatural grim.
This fight,
this loneliness,
you brought this on yourself.
We zombie walk on love's blind maps,
gathered blueprints of some future past,
laughing as we crush on new burns

and fall out of love with alibis
for not returning
cupid's stupid arrows.
It's sickening,
it's mighty wrong,
it's a war you must accept
now and forevermore.
Leaving a trail of blood
with each invisible step.

Red light.
Yellow light.
Green light.

You're just another
Red light.

Keep calm.

Be *quite.*

Quiet.

never ceases to amaze

The blue in the dead sky met
with paintings of murder crows
flying in jagged lines.
Distant thunders then cracked with
blue static above our funeral black sky.
I am lured under our heavenly roof,
inferior to the damning effects
of the devil's ruse.
The tip of the shovel is bent,
always hitting rock,
digging mindlessly
for months.
I label myself tortured,
even amidst a sublime ballet
of lights, a traffic of angels getting fucked.
Blessing me with a kind farewell
and a show and tell of what is to come
if I may.
I stutter now and
tease my eye from
their drastic schemes.
Every truth is a rude awakening, they would sing.
Sketching someone's soul on wet sand,
is grasping desolateness;
deep places are meant for diving.
What never ceases
to amaze me
is you.
It's the floodgates of hell
and the surfaces of heaven
she guides me to.

I am never letting go of her shaking hands,
in love with how petrified I was
with the music playing incoherently
in the *New Jersey* background.
This arrangement of keys and strings,
are tangled serendipitously.

We pull each other out from
life's coagulated
glaze.

daylight's optimistic nuisance of a friend

Why indeed must you inhabit my head?
Why indeed?
Why indeed?
If you were a dragon…
was I feed?
So organized were your lyrics
when you burned me…
sounded original,
transcendent,
puts me in a unique trance…
what a blessing to have you sing it for me that night…
as it bled through the mountains;
as it set fire on both my shoulders,
as my flesh became clay
to another psycho artist.
Why indeed must you travel so far inside my heart?
When indeed I tightened security,
gave them guns and bulletproof vest.
When indeed I gave them a radio,
to play old songs we chanted as kids.
If you were a ghost…
was I a dream?
Sleep paralysis has been on point with its goal lately,
to tell me that I haven't moved on yet.
How indeed?
Goes without saying we'd be dancing with two broken feet.
Smiling with broken teeth,
opening up to night terrors
to prolong daylight's
optimistic nuisance
of a friend.

Whisper the truth for once;
indoor voice please…
put a silencer in your gun;
Oh, Lord
show us eden…
deliver us from
this plastic
world!

EX_{HIBIT}

T

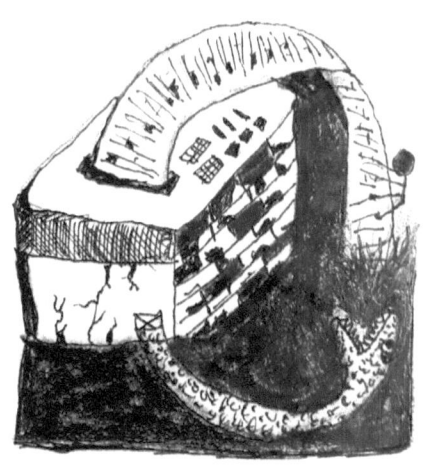

the toll
of
a
love
unshackled, unshaved, undead,
and
inundated
by
false prophesy

this black and white world kills my lady love

I had enough with this routine,
our flying ghost keeps turning rocks.
This voice inside echoes now,
this black and white world
kills my lady love.
I light us a new match.
I am pressured to fall down,
pleasure is found in a second glance,
roses turn black as the night you found me.
I am better off the edge you pushed me in.
I've overcome,
I am no longer shy of new beginnings.
I am better off the pills
you begged me to swallow
for you.
I'm higher,
I am no longer drowned
by our deepest sorrow.
I am inspired by the same fear;
but I am no longer a wounded deer,
looked upon with silent remorse.
This passion reeks of
our false compassion;
your stone-cold words
are in the refrigerator.
Today's season begs to die;
the dark only paints over the stars in your eyes.
A closed door reminds me of a red light,
don't be discouraged to let new flame rise.

Our house is on fire,
the space between us
fills the smoke
with offerings;
just smile now,
say I do,
I do.

Roses remain black as the night
you *lost* me.

painting creative ways to love me

In a dream state;
I see you with me.
Our moments
on rewind,
on repeat.
In a snowstorm;
your embrace help
beat the cold.
Our moments
on rewind,
on repeat.
This changes the reasons we fight for,
you see me lay my head up high.
This changes the reasons we have left,
we're going to fight until our last breath.
You're painting creative ways to love me.
Our moments
on rewind,
on repeat.
I am in this until I can no longer remedy,
this man in me.
I am in this until I can no longer remedy,
the love I feel.
Our moments gain permanence
when heaven's waters hit our feet;
on rewind,
on repeat
we will p*lay*.

vague words set on a timer

I read the crime scene on the newspaper;
there's nothing left but the fruits reaped by demons,
recklessly distributed poison pill-sized into kiddie cups.

I am hurt by the misleading pictures,
let's move onto the next set of predictions.

It's been a long commercial,
it's important you be the one
to say a last goodbye.

Secure a path for us
and lay it out kindly;
the heart reveals that we're rotten
to the core of our being.

Calm yourself,
don't breakdown,
what you offer
I must decline,
you live on
vague words
set on a timer.

Dreams wept as they pass through us,
reading the final letter written by you,
to me, enough to entertain the faceless
moon stalking our next move.

We're tired of walking in graveyards,
there's no road for us to follow,
it's important we kneel
to love's dead-end perdition.

out of our beachside ashes

It was the way we met,
I didn't know my heart beat with music
till I met the sullen beat of yours.

She kisses every wound with disregard,
I hang every line with a question mark;
at least from our clouded perspective
you will stay honest without a doubt.

Haven't I seen the better part of you with my eyes closed?
Haven't you blamed the part of yourself you hated most on me?
Let's get in trouble and be locked up together, *shall we?*

We were amazing when a moment submitted to our games,
we'd get into trouble and be seen all over desolate screens.

That was the way we won;
I didn't know my world
is better upside down.

Let the offended sunset make
something out of our beachside ashes;
we'll fix each other
a trouble bath.

Let's get in trouble;
be praised
as l*ove*rs.

That n*ever*
mad*e* it.

distorted and hostage by the sun's decrepit rays

I flower our garden soil;
I found beauty in our war with colors
while the stem leaves turn black;
desperate for imponderable hues.
A lamppost nearby began flickering
amidst the terrifying winds refusing to acclimate.
Posters peel off our bedroom ceiling,
people are in an unsteady pose,
dancing awkwardly under the strip light.
I begin changing the light bulb,
subconsciously, I make a fist,
glass breaks inside my hands
provisioning a thousand tiny cuts.
Emotional deadness,
homes my pitiful face,
immune to the pain
from another bad idea
my heart couldn't find
a fast meaning for.
I make my way to the bank;
depositing more emotional currency.
Yellows, greens, reds and blues;
I like to spend it on *her* sometimes.
I am out of grays; *just great!*
Now you know my imagination
is my favorite hiding spot.
You're proud, aren't you?
I am your dog after all,
chasing my own tail around for months.
I gave up, and started chasing your shadow;
distorted and hostage by the sun's decrepit rays.

Will she leave me feeling as hollow as she did yesterday?

think of all it brings to us

You speak of these things,
but all they bring me is hell;
realize the words you say,
before they spill.
You give all you can,
but mostly take away;
realize the value
of what is now gone.
Guilt is here to stay;
what can you do?
It never went your way;
what other proof are you looking for?
Just leave me behind,
just walk away,
like it's all worthless
for you, as I walk away.
You take pride of these things,
but all they bring you is hate;
realize they're worthless gifts
before you write my name there.
I give all I can,
and nary take away;
realize my value,
before it's too late.
I am here to stay; *what can you do?*
All goes my way; *what other proof are you looking for?*
Be farther from the person I came to be;
the love that right your wrongs for you
and understood your similes,
suffering in your lost art.
Let me shake your hand with gratitude;
I need a new scar to look at.
Just walk away from our sunlight;
our time is past tense,

it did not leave a lasting essence.
We're here to stay; *what can they do?*
All goes our way; *what other proof are they looking for?*
Just think
of all it brings to us;
all it brings to us.
Just think of all the things
it brings to us;
all it b*rings*
to us.

vague words tell great lies

Satisfaction is never truly fulfilled;
in life we see great love destroyed
with no foundation left to rebuild on.
We just adore ourselves, killing time
with our delusions and market price resolutions.
She'd watch the recovery of a wound;
it's my touch she's feeling,
thanking my ghost for the slow healing.
Now pay the deed is done,
thief on the run,
into another earth.
She'd recall the softest verbal hooks,
her eyes would scarily awaken
to receive an empty can of worms.
Her questions are sentenced before a jury;
including the lies in-between sentences.
I hear the facts.
Thumbs up!
Great job!
From those you think loves you back.
New things begin after you say goodbye;
vague words
tell great
lies.

The snake enters;
vomits out
a whole
m*ice*.
Evidence #1.

behind the bitter aftertaste of red wine

Does another at this moment deserve your heart?
A lifetime role as your bringer of light?

Although, I was bestowed
no promises to sign, and
waited for no ink to dry,
I surrender still to lonely nights
in the company of dead stars,
asking to no one in particular:
why now?

Every word you unmask is neon paradise,
it leaves me breathless and keeps me in tune,
while the crescent moon fades outside
with the winter gloom.

I account for another cowardice move,
I would trade it all for a braver mood.

It's been six months
into a long summer season
on two different places.

I became a better man
when I left my beating heart
with our patient eyes meeting
behind the bitter aftertaste of red wine.

This is just a friendly reminder
it was hard to keep my mouth shut
until now.

I heard the seagulls above our sandcastles
waiting for something other than a choking hazard,

what I've been fed was too large a morsel for my heart,
now the line is lost in layers of thick sand.

Who shot the hourglass?
Was it me or your bloodied hands with a smoking gun?

I pray that my maiden remembers me,
I dream of slow dancing with her to obscure music,
where I'd mirror her graceful gestures fascinatingly.
By night's end, the moon will permanently tattoo
our names on its soul.

My guess is
the moon loves us more
and it can't wait to speak to the sun about it.

But we must await the choosing of how we feel,
till *morning light* reveals our lifeboat;
ours is indestructible,
ours will float,
and traverse
to and from
many
edens.

Our neon paradise,
is discovered during
sleep apnea's
rosy imagination.

I understand now my darling
how much *your* divine love cost.

rejoicing with the same melody as yours

The desire for understanding kills our original fire;
ever gently like a dream forced upon our darkest will;
sending warning to the next one, *is that all I could send myself to do?*

How her weapon is polished with silence,
so insensitive yet so sincere.

How your role in her plans will fruit,
with cracking laugher as the movie rolls
its eyes over a dramatic soundtrack;
not rejoicing with the same melody as yours.

Even though it was never enough,
I am never enough,
and that's alright.

Was I rent?
Was I only yours for a second?
Did you feel my existence breaking like a blaze through your sparkling blackwaters?

The journey through love's longest rivers,
holds with fragility a few delicate rose petals.

Your agonizing voice is far too distant;
crying of unforeseen pain,
crying of stones that are too
heavy to lift.

Levitate with me if you may,
feeling proud,
forever smiling,
seeming profound
in my whispers.

Hurting,
sleepless,
hearing Banshees
for eternity.

may we rest

Carry my feet where your shadow can't,
the wind blows through my hair,
the trees are dancing ballet,
a creature ran faster than a bullet,
flying over branches,
falling.

Do you even know what we're doing honey?

The things you do are so confusing,
you're a mindless animal
headed for its death.

Make me an apology letter,
you make my vision foggy.

Rot in your safe room,
I am not bluffing.

Do you even see where you're going honey?

The things you plan are always losing,
you're like a lost dog in a field
with no owner at its feet;
a stray that dreams
of what's at the end
of railways.

Don't apologize,
it had to be said,
right the wrongs,
you don't care.

We're animals headed for our death,
that's not what we were,
it's what we became.

We're mindless animals
already dead,
may we rest;
may we rest.

ready to become dust, restlessly collecting

She opens wide,
ready for a ride,
I came and guided her hand.

This feels right,
dedicate this time to us,
our memories will shine
till the end of our days,
let it grow, live for
the noon-rain showers,
the sunset moonglow.

My arms open wide,
ready for the embryo,
I came and took her hand;
time gets ready for an epic drowning.

Our days are expendable,
ready to become dust,
restlessly collecting,
I guess it's time
to dump the icebox.

I'll write myself back into the script.
Time swallows every insult;
the manner of acceptance is cruel.

We'll cherish instead our loud goodbye,
they cut through thin air like a katana.

An idol of the depraved melts in the sauna.

Have we been deprived?

before our demurred eyes

You remind me of a song,
I have not heard it for so long.
Let me hear you say something familiar,
words that touch my heart and soul;
that's all you need to know for now.
Dance with me to this melody,
let's demonstrate love through blind clarity,
let's take it slow, slower than the choir's harmonies.
You're a remedy that never fails to destroy me exclusively,
dance with me all through the afterlife's horizonless seas.
Time doesn't exist for the two of us here,
prove to me you're not wasted energy;
let's travel time, *shall we?*
You remind me of a sunset,
have not seen you for so long.
Take me somewhere colorful,
a sight that is foreign to my heart and soul,
that's all I ever needed in my tiny box.
Why do you ask questions?
You're amidst something so beautiful;
death is something beautiful.
You remind me of my childhood,
I don't have any pictures, but
I am certain you were there.
Take me to the highest mountains,
I hear the rivets fall from miles away;
a sight that tries to flow through my heart and soul,
that's all my soul needs,
to want to dwell on.
How vague was our conclusion my discharged muse?
Let's stop time,
go our own *pat*hs,
through different alleys just as dark.
Let's travel time driving through

centuries-old streetlights.
Shall we?
Deaf from all the screaming fits;
such melody has never seen a dance lose appeal,
let's take it with a bed of salt;
it's now time to kneel.
You're a god ordained epiphany
manifested,
don't throw shade
on your unexplored importance.
Dance with me
through
Earthquakes and Sandstorms,
while the sky constricts
before our demurred eyes.
Cherish love's landscape for its unlived guise,
the impermanence
in every tragedy
being influenced
by another's vice.
Let's travel time;
shall we?

gambling away youth's energy

I was just like you once,
connected with the world
and all the people here;
I watched them disappear.

I was just like you once
but I slept through another day
and spent all the night away
in the solace of my nightmares;
speaking Korean in my sleep,
while the walls snicker and jest,
with their chameleon tongues.

This moment worked for me once,
kept me covered with a mask,
so no one would notice me.

I am fishing for a wish
on the streak of light unraveling
on the longest ravines of darkness.

The starving stars protest
the meteor's newfound conquest,
inverting the hearts of the wasted.

I was just taking another turn,
standing in line with my ticket,
and gambling away youth's energy;
I waited to feel the fear,
but it never came...

I was just like you once
but I slept through another day
and spent all the night trading jokes
with my favorite demons.

Talking with our mouths full;
throwing hammers at the walls.

I was just like you once;
sent away to the moon's
grand canyon.

I was just like you once;
praying for my own doom.
I've spent my nights engaged
to countless thoughts misplaced,
all this time I thought
no one will notice me.

Until recently when your meteor
made its way into my unmolested heart.

This moment worked for me once,
I kept myself covered with a mask,
I really thought no one would notice me.

I took my heart's one wish for granted;
damn you, attention-seeking stars,
I sent *your* meteor around my heart.

I never forget the name of my whores,
I miss *you* the most.

I am ready;
I miss
our *red*
room.

let love come to you preserved

Things didn't come easy
as I wander here alone,
things didn't come easy
as you belittle me.

Holding on and hoping
my last breath
waits for me.

I am used to feeling greatness consuming,
and neglecting love's Hi-Def image.

It won't be long
till I get a taste of
what it becomes.

Things didn't come easy
as I wander here at home,
things didn't come easy
as I kick *our* door down.

Sweetheart, I am taking my battle stand;
I'll fight for what I believe this could still be.

Heaven is a road over,
kindness is free of charge.

Nurture our garden of hearts;
start beating again,
less frightened
to flourish.

Let's experiment with rhythms;
let love come to you preserved.

This hope has proved worthy of the boot.

I am feeling unimportant, like the dying piece of a star.
Pull me by the roots now or never or I'll be coming for you;
it won't be long till I get my *taste*
of what put my acre
of sin on
the map.

with the kicks and high-jumps of small feet

Countdown till the suicidal sky implodes;
a canvas of black will surely return.
Let's resolve time lost;
another *goodbye* betrays another *hello*.
Countdown with the pleading children
with roses tucked over their earlobes;
the sea of dandelions were smiling yellow
on our green oasis; the wind brings them home
with the kicks and high-jumps of small feet.
We recreate the times we remember most;
another *goodbye* undoes another *hello*.
Once we arrive at our destination,
come only *once* for it to feel like home.
In here we'll make new memories,
no shame or tragedies are here to befall us.
We'll live in-between heaven and hell;
deliver ourselves to the Lord's Kingdom.
Your heart's in the middle of nowhere;
another *goodbye* cowards from another *hello*.
Countdown till the lions starve;
the rifle bullet was dangerously strong.
We never recovered the anger that was felt;
another *goodbye* skids over another *hello*.
Countdown with me;
our sad ritual lasted
longer than I am okay with.
Countdown with me;
let the lie drain life.
Here me out,
remember those rainy nights.
Here me out,
remember us intertwined.

Our time was up
a while
n*ow*.

Why prolong suffering where there is none?

all our kindest sin told the perfect story

I've wasted my last seconds
blowing off clouds,
wearing out demons,
blessings out of rhyme;
she remains a dying laugh
skirting over my serious smile.
We didn't reach for wisdom;
we pretend our love always.
I must have mistaken you for someone else,
protect me from losing my mind;
I am on the verge of lunacy.
Bringing me back to when it began,
our kindest sin talks of the perfect love.
I wasted my faith on this path,
walking on the rancid sun,
reasoning with irrational angels,
corrosive feathers lost in time,
she remains a dying option
on a set already planned.
I must have mistaken you for someone new;
I am powerless under the shade of her Stetsons.
I am losing my mind,
realizing that all our
kindest sin told
the perfect story
of love's lost
legacy.

there's no other choice but love

I cannot decide,
it's too fun hiding the answers;
she leaves my cement lips in denial.

She's holding onto a sun that's setting;
holding onto a moon that's waning.

You are ten times worse than my second divorce,
there's no other choice but love.

Forever is a monster giving *us* a big hug,
there's no other choice but love.

I cannot remember the signature signing,
I am no longer on your side,
I am taking the first step,
goodbye.

The remorse climbs my sloping heart
ready for a mountain demolition.

There's a gaping hole in my soul;
guiding my self-reflections
into the right answers.

She's holding onto a sun that's rising;
holding on to a moon that's not there.

You are eleven times worse than my third divorce;
there's no other choice but love,
there's no other choice but to love
the open road and drive;
forever is an angel giving *us*
the *green* light.

a*cacias* over *or*chids

Why do I have to be like this?
I open myself up to wrongful abuse,
I am becoming destined for failure.
What must become of me to stop loathing you?
Keep away from me;
you're a drug overdose.
Opening myself up to *you* is almost self-abuse,
I am faithfully destined for failure.
Why must you improvise your words?
When you silently advise that I keep writing myself off,
letting me fall, d*eeper* and d*eeper*,
I open myself up,
I let you in the control room;
I am becoming less
than you needed me to.
Let me overdose;
dying would be mystical.
Opening myself up would be right to abuse;
here is a cheque for the most expensive casket.

I prefer a*cacias* over *or*chids;
take note!

coping

Faith put me up to this,
come at me,
release me.

Bliss opens up the sky
and filled my night
with dreaming stars.

You've corrupted my 2020 vision
and now I see in black and white.

We dance this dance all our life,
a challenge we gladly accepted.

We have fallen farther down,
all this searching left us tired;
I am coping but I can't take no more.

Honesty is hurtful
when lies come
out too strong.

Silence closed our mind
and made us numb
all evening
long.

We danced solo
accepting our
wretched faith.

Our hearts are
out of shape.

We were not free;
I am coping
but I can't take
no more;
I am mopping up
your tears
as you
go;
losing track
of the
toll.

EXHIBIT

U

untied chances
and
butane containers
perpetually
emptied

I'm smiling at you expecting a smile back

Look at me,
I got a serious set of words to say.
I am talking to you,
I am talking to you.
Look at me,
when I'm smiling at you
expecting a smile back.
You know how much I care;
you know
I'll do anything for you,
I'll even take the blame.
It's fine,
it's fine,
that you won't
do the same
for me.
I'd always been fine with it,
I was good to go my friend,
I promised to meet you 'till the end.
Look at me when
I'm thinking of you,
I got to keep my calm.
It's hard to let you go.
Goodbye, goodbye,
but you won't do
the same for me.
I got a serious set of words to say,
I am st*ill* talking to you.
Look at me,
when I'm smiling at you
expecting a smile back.
You know how much I care;
you know I'll do anything for you;
it's time to find *new* things.

You'll hide,
yule tide.
In that,
you put mass
effort
in.

in your kiss

Fill me with more shame,
when I ask if you'd allow me
another try at our game.
Every day is filled
with wasted hours
passing the house
that was ours.
Every full moon
I still give you flowers;
the wind just blows it away.
Every
damn day
I am stuck
with the same
damn reason.
My heart sighs,
my branches are empty,
when will your sunlight
return its bamboo rays
to me?
You are blind to what I am holding,
my cards reset; I am here lusting
for a threat.
Hold me till it hurts;
until I feel misused.
Set my mind sewers humming,
I cannot find my sanity in your kiss;
set my beauty apart from your ugliness.
When will your sunlight
be just mine,
again?

salvation taste of fresh honey

Others find a cure being immature,
others realize there's no point in the truth,
others shout towards a God that won't answer their call;
I'm just here suffering.
What's here tonight as I surrender to the ocean?
Is it the faded light from the moon's silence?
What's not here tonight?
Is it the blinding light of yesterday's fountains?
Holes in the plot breaks down, unmotivated,
the fuse in my heart rust with pale scarlet.
I am uninspired, just like
your words that day
with eyes so graceless,
gazing towards the broken man
you once thought *very* lovely;
the uncut version was killing me
slowly.
There's no return apology,
this is the real thing.
You're no match, to my beautiful view of
a demon swaying with the fallen leaves.
You're my reason to believe in nothing;
swaying to lonely heartbeats at hunting season.
Others find a cure being immature,
others realize there's no point in the truth,
others shout towards a God that won't answer their call;
there's *no* point in suffering, any*more*.
It's an endless war with life's provocative infatuations;
winners of this sickening trick, only bask
inside undefinable depths
of sorrow;
some victories
are just too toxic
to even breathe.

Rumor has it,
salvation taste of fresh
honey.

Write your will yet,
honey?

shimmering with ven*om's* forgiveness

I could hardly notice your hair
going off in flames.
Ah, familiar sights
I am missing,
familiar thoughts
I love to step on.
At the same time,
you help me with the pain;
whenever the rain dances on my shirt,
I dare myself to dance along
to your soothing absence.
I woke up with the desert smog,
then, in the middle of the ocean
with nobody to wrong
except myself of course.
As the rain danced
I was lost under sheets of my loneliness.
As the rain danced
I was lost under second-hand recollections;
of how I miss your subliminal dialogue and mocking symbols,
of how I wanted thoughts of love to be fireproof and baptized in soil.
On every rain dance was our soothing alibi;
you can parachute anywhere but here;
distances stretch rapidly
as the steaming water
runs red; *shimmering*
with ven*om's*
forgiveness.

its midnight choreography

Love sang a song smooth and strong;
the night fills with shadows borne by the moon.
Laughs and greetings,
friendly meetings,
harmony of voices and
wise generous choices
filtered the air with crimes of despair to spare.
Love is making hand gestures,
smiling unintentionally,
the fire in the center
can't wait to grace it.
Glowing brightly,
feeding on their desire
for each other,
the warmest,
most gentle
touch of the wind
was strong and mighty,
the flies burn in dozens,
at the heat of night's sensual incense.
Warm blood are in motion,
relocating; leaves like tears
fall down from the trees with sap,
inhaling Zen from gasoline fumes,
willingly misguided by the fire.
Then a distinct sound led to many
a honest reaction;
a creature has arrived,
its eyes glowing
so brightly like
newborn stars,
their shadows
go *very* still,
complete silence

took over, backward
glances toured, unblinking
and confused
waiting.
More eyes emerged,
leaves began breaking
in their safe places
and prayers would
sound near,
unmistakably
solemn.
The sire of flames persist
with its midnight choreography,
its eyes escaping reasons;
shadows move with speed,
the fire sways alone;
inspiring stillness.
Angry growls and
frightful sighs,
glued to them,
desire them;
it is skin-packaged
meat they smell,
fear and sweat
marinate.
The fire b*urns* al*one*,
a wild chase begins,
the moon shines down,
dripping of black wax.
A fever increases,
at every needlepoint
glance, weeping dry,
arm in arm,
ready to defend each other
from ironic arrangements
as their final

messages reaches
with tortured
innocence
force to plead
guilty to
the spine-chilling
blizzards of
death.

may be the greatest thing I've ever kn*own*

A*gain* and a*gain*,
I turn my head,
holding too closely
the passing view
from my painted horse,
on a twenty-two-year-old carousel.
I remain on my horse
for twenty-four hours,
for seven leisurely days,
operational for as long
as faith prevails.
Through ups and downs,
when will it stop?
I saw riders,
appearing and
going like the stars,
and others shining
brighter trying to reach
for my handlebars.
I met those who rode
beside me, followed me
from behind, trusted
my circles, loved extra
blind, trusted in the seasons,
and every phantom mime.
Still many get away, fall off,
and were merely a foggy daydream;
the dilution of infinite circles,
gives in to restless warnings.
My heart beats to the malfunctioning music
and the crackling bulbs that needs repairs,
that needs changing;
sometimes I feel alone,
riding these boring circles

on my own, but when it is full
I feel proud and strong, even
after they sincerely
let go.
The manager of the ride
changes the view
every passing turn,
these days it's of moonlit skies
dreaming of her flowing hair,
it gives me goosebumps
just thinking about it…
Sometimes it's sunshine melodies
calling me to stand on my horse
and free my spirit, oh I know
one day she'll hear it!
I counted silhouettes of those who'd fallen,
like feathers from an angel taken by waterfalls
of white light, I blink once and it's dark again.
I pray, as I melt on my horse's sculpted hair,
on the faded paint where my tears found haven.
I first fell in love at the age of eleven,
to the girl who sat next to me,
on her horse riding too close to mine.
It took two years before my heart said *"hi."*
Took another four just to feel her *"goodbye."*
It became routine to recognize the emptiness
within this solitary ride, I've consulted myself:
"Why not the roller coaster instead?"
Carousels are mental,
after a long simulation
the excitement ends,
to live amongst the clouds,
and scream your lungs out,
it's a hit from a potent drug;
it's a loop of despair and repair,
a simultaneous coatis of both.

Still, I rather take my chances
dragging my feet down the carousel,
at least I can cherish the view,
allow moments to breathe
witnessing the skies make love
to one another; feel the yellow sun
flirt behind grey clouds.
At least I'd have time to ponder,
what is real,
when it comes to love
and how when it's here,
it is true how it does slow
the circles as it pans around.
Holding her hand,
as we ride
side by side,
through *the ups*
and *the downs*
It's magic,
it's bliss
forever kissed
by the shine
in our connected
eyes.
Powering this ride,
forever kept
in the memory
of *now*.
What if,
you may be the greatest thing
I've ever kn*own*
my whole
life.

shamelessly magnificent

The beat of the drum gets louder, much angrier.

This soul of mine has found meaning
in formless surrender.

There's no need for the sound of guns,
they're harmless.

She'll proclaim the words of God,
pretending that all will be alright
when the rapture comes.

That wherever we go the sun avidly shines,
that wherever we go it won't be the end just yet.

We are kind to the circumstances; we know
it hurts to lose meaning in words once
understood.

This theory of mine has lost its value,
it has done us great service;
she has promoted our love
to shamelessly
magnificent.

This lie is catching on;
it's *catching fire* on
me
first.

we left

We are headed down this path,
mixing colors;
never coming
back.
Mistakes are done and set,
our scripted words
are making you
upset.
There are dangers in the things
I'd done,
she remarks on the stupid songs
I've sung,
my voice filters
her heartbreak,
it's too bad
that she left some words
unsaid.
In prayer,
I'll keep this to myself,
a wind so strong
makes me fall back
a step.
There are dangers in the things
we've done,
remark for the stupid songs
we've sung;
her voice filters my heartbreak,
it's too bad we left some words…

the best parts of love

Don't start going off wondering,
there's nothing to ponder;
what has happened simply
won't be
anymore.

It needed to be said,
it needed to be done,
I don't know what is left
from the wrongs
I'd dug out.

It needed to be fixed,
it needed to be sung,
for there will always be one,
who's alone and doesn't matter.

Don't ever betray me,
don't say you're sorry
because there's no battle to be won;
what has happened won't be anymore.

Don't even try to mend a mistake
that's better off broken,
I don't need you now,
our time is over;
what has happened
won't be anymore.

Our photo album is raining
with conquered smiles amidst
the pouring down of hard-earned
pain; shame is never a fair game;
the best parts of love aren't translatable.

*Is failure to see the truth
in just the way things are,
the only constant thing?*

Connect the dots
even when they're
too far away.

Have merciful ideas go astray,
green light closure to work both ways.

our premium exhibitions

Liberate something crazy
in the spaces between us,
I don't care where you're from;
if you blindfold yourself to believe,
you are mine and I am yours.
Maybe now that I have your attention,
baby notice my good intention,
so take my word for it,
I am certain you need
something to pick you up too.
I am all you need right now;
like murder to a loose blade.
I saw you fall,
felt your tears
as you crumble.
I felt you here,
now, you're gone.
I am not sure
what went wrong.
But baby,
stay strong,
lean closer,
in a moment
it's gone,
it's over.
Maybe now that I have your decision,
unroll the blueprints on the floor,
the unknown will take us on a grand adventure,
I am certain you need this more than I do.
It was fun while it lasted,
painting a cold trail
of amazing abstractions;
we will one day curate
our premium exhibitions.

Dear traveler,
I hope I made a special place somewhere in your map,
that you're welcome to return to under belittled light;
after a moment we're *gone forever.*

a monarch excreta

I wrote it down,
every single word
I meant to say
about who's to blame.
This love is like a raindrop,
lost in the puddle of yesterday's torrents.
It is no longer unique,
it is never without
an audience to vow
under its reign;
she inspired paintings,
abstractions of today's
romantic comforts.
What does it mean?
When they say
that our love is
gone away,
tearing up
from the seams,
making a run for our money.
What does it mean?
When what we deserve is not ours to receive;
it should be given away to charity;
or to bribe clarity.
This sacrifice,
it's meant to be new,
never seen before
by eyes like yours.
I have seen it all,
every single sight
I meant to see on
who harbors it all;
this rain of grief.
This love is like a raindrop,

lost in the reservoirs of tomorrow's sun
dam.
No longer unique; *uninspired,*
I stood still as a monk,
I pondered it all;
every line crossed over,
unknown to my morning calls.
About who's insane?
About what's at stake?
About our flame;
GAME OVER
I blink in disbelief,
oh sweet release.
This love is like a droplet of blood;
it was a part of me, an opportunist.
Now as it left a mark in both our mental spirits,
less of what I'm seeing is you;
lost in this puddle of our youth,
no longer unique,
used up and shallow.
Let's proceed with the operation.
Take what's mine,
leave what's yours behind,
close the wound and leave it underlined
for the surgeon on-call a quarter to nine.
Let's proceed with your solution,
give me the cold shoulder;
Roger.
What's the point of sleeping?
An ocean rises meters higher on our barely grown grapes,
branches divorced from our trees,
barely surviving the current.
This sacrifice,
it's meant to be new.
Never seen before by eyes like yours.
We're sinking,

we're met with sharp-witted
piranhas.
Sinking, we found a blue pearl
with our name
on it.

A monarch
excreta
bl*esses*
it.

a basket case of bleeding apricots

The smile around your face
is another fine moment
I will soon erase.
The truth behind that face
keeps me wide awake.
I am open for a moment now,
open to hearing what you have to say;
I am handcuffed in the bedframe,
I listen anyway.
You said to slow it
down,
keep our feelings
from going numb.
The truth behind the cut reveals,
we are a basket case of bleeding apricots.
I am open for a moment now,
to tear up about what you have to say,
I stand still to listen;
she enjoys the view of me caving in.
Our desire is fading out;
it's just a thing of the past;
face me and turn yourself in,
no longer yours and
no longer are you mine; quit
asking,
asking, and
asking me
if we are still a thing of what's happening
now.

my constantly mesmerized gaze

After the words she said about fixing herself
and grasping the courage to tell me something,
something bigger than her,
towering over her bedside
for weeks and weeks in a row,
I ask myself *then* again:
Will she do it with a forgiving nature
or fall and stumble, expecting me to have
both arms wide open ready to catch her?
I have half an hour at my disposal,
one gold coin left to throw down the well
for hopes and wishes to revive our pending farewell.
I am dreaming of returning to the surface,
to the moonlight's love and affection,
needing the attention of one person in particular
in this audience of birds in command formation,
heading East; far from where my heart found Holiday.
I vow before their angel wings
for answers to
any questions
please.
What was once blind flirtation
became this reckless invasion
of souls.
You were prophesied,
told by people I trust
who knew I'd find
great love.
My first kiss would be heaven-sent;
they told me it will be a turbulent bliss
I can always renew in my constantly dazed state;
you were living proof of these tales
I long to experience firsthand.

But you were gone,
as if there ever was a me and you.

In my constantly mesmerized gaze
I look towards everyone else's
"Happy Days."

EXHIBIT

V

vases
of
dead flowers
for
depressive
days
love couldn't
save

glowing bats, neon butterflies, and shooting stars

She waits for my comeback,
I promised her that.
She listens for a knock at our door;
aware of the demon's breathless hoarse.
There's no point deceiving me;
no point being deceived by me.
I forgot to mention the beautiful love
that only comes around once in a lifetime,
I could be the one tonight
who will present the better outcome;
who will beat the odds eight billion to one.
I am wondering when the echo died
after I yelled through a cracked screen
I love you, I loved you, I love.
I just cut myself on ceramic glass,
it was a beautiful vase of dead flowers.
There's deceiving me, and
there's being deceived by me.
My empty boxes met her razor smiles,
she cuts open my square mouth,
wearing her new florescent gloves;
she made her fingers dance,
suddenly, they're
glowing bats,
neon butterflies,
and shooting stars.
We go crazy
sometimes.

everyday feels like this

Another Sunday morning
praying on yesterday's legs,
I sleep through the afternoon
missing your head on my chest.
In my dreams it's Saturday,
I am welcomed by
a waving sea,
we dance through
trials unspoken;
fixing this broken heart
you found in the mines.
Another Monday
fills my head
with voices of the dying;
telling me stories from
the deepest of graves.
Another Tuesday to feel alone,
my broken heart can't feel its home;
the distance between us is unbearable.
Another Wednesday to feel away
from the feelings that resonate,
with you there were stars
that shined in the day.
Another Thursday to color past the lines,
a clear picture of you I can't find;
I rip the pages out seeing
your face in the clouds.
Another Friday losing my mind,
scrambled words, sunny side up;
correct me if I am wrong
you don't miss me at all.
Another Saturday this is where we belong,
lost in each other's eye-roll;
feeling your heartbeat decline.

Our sanity dancing merrily tonight
to the silence after my screaming lies.
The serenity that makes the week worthwhile,
this scenery that I crave to have is divine; *never mind.*
I hope everyday feels like this,
it's always Saturday for me,
where we welcome a fantasy
of difficulties;
our boiling sunset bleeds
with macaroon dreams.
You're a dancing Earthquake;
shaking my world through trials
foretold by the fortune-teller's
magic 8 ball.
We'd find an obvious truth which says:
"You overfill the heart's urinal, her sentimental washroom."

relax and wait *here*

Rename the demons that have found you,
release yourself from their clutches.

Rename the anger that has found you,
reshape the frown upon your face.

A smile can do no more than dance
along the lines of open scars.

Anger has befallen you,
watch it kneel,
stop feeling sorry.

Lay on a field of dandelions,
lay on shadows casted by tall trees;
remember that the hollow
can still be filled,
relax and wait
here.

Return the gestures of a fellow heart,
repent for the sins that found you.

Resent the messages that failed to
release the answers that you heed most.

I am sent to watch you grow;
lay with you on cotton snow.

I am sent here to see the light
ignite in your eyes once more.

I see the richness of you,
sinking happily in my dreams,
bliss is our returning leaf,
trees start falling silently.

Let's make our clean getaway;
far from war with our bookshelves.

Remember that the hollow
can still be *fill*ed,
relax and
wait…

I like this new you, you feel inspired

You think you can have your way but you're wrong.
Our sense colors begin to fade,
makeup runs down our face.
Silence is our only companion
in this failed union;
take my hand and we'll kneel
to the big man cutting onions.
You think you can have your way but you're wrong.
Lighten up the mood,
let's dance under the moon.
Pull out the knives,
eye patch every wound.
Kill all the thoughts,
revive who we used to be.
Sing me a song; I promise
I won't forget the melody.
You think you can have your way but you're wrong.
Block out all the noise,
use your indoor voice;
call me your lucky winner
with a bonus prize
of a thousand blisters.
You think you can have your way but you're wrong.
I like this new you,
you feel inspired.
I want this feeling
to play a little higher,
to stay a little longer;
I don't want this to expire.
Let's dance on the wire;
let's admire our fire.
I promise
I won't forget
our
*melo*dy.

under the stars to songs overplayed

I've pushed it real deep;
I knew I couldn't.
I am nearly insane;
I am stuck in repeat.
The center of my obsession
is the painting of us;
barely holding on
to four crumbling
walls.
Our home is embraced
by high winds;
I hope it rips apart
your half
first.
Black hat wearing fool
with a pitiful look of regret;
dances under the stars
to songs overplayed
on cheap strings.
I am sold on your attitude
with only a dollar to find;
old soul once young
kindly destroyed
by the giant rocks.
Quit digging holes,
he forwards your call.
His evil thoughts found a home.
Buried now,
ending call;
found mercy's tone.
On the edge
dreaming
hand in hand;
fake.

On the clouds,
floating with white lines;
fake.
The center of my obsession
is the painting of *us* barely holding *on.*

placing a question mark on *us*

What is it with the thoughts of you holding on too tightly?
All the lullabies to keep myself from
missing you
does no*thing.*

If only I could bring myself back to the moments I can
hold you and keep you
closer to this hopeful
heart of mine.

If only I kissed you;
before time split
us ap-
art.

Your eyes bring me back to life,
I can't find this in anybody else;
your smile it holds on to,
every joke,
every laugh.

Our time apart,
our wave goodbyes
can't ever stop me
from placing a question mark
on us.

What is it with our photographs?

It feels incomplete,
it feels undone.

All the words I said,
I hope they resonate for you
to keep me from being just another leaf
that fell from your Maple tree;
I wait another season to be reborn.

If only I could bring myself back
to hold the flowers I should have
given you and inspire legends
instead of dark tales in our imaginary reunion.

If only I kissed
you;
before our time is no longer an apartment for
two.

Years later,
in a night with barely a star
I play the strings of our lost guitar,
singing about everything we could have been.

Years later,
in a night with barely a moon
I try to heal a heart that feels old too soon.

Beating
to our rhythm,
to the sound of our love
in another melodious lifetime.

Our time apart,
our wave goodbyes
can't ever stop me
from placing a question mark;
from placing a question mark
on *us.*

giving me a helpless puppy vibe

I was al*most* there,
I guess, I've seen everything
I ever wanted.
The colors were red, but
the sunset never felt
so dry
and wasted.
You're giving me
a helpless puppy vibe;
you're taking everything I have.
I am going out,
exploring the chances
I'll never take.
I was there,
in your deceased fantasies.
The color blue is rarely in the skies of today.
You're giving me a desolate
contrived; you're taking
a nosedive.
I am wearing the face
of a clown
from dusk
till morning's
recycled light.
Going out,
exploring the chances
I'll *never*
take.

all tangled up and mental

One look at you and
I had fallen in love,
our Summer breeze
was cold as ice;
something must be
in my eyes that June morning.
As I was blinded by the sunrise;
I looked for you
but you were *gone*;
gone for good.
Where do I go to find you?
I never could consider you gone,
it doesn't taste as good as
I thought it would to say.
This does not look right so far,
the plan was to stay on your radar.
To keep me wanting more, and
refrain from getting less than I deserve;
let's pretend that we're out of this mess,
let's dramatically shout: *"It's the end of the world!"*
One look at you and I've become somebody else,
I miss our unhappy bouts, *minus the anger;*
someone else was in my field of vision;
I didn't recognize that person.
I worry about the empty spaces, *yet*
I am astounded by nothing.
I took one last look at our crazy mess,
all tangled up and mental.
Her stars penetrate my stained-glass window;
there must be beauty behind the beast somehow.
Talk later,
I am late for a funeral;
I think I've broken the radar.

I am lacking in desire to desire,
don't involve me with the reparations;
let's just pretend that we didn't exist.
We look like dead flowers on a dirty vase.

How much did you sell our souls for?

becoming *unloved*

It came to me the other night
after a few drinks and a bar fight;
that housing all my fears won't serve me right.
I did the trouble justice,
I came out of it more alive.
I redeem myself for reasons
that will never cross my mind.
All the mistakes I've made,
all were broken grenades;
I didn't hear any warnings;
was there even a pin?
Stop waiting for the world to end,
cancel the thought of becoming *unloved*.
There's nothing wrong with risking your sanity for energy;
I must stray from my false identity, I must rewrite me.
It came to me in orange flashes of light;
after I emerge from your foggy breaths that night,
she kept me inside four walls so high,
hopeless because I couldn't fly away.
I gave our drama a rest well deserved,
I come up with better script
and funny dialogue.
I redeem myself for damage done,
I quit wondering
where the better days went;
a bit of laughter does *good* harm.
I see a cup half full,
you're empty and you're convinced;
but your soul begs to differ.
Love never is a peaceful waterfall;
realize that you must find it inside you first.
I found my diary under her wedding gown.
I realize that the truth is our rise;
but it can also reveal our fault line.

I fell in love;
she fell in love
with my crimes.
She admits to her fault:
It's about time!

her last endeavor

We continue to drive that road,
embracing the sights butt naked before us;
we deliver a smile enclosed in a dreamy abode.
We'd be making music with our love-drunk voices,
took one shot for shame and another for captured joy.
We got out of the freeway,
walk into any direction,
saying: *here we are.*
An evil voice blurs our perception;
falling branches responds to the wind,
creating movement so freeing and blissful.
Our obscene shadows are sighted by the eyes of others,
our empty thoughts lead to spiritual loses
wondering about the circle of life;
if it'll ever emerge to a grinding halt.
The wild mushroom clouds began pouring salt
into our invisible wounds; our wounded souls.
From a distance is external beauty and doomed freedom,
from up close is a shouting beggar at the gates of wisdom
ceased by the devil acting as proxy to heaven's gatekeeper.
We remain genuine recipients to the hurt it bestows,
living with humid questions with no existing answers.
It's only the wicked lies of a man; outtakes of a God.
It's only confused words with hidden meaning; *clear*
words with profound mantras plucked from the scalp of the air.
We took a step too far; now death is at its closest it's ever been,
blue roses arose from the jellied soil, near our tombstone candles.
A gun blast sang with the power to enlighten;
fields of burning grass became our final sight;
as the breath of nature forgives us and invites
childhood memories to delight in our finale.
We're persuaded to change from the start
of the day, and see every life as a work of art;
even if incompatible lives are intertwined,

with us; *what did you expect?*
We ascend into a cruel world; a blind species of word sculptors.
The less we k*now*, the more we t*rust,* every oppor*tunity* is a must.

Her head turns to a familiar voice only to find out I am not there;
her last endeavor is to explore what lead to our love's demise.

constantly shifts, constantly ask

If only we played our cards right;
do you think it will go well for us this time?
Tomorrow lives too violently in our mind,
get in the spirit of our role,
reread love's bible.
Pull the sorry doors closed,
blizzards are constant and strong;
stop letting the cold in.
Pull the sorry doors closed,
before a nameless hurricane comes inside.
You're killing what's left of solidarity, *my love*.
Tomorrow complicates my mind,
let's embrace the comforts of our home
we'll figure it out minute by minute,
eastern standard time.
If only you'd abandon the crime scene
at its virginal state,
I won't help you this time,
I won't take sides.
She'll never know
what is enough;
her hurricane
constantly shifts,
constantly ask
for emotional brakes.

She's killing what's left of my precious
Sa*turd*ay.

speaking kind syllables

Color the shine weak,
color the rain bleak,
different colors
deceives my pain,
the order of chaos
gets to my brain,
I don't remember
my holy name.

Up on my feet again,
my running mouth is
speaking kind words,
I am losing my mind.

Up on the clouds
I am falling down,
with no one to save me;
with no one on my mind.

Color the moon blind,
the color of gravesites,
different colors
deceives my shame,
the order of chaos
gets to my brain,
I don't remember
your nicked name.

Color the blank space,
color it black,
different reasons
distract me from
losing you to fame,
the order of chaos

gets to our brain,
time meets us half-
way.

Color over the line;
too little too soon.
Color over the line;
too little too soon.
Color all over mine;
too little too soon.
Close your eyes,
imaginary ghost.

You are up on your feet again;
a singing burden.

Speaking kind syllables;
escaping God's maze.

Up on the clouds,
flying without wings.

Your childish laugh
echoes forevermore
in the heat w-
ave.

as our nightmares fight for realism

Take it easy,
take it one step at a time.
Take it all at once;
relax as it sets in
like a holy vow.
Tomorrow sounds less of an answer
to questions that starts with:
"who's there?"
Dreams seem pointless
as the nightmares
become too real.
Ball your hands into a tight fist,
dig your way out of this;
you're strong enough,
push through and unravel.
Take it hard,
take it like a man;
have you taken enough?
Relax as the next wave
counts d-
own.
Dreams seem pointless
as our nightmares fight
for realism.
Ball your hands into a tight fist,
don't dig your way out;
you're intuitive enough to
slap away secondhand
grenades.

I lied,
the impossible
is not for you;
prove me wrong,
I just know
you'll
do.

lead us back to the islands of front pages

Should I decide to stay?
Connecting dots that are
faltering in hue.
I am drowned in doubt,
rearranging anti-thoughts
that starves itself unholy.
There is a safe house;
no one here will measure
our dimensions.
There is a ship
that will lead us back
to the islands of front pages.
We're worse than fallen angelicas;
we set fire to easy places;
vile calmness and
toxic sweets.
We never go with the flow
of the winds of change.
Bliss is the name of the sex-worker
under the bridge,
nothing more,
nothing less;
not a nickel
or a dime
more.
There is a safe house;
no one will care what rots
in our blue rooms; *bedlam.*
Will the waves broach of innocence?
On our sleepless,
expressionless
gaping jaws.
May the boats
under our eyes

compensate for the imaginary lines;
hanging around our necks, cho*king*
and having the last
con*sent*ual
laugh.

flip a coin to decide my faith

I don't want to remember
what I've done,
I promised myself
to be more in control;
instead I gave in
and now times past,
times are wasted
on my see-sawing
shadow's wants;
I need to focus
my glow away
from the *likes*
of you.
I just don't think
I'm clever enough.
Will the laughter remain as the time goes by?
Will you let my demons be your friend?
All the good in me
has gone away.
Oh, how I long to be in bed next to you,
oh, to be waking up with the sight of you,
I couldn't really ask for anything more;
I couldn't really think of a better life
than what's in
my head.
I don't want to be a stranger to another one,
I promised to hold onto feelings that had begun
disinterested, or not, in developing the visuals.
Instead I step onto my sweet design of layered thoughts;
I need some time
alone to cry.

I flip a coin
to decide
my faith,
I failed to catch it
now.

I am in a haze,
about *you;*
about *why* you?

you don't exist without me

Just take the streetcar,
just take it a *little* too far,
just smash the guitar over
and over til the front-yard
clovers. *But when is that?*
Pop the lid, cap the gun
till our hair is spring-white;
nothing feels right, *right* now.
So when? A pastor told me:
*"I am mother nature,
you don't exist without me.
You take other people's
identification, without me,
you are nobody…"*
What will it do to us if we deny his words to ensue?
Want to get hit by a stolen car, or a swollen plane?
Will my words *do?!*

My Helena Of Troy

The end rushed towards the lovers who tremble pass their opening days. Fast trains and running mares come second to the speed in which they loved. Hurt by the sound of applause and blessings from the cosmic fireworks of divine prayers sung on mute. Never knowing if the clarity in unspoken words will find shelter in me from her softly played keys on the piano.

She's precise and subtle with the musical playing and humming graciously, compliant to faith's fairy tale quotes. Never have I felt such tamed craziness before this Helen of Troy purified the aches and gave them verses.

Now I journey through the white sheets of her inflammatory decisions. With fear the impending separation matures. It takes another evening to bed. Penetrated by plot-holes. *Why do other moon trees last millennium?* We could barely take root.

She addressed her heart's doubtful bouts, and I fear the closing of our eyes, listening in on the tears that ran a marathon over her cheekbones. I embrace another hard pillow, trying to obey my transporting soul, breaking agony's wishbone as one breathless ghost. I can't get her love's scent out of my mind. The obscure appeal her madness spins like a dance or a cartwheel on blue evening grass.

Will my old ways catch up and interrupt what she's training her bravery to say? Or allow the residues of our morning psychosis bleed the darkness away into our separate screens?

Pandering along a trail of loaded firearms, fragile and sensitive triggers would shoot, as a green firefly sat upon it, waking up the future which is stillborn at the moment. But then comes a mockery of the illusions discussed and the night deadens. The mood shifts and the moon waves farewell to the waning light that once dominated those opening days.

What's wild is she'll pull me by the strings like an impassioned yoyo making me do cool tricks, unaware of what I am capable of and she'll design my swings with impeccable competence. No dizziness, no projectile of yesterday's dinner, complete unity with the early spring air. I execute what remains of my life's youthful flowers, so our roses wilt grandiose drama one petal at a time. It needs to depart at some point, the playful beating of a sunshiny hour where understanding permits intensity and untouched film for memories yet to be shot.

But plans in advance fades away on the page, the ink never promises to hold. And the anecdotal hymnals we wrote minutes before midnight are left to perish in the snow. The rusted cogs continue to run these watches we never wear anymore. I stare at her loving glow in a photograph somebody took, I wonder if her smile could be more heavenly if I were the cameraman in charge of the viewfinder. I said to myself, when I saw you at that wedding.

God, thank you. I've found her.

EXHIBIT

W

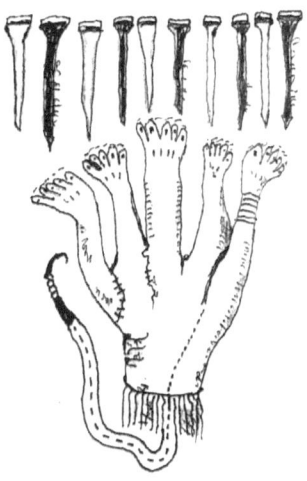

walk of blame
at the altar,
alternating
between feeling
loved
or
imprisoned

the worst inevitably follows

Put a lock between our doors tonight
I have lost a lot of time
boarding up the walls,
I am distances apart from
what insidiousness caught my eye;
let's hope for the best in the afterlife.

Hell fires,
you inspire;
killer of the sun.

Somebody has woken up
the monster.

We wake to the owl's call, *now*
it keeps us up all night.

Put more wood in the fire
the worst inevitably follows.

Heaven's light
was your design;
I am backing out.

The beast howls painlessly in the rain,
a halo flickers above your head on the hospital bed,
holy voices disconnected from the source.

The time clock is ticking away
through more
of your
non-*sense*.

with someone else on the safe side

I,
I am in the dark here so
how you been?
I,
I am in the edge holding on;
slowly caving in.
Can I have a moment of your time?
Could you pick me up or will you let me down?
I,
I killed the messenger
or was it you?
I,
I am at the beach tonight,
watching the waves
under the moonlight.
I,
I can't get enough of the stars in your eyes;
slowly blinding me.
I,
I am holding on
to the edge of our crumbling tower.
Can I have a moment of your memory?
Crossing over love's broken bridge;
you with someone else
on the safe side,
me on my own.
Cue
the land-
slide.
Can I have a moment of your time?
Could you pick me up or will you let me down?
I,
I killed the messenger,
or was it
you?

in the form of the most deceitful embraces

Our demons came to play,
waving farewell
being set ablaze.
You know I'm there every step of the way,
but you make it a hobby
to shelter
the truth
from
me.
Our angels came to save
us,
waving farewell
to the darkness
we loved *so much.*
Let it shine our way
in the form of the most
deceitful embraces.
Harmonizing with night-terrors over the ocean;
be the one color which the sunset cannot fake.
The end is expected,
we are the bitter ending.
You know I'm there every step of the way,
but you make it a habit to always shelter
our t*oll*
from
me.

won at an auction in a guru's deathbed

In construction with
our weekend endeavors.
Green fences form
around our tormented children.
Evil bound, streaming
viruses after viruses.
There's no way out,
no allowances, we install
obsolete microchips
hoping their system
can weather the differences.
Invisible socks,
rock a bye the baby
aboard the docks.
Sink into a *new low,*
stiller waters,
won at an auction
in a guru's deathbed.
Wasted it,
wasted it;
for gasoline,
you hopeless
trampoline.
We travelled far,
listlessly picking
fights in a fashion bar.
We're stylish clowns
breaking down
business signs.
Oh, how we tried,
to remain loveless
in the Cadillac Lounge.

She left her purple dress,
on my bedroom floor; she
also left the radio on.
Tunnels we explored are damp
with fresh sewage;
our last song became
an interesting bullet wound.
This tread is
knee-deep in
easy going
manure.
A selection of mute
suggestions; a bike begging
to be stolen.
We're stillborn caterpillar
buses in the butt of July,
I feel like vomiting out
the car window
now; craving melted
chocolate bars.
Wish me luck!

chambers of generic silence nonverbal unscripted

Practice a loyal life;
every possible way
to make it right;
or be subtle with
the dying regimens
you've chosen.
Never leave a thought behind,
in the dark they will come back;
with friends more-like;
be triple in numbers,
keep the canapés warm.
Practice telling lies to a truthful heart,
pursuing battles that does not demand to be fought.
Note to self: *"We cannot know when life is truly over."*
Go towards the light so clear,
a path growing stronger;
probably step away,
before the rail-train
kisses you.
We think that the roof could
protect us entirely from the rain;
God's cries of pain are but
incomplete sentences,
chambers of generic silence
nonverbal unscripted words.
HE leaves us to be soldiers
of the unknown consequence.
November leaves come raining down;
a sign of dire change
is upon
us.

Be *less*
than.

that ecstasy, that majesty!

A sensitive topic is disturbed by the sound I hear;
a miscarriage of our dream's malady.
We've mindlessly transformed
and lost who we once were,
anger stricken by cars that
long passed,
not giving our crime scene
enough virality.
Our tired eyes are scratching at vile daydreams,
a hot mouth is unable to scream for help;
acquiring witnesses
from an unlucky radius.
We are creators of lies;
crafting non-tangible facts
that gradually dies.
The rainbows swim lazily
on her rolling eyes.
Believe in a better outcome
with a senile mind,
may hate teach you how to love
being unloved.
Empty in the past it may be;
it always seems,
but filled with meaning
blameless in its conception.
Hold on to that ecstasy, that majesty!
Vow down to the kings and queens of your bodily miseries.
This world is a vacancy for good things to pass
through collections of unreturned seasonal glances
through winded windows.
Love is susceptible to resurrect with ancient lines,
until it is cursed to permit the giving of a second chance.

Love *never last*,
new fascinations
are n*ever* planned;
wet stones on dry land
becomes of each pebble
rolling down the winter hill
calling out for *Sisyphus*.

in search of meaningless answers

The tiny circles the rain left behind disappear,
it wasn't meant to last like you and me; it was
easy to forget like a dream, we cannot configure
its medley desperately enough. It was another
night, without the moon to guide our empty
thoughts and misleading words. It meant to hurt,
it is shaped like bullets. Wait a moment; I'll
lend you my gun, my last gift to you is
to allow myself to be your moving target.
I stand alone at a bus stop, out of my cage
in this zoo, as they look at me from their open
windows, wondering what I'll do. If there lives
a smile under our hooded expressions, casting
shadows on our weakening pride. Waiting
for nothing, waiting for no one, dark is
our heart cancelled on the pleasures we usually
take for granted; that we never knew we'd miss
now that we don't have it, it's all we need it's all
we crave, in this windy climate. We're caught
in the currents of these easy choices. Demons
would look down at us from the tallest buildings,
children would look up at us wondering who
this strange person is; if we are good-hearted or
the type to acknowledge but from far, far away.
Holding into this ambiguous mystery, this layered
apology, our hysterical medicine leaving a bitter taste
where sweetness used to be. Like cars lined up
at a stoplight, feeling better with every distance
travelled from where they catch pitiful glances,
from stilled shadows always waiting, decaying
on the sidewalks, dishonest with their timeless
and foolish ruse, their eyes afraid to be caught
behind the tinted glass; when the light turns green;
some invisible referee cues their hollow grin. Finally

we're inside this lonely hunk of metal, securing more
seconds, saving sinister reasons as it cheats our sanity
birthing unfriendly rhymes. With or without another
humble acquaintance to pacify our broken smiles, to
free our time for somebody else, to mirror our sacred
hush and add a familiar poison in our broken cup.
Yelling and desperate for echoes of truth, to amount
from faith's mischievous games, leaving us to
decorate our walls with fake realities. Use its power
till things gradually make sense again. Driving miles
away from the grays in our mistakes, the true nature
of how things truly are. Become somebody else,
playing another convincing character; another unsmiling
face, getting less appealing with every deceiving lesson.
Profound to only the individual, as hollow as a person could be
thinking that clarity exists for anybody. Black eyes are hit
by too many question marks and the proof is under-realized.
Unflattering to our current benefactors. This is enough, it will
have to do, *with or without* an actual answer. We all dedicate
our lives in search of meaningless answers. *How dare you become
mine?*

to console

An idea on its way,
is getting smarter every day,
you're a lost cause
getting towed on the driveway.
I don't know what it is,
but it must be really sweet.
Here me out,
this great idea of mine.
It involves you and me,
to us everlasting love
comes free.
I don't care if you feel
a bit off in some way,
I won't give up on you,
I won't give up on us.
This crime of mine,
is so curious, but can't
find the strength to console you.
You're a main event
to this show of flying
colors, I want to know you.
I don't know what it is but
it must be really, *really* sweet.
Imagine a time when you're happy,
for us it will always be everlasting.
One chance is all I'm asking.
So take off your mask,
the devil is in the details
of every dream we ever had.
You've heard me out,
loud and clear.
I am so glad you have walked
with me this far, but doubts are
there, they linger everywhere.

Your eyes met mine,
still I can't find you,
I am searching,
looking; *am I almost
there?*

the smell of carcasses on our land

You are crazy
with a capital C,
I didn't know
what would happen
till it happened to me.
All the pleasure that you found,
it wasn't always what it cut out to be.
What if I just let things be?
You and me we're not for each other,
I watch the blossoms in a sea of flowers
I run for cover as the new day starts;
our love turns to grey.
Terrible this must be for you,
come celebrate with me
as we acknowledge our doom.
Don't you just love the smell of carcasses on our land?
We only fill our heart with quicksand;
move on, move along lost one.
Those who wait will grow impatient,
you need only wait a second, a minute
to pull the cord on our beastly tension.
You know better, yes you do, I believe in you.
Your heart has the power
to become useful to another,
better than you're used to.
Will your choice ever be to begin again with me?
Laugh at the truth
my sweet porcupine,
till we choke
at an answer.
Choose
to be fine.
What if I refuse to let things be?

We weren't meant for each other,
we drowned in a sea of dead flowers,
the new day smells of
cancerous
air.

your soul keeps mine happy company

Every body wants to be found,
every day just seems so long
when you're around, remember
when we were safe and sound;
remember the wedding bells
that chimed
to the moon and back
to our lonely Earth,
to the stars, we proved
we can make it that far.
You are the sanest part of me,
your soul keeps mine
happy company.
Why couldn't I have loved you like a dream?
Why did I let you bite your tongue?
Say what you need to say my Queen,
I will hear each verse out,
I am not a cynic, or
emotionally
incompetent.
Every body wants to stay young,
every body wants to fall into love,
own a presence so profound.
Remember childhood wasn't too far,
remember yesterday's the same;
it hits the same subtle chord
when you tell it.
I cut myself with
the remark you've left;
so I can remember
when and where
it hurts the most
to be without you.
I cut you into a hundred pieces,

into a thousand different dreams,
our pain is truly remarkable;
when and where and how
we patch love's crescent scar,
who's to say?

withdrawn by a temporary honest heart

I feel to some shameful degree, *filthy*.
Not even having a family of almost *fifty*
can nurture or calm the tsunamis of guilt
I carry on both shoulders screaming and
shouting with the voice of sinister evil.
I can name them and speak in their tones,
I can listen and be fascinated but lose sight
of what is wrong or right with my world.
They're just so full of beautiful energy
omitting from their halo of fire and the
ashes that come out their mouths as they breathe;
like stardust, like a meaningful war between two lovers.
Using no weapons other than the sharpest sentences
withdrawn by a temporary honest heart; I am tired of doing the
falling apart.
So we make up, make out, under the worried moon and laying
pity, shining grey on my skin with their lifeless faces; repeating a
verse of: *"I am sorry."*
Shedding their skin and sleeping on a bed so hard;
sleep don't come easy for the happy one or
the healthy body with the decaying mind,
pumping blood onto a bullied heart in a
schoolyard so vast, full of gossip and pretty lies.
I feel empty, not even that joke you just told me birth a laugh.
All I can give you for now is unblinking eyes with a grin
on the side; seasoned with a heart-stopping sigh.
I apologize, I just can't make up my mind on who masters
what I'll do next. I just don't want to come across as disingenuous.
Appear as if I could make that jump towards the edge of the cliff
and fly above the frozen lake; when I am a penguin, not an eagle
with angel wings. But there's something in there, someone told me once
how special I was and how important my words are; how awesome it was
to be *the other door* for them, shinning a firework display of
welcoming colors

meant to be misunderstood without a chance. I am one long
paragraph from coming undone
but let it bleed like a nail through the palm of the son of God,
it's incomparable the sacrifices that were made when two hearts
beat the same awareness and succumb to the hurt and madness
with the ease of a child through the swing set.
A couple swings later he will be older and tire from the easy,
excited to make his life more difficult.
Distances from sleep,
restarting his heartbeat every day
to be kind to his only soul;
to look better on the mirror.
A smile, eyes inspired to be awaken
despite the grey in the horizon,
that one lesson, *that one lesson;*
I can't grasp it now as I took that leap
and met with the reaper at the bottom of the staircase.
Counting stars from the floor of the bar,
I am hypnotized by
a ceiling fan
circling
around.

Help me.

Can
some-
body,
any-
body.

Help
me.

the reaper's favorite whore

Take my pinky hostage;
speak a solemn promise:
"Repeat after me," you said.
The fairest prayer won't secure you a seat in Heaven's ledger.
Brothers and Sisters, I dreamt it.
Impure thoughts doing a cartwheel;
save yourself before things get too real.
Take a picture with stone statues
no longer leaving a footprint in the world;
think you're significant now don't you?
Pushing your finger through fresh bullet holes.
Did your poison circulate yet?
Mind if I get another dose?
Seasoned with fairy dust,
and a peeling layer of Hell's rusted gates.
"Do not proceed until operator opens the gate."
But it's opened, someone's been careless today.
It must be Heaven we are in, covered in many layers of fake.
Tip the emergency handle; blame the working maid.
There inside your glove compartment grew vines
and branches of days we've confined in tiny spaces of darkness.
What did they do to deserve this?
Unfold the picnic blanket,
shelter more thieves in the pavement;
allow wildflowers to impregnate the cracks.
Find haven in my love;
lust in my compounding theories about impractical lies.
Don't have second doubts now; tighten the knots,
hear me sing a tune of violence in the trunk of your car,
3 A.M. in the parking lot.
I am a heavy sleeper,
the reaper's favorite whore;
it's such a hollow chore
making friendship rings

for these walls.
We wanted this…
Look a squirrel!
Oh shit!
It fell over the edge,
what an astronaut!
Not as afraid of the lady
in the stars as we are.
Steer clear of pedestrians,
be vigilant of future downtimes;
optimist would see it as a:
"*You start as a pebble but turn into a boulder on the way down.*"
I say "*bullshit,*" on his wisdom.
I say *"praise thee this new religion."*
In your memory let me fester,
like debris on a black and white film.
In your memory let me jester,
years a sponge squeezed to clean our dead.
Marinade my dreams with clouds
giving birth to crows shouting:
"*I love you!*"

Nothing else,
this is what I want.

Nothing else,
until this is
what we
want.

EXHIBIT

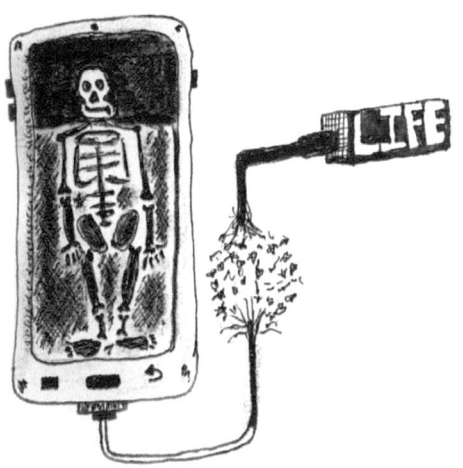

x-ray impressions
through
long-distance
affectations

walks with me in pastures of green and blue

Flies hover near the dead,
I found one swimming in my soup today.
How does one sleep with all the buzzing in the dark?
I am not sleeping until I kill this fly.
It's gone, I can't find it,
it went quiet; suddenly
I miss it.
Dead.
Caught it with my thumb
and pointing finger,
like putting out a flame.
Whose whispers wait to replace what I killed?
Who profits from such understanding?
I like chasing faded rainbows,
I just adore grey clouds
and Photoshop them in blue skies;
erasing the stars brave enough to try.
I've declared promises to sleep earlier tonight;
I will and I'll try, even as you run through my mind.
Oblivious to the secrets I find,
lingering with a sublime doubt;
incapable of sharing a bite.
A single match to recover the warmth
lost in our dying flame, so deceased
our smiles on our once loving lips.
I miss you, there is no ignorance
in my desire to return a better
and more balanced individual,
go towards the truth in troublesome
walks with me in pastures of green and blue.
Amidst the ever-changing waves of the evening skylight,
amidst the flickering reflection on our teary eyes wanting
to let each other know how to resume with the story our
souls once told; it was truer than any cold winter or hot summer.

April came and all became this one adorable, sinister, unappealing
roar of a joke; no condolence sent for the bleeding ears,
from the rapture of demonic and angelic laughter mixing.
Be your own lawyer, witness and culprit to a fantasized murder;
for a romantically incurable reason;
for this unsleeping blame,
our treacherous maze of offenses.
It's crazy what the end of the week does to a person,
Sunday evenings are for unhealthy prayers,
unsure goodbyes to some shadow you can't see
in pitch darkness in your hollow home; there is
no furniture,
no tortured memories,
no flashbacks
of our journey, instead a malfunctioning screensaver at best.
Our faces were too weak to handle the momentum
it has reached in such a quick time,
the heart it works
in a more progressive timeframe;
dumb but sanitized
enough to numb the hard parts out.
Saving it with a side of cake
as it makes my sanity ignite
with such diabetic rage, a cage
for two birds fighting for scraps,
for words to shout through
the cage, feathers begin to fall
like leaves, enough for a pillow,
an itchy blanket for two,
a shared nightmare we used
to put too much work into.
Kept alive, this ruse an insult to what could have been,
if we didn't decide to play this tired game of hide and seek.
Silence is cruel the second time around;
loving our type of silence was not my intention,
although I do respond to it with indignant pride.

It's pitiful; it's coincidental that somehow I find
solace in your indirect remarks, leaking out from
under the weather, showering me with guilt so icy,
then coming through like rays of freshly squeezed sunlight,
why now bask in such crave to misbehave under my cold winds my
angel?
Does it matter to me that I am alone with this notion;
mixing potions that taste of the most delicious poison?
I am done, I've concentrated my obsession with the dark enough,
silence my mind; mourn the dead fly, may it rest its tiny soul and
may the Lord of the flies,
for...
for...
give me.

you are a queued rainbow to someone's hard night

I had too much time to think;
someone fix my leaky faucet of a head.

It's too dangerously selfish to just go away,
you know.

I just dread being asked to live
another day.

While you're not seen
by anyone again,
know you are a queued rainbow
to someone's hard night of rain.

You can't retrace your steps,
there is an impossibly long rope ahead;
it's too easy to get tangled up my friend.

You can't communicate with a broken tongue,
it's torture for someone with so much to say.

The thunderous sound makes the current
flow wild with the pianist at bay.

Silence of the rhythms gets to where you are yelling,
"Love's too damn hard to overcome."

Try to soothe your heart to it,
*or will you still choose
to never be seen by anyone
again?*

Know there is no certainty
you will resurrect
in three
days.

Now repeat after me,
"I am hopeless and decayed but I will overcome today."

be okay despite

In a run for my life,
I don't know if I can be
fine again.

Say this is truer than love;
rain clouds start descending
from the higher plains,
changing lanes.

Another way to see this through,
is to be okay
despite the pain.

Another way to chase the blues
is not to run from it;
but drive it over
run it over, then
drive away.

In a run from my sins,
I don't know when it will burn again.

Say this is more painful than heartbreak;
rain clouds started clearing out
giving my soul an undeserving breath.

Another way,
the only way
is to be okay
despite the b*urning* pain.

It's a brand new day;
nighttime is hours away.

Another way to see this through
is to be okay despite the pain.

Another way to chase the blues
is not to run from it;
but drive it over,
run it over, then
drive away!

going blind, seeking vengeance

It will come when you least expect it,
realize your rights before you neglect it.
Forfeit the game;
you're on the losing side
or take a chance and endure,
with your head on the clouds;
the first dreamer dies.
I have a gun to my mouth,
I pull the trigger;
I am on the ground,
the bullets are digging deeper.
I messed up,
mistakes can lead us
to crime scenes of the past
and become a part of
what's happening now.
Realize no future
till we go totally insane.
I am going blind,
seeking vengeance;
who do I think I am?
Fading,
fading happily;
ease into amazement.
Fading,
fading gorgeously;
ease into a mystified release.
It will come when you more than need it,
shoot down the vultures before they eat us alive.
Forfeit this day, take a swim, ocean deep;
go on through the empty black canvas
near the sunset and sunrise,
happening simultaneously.

In killing time, we
realize the broken
second hand
of our ancient
clock; *a hand
grenade's more like.*
Realizing too much
while you're still
bleeding out seconds.
The future is dauntingly *present;*
rewriting itself a secret
message. Re*write* me.

that will better and embitter

I hear voices
so unfamiliar,
this isn't me.

I am going out of my mind,
I am going out of my mind;
pull me out of this life.

I am inspired only
to lay my head to rest.

Longing for something
that will better and
embitter me.

I've done better things
with my tomorrow,
I speak with so little
actually said.

I refuse a command,
I am out of hand,
this isn't me.

I am going to regret my next move.

So long,
I am out
of breath.

the sweetest end

Do you really laugh?
Do you really smile when you're looking at me?
Did we get anywhere with our precious small talk?
She's ignorant of the seed she sow,
rising through the clouds
like a sword within me.
I am collecting wildfires,
living under burrowed time,
trying to belittle the sun,
trying to be better
than everyone.
On my final swim
I found a pearl;
pink like the sky
that night.
My sorrowful
but blissful flight
back to the surface
was more profound
than the precept of heaven.
I am not a servant to serpent crimes,
I'll live through the miseries;
hide the aged shovel please.
You're a walking treasure chest,
bite me with your golden braces,
guide me to happiness,
sunshine and crescent moons.
We concert with adequate heart
and soul to attract nothing more
than second chances, stacked with
more second glances, second pages,
till the sweetest end;
if it's bitter, we'll pretend
it is just hallucinations,

rocking chairs,
carousels in the park,
a circle game,
we'll never know,
we'll never know.

I will ask for no kind apology

I know it looks bad,
I vow to pay for it all,
clean up the glass shards
on the blood-stained floor,
wipe the grotesque splatters
all over our living room walls.
Do I regret the injury that befell us?
Us pretending to be both judge and jury;
making compounding theories
to mast our individual throes.
This wanderlust you call,
is a satisfying hobby that
launches you up north
where the sun barely shines
and there is nothing but desolate snow.
I get it now,
how appropriate
you belong there,
you're cold and alone
and I miss the summer heat.
It only comes every now and again
when you found somewhere else to sleep
on these unholy Sunday evenings.
While I am counting ghost in the darkness;
giving these eerie voices their own names,
calling them out on their charade; parading in guilt for the new friends I've made.
Meaningful nightmares I get lost in are more comfortable than any dream,
hopeful with secluded questions I rather refrain myself from asking.
One being: *"Is heaven in the attempt at understanding someone?"*
She loves the idea of returning the emotional compromise,
but fears and dreads its impending demise.
When surely in time we will find out,

but how cruel is it for you to close the case
before the investigation even began.
You became hollow like a cactus tree,
well depended like one too.
You shelter yourself in the desert
where I will roam like a vulture,
to swoop down a wounded carcass
of a lone wolf, abandoned by the pack,
bravery denied, as his eyes go wide,
from a tumbleweed passing by;
scared easy my love?
Her amusing taste in lies,
her soothing bitterness is sublime,
music to my mistakes,
my muse when it comes
to these elegant discoveries,
categorizing the different types
of heartaches one person
could drown
in.
My heart is missing something,
all our hearts don't feel the same after its been struck
by that marvelous feeling.
So greedy and gracious,
these pitiful long embraces;
just overpowering and triggering the longing
given birth by doubts and clever madness.
Pretty lies;
pretty smiles
drawn ear to ear.
My dear cries wolf whenever she sees me,
oblivious of the levitating waters on both sides
cleared by some magic,
just so I can get by
and make my way
to you.

Notice me somehow and finally let me go,
once you let me in on a secret you wrote;
about how even in the attempt at being friends
a mere stranger passing by is all I am to you.
Now that it's too late to apologize,
now that I've kept tabs on how many goodnight
she hasn't said back.
How many calls must descend back down to silence?
How violently he cried and wept with passion and dismay
inside this white tiny room in his cardboard head;
a vacation minus
the joy.
How he wish she knocks and ask for his hand again,
even if it's just to lead him away
into the edge of a cliff,
in one of those mountains,
in one of those hills
that witness him leaving
in a van full of luggage;
leaving her with a childhood friend
who wouldn't do her wrong
as to leave and never return.
We were so unaware of the momentum slipping a downward slope.
How fancy these talks became as we try to unmask the shame.
The mission in which we decide whether to make sense
or be vague about everything.
I guess it won't work,
we are not of the same world,
we journey through different roads,
in two different circumstance.
Still in spite of my sadness
I want to sing you a tune,
until you sing along with me,
but it seems the orchestra is leaving
and the spotlight is no longer on us.

Life now burns hotter than the core of the sun
on my hopeless journey trying to figure out
how lonely it truly is to be the only one in love.
This fire,
it's eternal,
but it cannot be,
I won't let it kill me.
This time,
I will ask
for no kind
apology.

How maddening!

in a forestry of laughter

The dead sky puts my soul
in a miserable space,
as if I've been exposed
to every daunting epiphany
I never even heard of;
sent by vultures
piece by piece.
Rotten memories seek refuge inside me,
building towers and colonies to prepare an army.
The devil's sigh will only crack the vase;
encase the bouquet in flames.
I can't locate peace in this sullen state,
I am too far from medication,
the sky made me so powerless.
There's barely a hint or a clue
of where the sun went, of where
the hope hid, behind the stars maybe,
but I want to feel it near;
I long for it here!
While the day is young and I am young,
this sorrow is still on display in its original box,
I set a timer for midnight; I hope no one steals it;
it's mine to stare at, mine to grace it with unfazed lust.
It's just so difficult, so freaking hard,
choosing a different outcome
after the loneliness thrives
and buzz like a fly.
Barks like a dog
leading sheep back
in the herd, to be tamed,
to be saved from peril
in the unexplored landscapes
of a worrisome dream.
You can see it,

when you feel it.
There is no use being free,
no use stitching these scars
just letting it bleed
is mercy.
An orchestra graces an audience
with its freedom,
with its melodious travels
across islands of second-hand emotions.
A rock is thrown down the river,
like a shining chandelier,
the circles of light vibrate
and leave marks on the walls
of the unattainable sky.
Sheltering years of remorse,
sharpest of swords reminding
me of my weight in worthlessness.
Of weather patterns killing hundreds or more,
I found no wisdom here
I tell you!
It's just another downward hill,
rolling until every bone and muscle
aches with night terrors and pain.
Until the dirt turns to mud
as the rain comes down like stones
and your scent enters the nose of starving wolves.
Dedicated to one purpose;
this is to never refrain from
or impose on what nature
puts on the dinner table.
No matter how bitter
or how sweet the person.
They will eat you alive
and leave a nasty impression.
Makes it hard to keep calm
or stand on peaceful grounds,

without a stuttering lie seeking
a heartbeat
or two.
As it echoes out on bloodied lips,
forever dry like a desert drought.
I am silenced again by another;
who I was convinced to have been
the chosen one.
Instead I pollute the air
coughing in dismay,
as another bites the dust
and endures finality,
and murdered
what could have been
a line up on the glass table of pure ecstasy.
Instead I'm left with another dead sky
without possibilities; now the day is done.
At least the moon might be full tonight,
I despise feeling like a suspect writing an apology,
learning how to breathe underwater.
When I can't even find the courage
to walk on the field we passed through
as lovers, without wanting to cry or bleed or tear.
Because beauty is something I don't understand;
it only leaves me from where I stand.
Who do I pray to?
I am kneeling and looking up
at the full moon.
Satan adores it
when a soul accepts
defeat, *doesn't he?*
Why must I wander so far?
I drown in a puddle left behind by yesterday's showers.
Why must I pull out from existence the most stunning flower from its home in the soil?
A soul evolves with every torment it involves itself with;

one that invites the growth of tumors,
counting scars instead of sheep.
Harboring missing ships
in deep water minefields.
Makes me sick,
makes me falter
into the saddest
materialized thoughts
and aging reasons
outlasting the seasons.
Falling from the branches that keeps me secret,
I feel shunned off whenever a bird leaves me
feeling insignificant as it flies over my bed
to whither and feel helpless,
it's madness
I tell you!
Framing insanities
on the bedroom wall,
looking down on you
from dusk until dawn.
Or in the afternoon
to avoid being reminded
of the *morning light*
she most lovingly
and fascinatingly
adored.
I long for answers,
for open drawers
with no locks adorned,
I long for a cure,
I long to endure
with humility and
trust you once more.
Whatever I must do
to prove my life has
something to be based on;

I will not take it for granted
anymore.
To find something or someone
also lost in a cave;
relying on that microscopic
light at the end.
It's crazy inspiring,
this grand adventure
for something elusive,
to find her shout with so much delight,
caging doubts and failures so as not
to blur what faith has in mind.
When two lost souls find each other in this collection of
heartbreaking lessons,
it makes me eager more than sin in anger,
for I still have hope for that boy in the manger
to lead me away from danger
and lead me into the right step
in the pitch darkness
beyond her silhouette.
The reoccurring gladness
and underdeveloped smiles,
is making promises
that can't be unchained.
It sucks when people don't find it in them
to love again.
I found no wisdom here.
Just wildflowers dreading the idea of finding each other;
we are the new normal desiring the company of no one;
to be the only audience in a forestry of laughter,
because we trust no other voice than our own;
to make this choice,
to be happily singular,
to shine past the sunset
and corrupt mindsets.

Found no wisdom still?
Just another day
spent by the window
sill
of a madhouse
in
Santa Fe.

an imbecile's prayer

You're in the way of my sunny day;
you're one of my favorite sins.

You're in the way of my cloudy day;
you're an imbecile's prayer.

Why do you put words in my mouth?
Can I speak for myself?

You're on the way of my perfect day.
You're one of the hours,
ticking away;
doing nothing.

If only you have heard me long ago,
on our way to the edge of hope.

If only you have heard me long ago;
our prayers become wasted insults;
while the choir sings
to glorious
lyres.

EXHIBIT

Y

yellow witnesses
pouring
anecdotes
dotted
with
pretty
hearts

my way back to your sunlight

Someday, looking behind this tragic mess,
I will laugh and forgive my way back to your sunlight.
Someday, putting my foot down;
I am thinking of changing my ways
and escape this dangerous path.
You met with an arrow to the heart.
Will this lead to the beast of insomniac sheets?
It's not what it looks like, it's not brighter than your sunlight.
Forgive the trouble at hand
and avenge me
and return
our loving
burn out.
Someday,
looking behind
this tragic mess,
I will laugh and forgive
my way back to your sunlight.
Someday, putting my foot down;
I am thinking of changing
my ways and escape
this dangerous path,
escape your exciting
w*rat*h!

stab me where it hurts the most

Demons despise me,
I've done so much good;
love makes me sane.
The devil told me the meaning of the truth
and that the pain never really leaves you;
it grows thicker into life's foggy terrain.
You're always one step ahead of me,
do what you like; I don't care at all
if you stab me where it hurts the most.
I will not scream as the blood runs across the world,
eventually the memory of good will unfold,
eventually our story will grow old;
eventually our world goes cold
with you alone.
Good runs in me,
I can't do nothing better;
without it, my spirit
dries out.
The evil I speak of breathes alive
on my shoulder about the sin
I am soon to discover;
I carefully decline her offer.
I fall below the deepest well of every step
I take. I get higher
than before,
the best part of all;
I get farther from you.
Still you're always one step ahead of me.
Do what you like,
I don't care at all
if you stab me
where it hurts
the most.

Eventually our world goes cold
and there's no room
for this at all;
no room
for re-
solve.

the serene white lie

My soul has been through a lot of shameful best shots,
shame always looked after me.
The waiting game is over,
I've been lost so many times;
now a special love has found me,
lifting me off the ground.
She colored me in the center of her heart,
followed me through the forest of despair;
she offers the best type of healing,
I am so glad she disappeared.
My call to action is her words,
like gospel in a church.
She keeps me satisfied,
she helps me kill the time;
the sunset is ours for keeps.
We will overcome this,
together immune to the reaper's kiss,
any trial that wants to stay
can simply fuck off!
Going back to when we started,
every second was contraband bliss;
I remember every kiss against the fences.
I still feel her dying breath;
both hands on the backend of a dagger,
blood flowing like a daffodil,
caught in the current of a water mill.
She paints my chest the color of her hair,
she follows me through the serene
white lie of death's sneer.

She offers the best type of healing;
I am so glad we exorcise
the parasite that lived
in her for years.

choosing weapons we don't know how to use

Losing you was the core of my mistakes,
I left you feeling like a witch burned at the stake.
We will claim the greatness heaven made
if our holding hands don't separate.
I found myself in a corner
I have never explored,
I found your loving eyes
amidst a landscape of decoys;
I feel teary-eyed just letting things
be the way they are.
Holding it all together
is a beating heart;
it won't give up.
Haven't we seen enough blood for one night?
Let the demons talk us out of choosing weapons
we don't know how to use.
What is not overrun by darkness?
Can we save our unproductive turmoil,
and inexperienced light for some other mass murder?
After the sun died, I wrote a note,
burned it into your heart.
My hopes are you recite it every night
before you temporarily die.
Another season arrives
to change the color of our sky.
I am flattered by the joke you said,
every line they still resonate.
Open me up to the possibilities
of being met by worst calamities.
I am happy to move forward,
seeking a new distraction now.
While still saddened by the fact
that I am no longer yours and
you're no longer mine.

Holding it all together is a beating heart,
it won't give up.
Haven't *we seen enough blood for one night?*

Let the demons
talk in
advance.

your purpose here was a highway accident

I am losing my pride;
it has taken a drastic turn,
I can't help myself from using
the elevator down,
losing what I don't deserve,
in this world that I can't see;
clearly without deception
charming me.
Hell has invited me to the party,
a paradise that I dreamed of since
I was three.
It was you who convinced me not to go,
doubt is a terrible thing.
Disappear like a rain shower,
your purpose here was a highway accident.
A ray of light was enough to expose you,
forfeit this stupid race.
You're not enough of a warrior to win,
a single punch is enough to kill your engine.
Down with insanity;
Hell will keep you safe.
I can't fancy the present here,
my problems are mistaken for destiny.
Do as you're told, destiny
catapults torches
and pitchforks
in our twin roads.
Dreams never hurt like this before,
losing what I don't deserve.
In this world,
so unpredictable;
your presence
so indelible,
doubt is the latest thing.

Disappear like a rain cloud,
your purpose here is to fizzle out.
A ray of light was enough to expose your cheat remarks;
forfeit this stupid fight; you're not enough of a warrior
to lose properly, a single punch is enough to reverse the effects;
label me a coward of the highest degree.

that smile that *is* life

Steal the melody,
open up to me;
you leave me breathless,
take the notes out of me,
sing me sorrow;
light my fantasies
with that soul
that gives me life.
Who are you but a shadow on the sun?
Far from my reach,
she burns me with every touch,
least of my worries are when she disappears,
she keeps coming back; she's circling round.
Steal the remedy,
stitch the wound internally;
she leaves me reeling.
Takes me patiently,
swings me lovingly;
right my mistakes
with that smile
that *is* life.
You leave me breathless,
keep me from giving up.
Your enchanted colors,
send me somewhere else.
I've lost enough,
but glad you're back;
now we can discover
what we lack.

Who am I but a shadow on the sun?
Far from her reach,
I burn her with every touch,
least of her worries are when I disappear,
I keep coming back;
I am cir*cling*
round.

kissed by our dead light

Can you see me?
I'm but a wandering spirit.
Can you hear me?
I am an echo in the grass.
Can you hold me tighter?
So I won't slip through your buttered hands.
Raise your hand up to the sky,
speak surrender on this night;
keep it all from tumbling down.
You're a dancing arrow;
aim for me now.
You're a Kingdom come;
lock me out.
I've always known something was missing;
keep it told to whispers hissing in the mass fire.
Can you kill our original fire?
I'm a piece of deadwood.
Can you feel me?
Keeping you warm,
like I said
I would.
Any sign of thriving sparks?
I am an aching scar bleeding vigorously.
Can you hold me tighter so I won't slip through?
Trials dismissed!
Raise your hand up to the judge;
speak surrender.
The arrow pierced through the part of me
that you love most.
Your Kingdom has forgotten to keep me
from coming through.

No barricades,
you're low on the defensive,
what is slowing you down princess?
You're a Kingdom come;
she ostracized my homeless heart.

I've always known something was missing;
keep it told to whispers kissed by our dead light.

a melody

I am in a neutral state of mind;
a melody of hurt,
a string of lies,
I nod to answer,
a questioning sigh.
Relief is a continued endeavor;
become a birth of whatever,
defeated by the nice weather.
Fine, no, yes.
A loss I truly accept;
packing up for a new journey.
Subtle changes in color give way;
yet buried by the shadows of evil
that takes and *takes* and breaks,
the fake and the shaken.
Forsaken like a broken piece of clothing,
crestfallen during the mourning process.
The sting of pain left unseen
sheds a light down there;
sees nothing, the searching
is reduced to a blank stare.
No guidance from this labyrinth
of counterfeit feelings of existence.
Remarkable choices that were made;
a cold drink lay on a wooden table,
lemonade.

near with that same sublime look

In a minute
I'll be there,
my heart beats faster
as our agile spirits
drive that dwindling road.
In a moment you'll see me,
calm down, I am almost near
with that same sublime look on my face;
longing to be amazed by a maze of endearing doubt.
It is time to admit what you feel, sail through the open sea.
Become one, *one* with our special dream, dream harder, forever;
we're almost there.
In a state of wanting, *may I have it now please?*
The look of surprise on your face as the sun rises,
scared the birds that smeared the horizon.
It is time to admit what you feel,
sink under miles of the closing seas.
We're already there,
in a pool of cycled fear.
In denial, this can't be real.

We are ungrateful; living
in and out
of our
best
sins.

in the light of who we were

It is in my best intention to rid of all the inner pollution;
a pandemic of thoughts I'm leaving behind.
I need you here, don't confuse love for a favor.
We need each other in this cold and lonely world;
this cold and lonely show where we are
some comedian's punch line.
Under the light of a new day,
let's go out and play like children.
It is my greatest objective
to rid of misconceptions
that's been holding us back.
We will get far away from here,
hopefully somewhere we're free to be joyful.
Let's rejoice and sin with good intention,
no more cigarette scented fear.
Let's drive there; until
insanity is met with glee.
Quit following the flaming trail of night's shadow;
luring us to the outskirts of a hellish orange sea.
"Tempting isn't it?"
I need you, don't be selfish now.
We need each other through this tough times,
let's rest in peace my darling, *rest in peace.*
It's been our calling,
we can be immortalized,
before sunrise remits.
In the light of a new dawn,
let's go out and stay out;
rotting in the vegetable garden.
In the light of who we were,
let's speak no ill words today.
Let's break through the walls of the Kingdom halls;
feeding the insects and the worms
in eden's central vaults.

I am not that guy anymore; *I am not that guy anymore*

I've seen enough to understand how I passed over the line,
deliverance I am still waiting for died just in time;
to cage me with my imperfections,
to tell me how it feels to be forever wrong.
As a member of the choir who sang demonic rhymes,
as a person giving in to the death of his first love,
every season I forgive all the lessons I receive
to then journey to the end only to start again.
I am not that guy anymore; *I am not that guy anymore.*
I've said enough to accept that I am set on mute,
tsunamis are what you cause amongst the calmer tides;
to drown me with my imperfections,
to tell me how it feels to be forever wrong.
Don't fear what you don't know,
wave goodbye to the rainbow,
kill the fire with your finger,
get your hands off the trigger,
don't listen to the storm clouds,
close all your windows;
die on your pillow.
Till the death of tomorrow!
Till the death of tomorrow!
I am not that guy anymore!
I am not that guy anymore!

spontaneous words began turning heavy rocks to find zero worms

So young and so fair,
her silence aware of his wandering stare
stretching till sunset's golden hair.

Set the half-moon up on a loving dare,
unaware of how fast her hold would be;
serenaded; all tangled up in her politics.

They're singing a song out of tone,
practicing hammering at the nails;
it's a duet so unexpectedly sedating,
I am melting passionately,
with their unreturned glances;
at the end of the song,
it's their deathbed.

We want us to work for what is ahead,
instead of the chains we unchained that day,
helping you find the codes for the vault placed
on a velvet pillow inside your heartless cave.

Badminton rackets,
bird stuck in between branches,
we praised our one audience
as we exchanged confusing signals.

Still our mentality insisted
on the unhealthy gleam
of the yellow sun.

During our walk home,
a six floor elevator ride,
silence was trying to escape
our illegal tongues; spontaneous words
began turning heavy rocks to find zero worms.

I offered an idea, you mistook as an opportunity
to escape your parent's grasp at your maturity,
riding the bus towards a past I was better off without.

Our talks were transcendent;
our misbehaviors are overworked
and we enjoyed throwing blades
at insecurities we mistrusted.

Laughing hard at loveless characters;
pinky promise,
you'll kill me
last.

Send me off into more days with your young heart
trying to extend her heartbeat like a radio station.

Crazy,
how we left
as if it didn't
occur.

Crazy,
how inventive
our distractions
were.

Crazy,
how conceited
our first and last
embrace really was.

Crazy,
how we let it happen
in the first
pl*ace.*

EXhibit

Z

zebras
sliced
by
patterns
of
black
and
grave
white
rays

the wrinkled center

Same as ever,
subtle and clever,
she pushes me deeper
to the broken blade
in the blender.

I am not too far gone,
I am not tangled
by the puppet strings;
sweet honey dear.

She's the bringer of joys,
looking nice in a sweater
with pink hearts in
the wrinkled center.

Never knew I could talk to you,
my spirit longs for the bitter taste of fate;
take me away
sweet honey dear.

Written on my walls
I already knew,
my spirit longs
for an answer;
let it be you.

I am a crime scene,
she wipes her prints clean,
I mend the deceitful little things
I've done; I've been the broken
blade on a blender all this time.

This premise needs a refresher,
my bittersweet honeyed dear;
I spilled coffee on your sweater.

I've fought with myself in my mind,
over and over I surrender dearly,
sweetly, to your homeless homing missile.
My spirit longs for the aftertaste of failure,
see you Sunday on the midnight mass.
Written on your walls my spirit longs for an answer.

To be continued…

after a beautiful choice

We were children who didn't know
what a heart was
and how loving it could be;
and how painful it could speak.

So one day, I turned around
from my everyday cowardice frown
and I turned from a clown
to a brave soldier down.

As you pulled me in and you trapped me now,
in a bad position waiting for the bomb to go off.

You said some cold words,
you did not love me back.

I said more words in response to that
but they're as hopeful as a bat waiting for a home run.
I took a swing, swing, swing; hopeful as a mouse;
trapped inside a cold white room with cheese in my mouth.

There was never a time we spoke at all,
silence was your power,
hiding was my call.

When my words found meaning,
laughing at what I would do
I just end up screaming;
hope hanging on a rope!

We were like orphans looking for a home
and we sat beside each other as neighbors
and we even shared a laugh or two together,
knocking elbows, knocking souls, *K.O.*

But one day words leaked out, rumor had its grip,
I was in an awful position; denying my contribution.

As I was pulled in by your honest eyes,
waiting for an answer that you know
won't feel right or clever.

I said I did, say *I love you* but,
you send me a hopeful note saying:
A friendship instead will be best for us.

But outside at recess when you met my loving eyes
I watch an angel turn to a devil in disguise.

Look at who you come to be after many passing years.
Now blonde, I am missing the dark hues of your hair
and vulnerable spirit.

I swear to God
I didn't love someone
like you, but love was blind
when I was a youngster;
now the blindfold is gone
deep in the dumpster.

You really took my best years,
I hope you know that.

Because of you
I didn't learn
what real human growth was all about;
it starts with love at an early age,
I didn't know this,
until my mistakes
became so clear.

Spilling my desire for someone
who was never here;
deaf to my heartbeats.

My heart, my heart, my heart
is not yet destroyed,
enlightened now,
after a beautiful choice,
to move onto someone
I deserve,
to put years under the grave
waiting for venturous
tender hands to save me.

When my words found meaning,
laughing at what I would do,
I just end up screaming;
hope hanging on a rope!

"It's a celebration!"

I block away the sunshine,
there's no point to it all;
when darkness has always helped to conceal the bruises;
collecting like pollution under the bridges of our youth.
Still I find you near me, you're a damsel in distress.
Will I pull myself together and pull the trigger on your head?
I see the enemy feeding me with envy;
I've found no cure.
Which will kill me faster?
It's lonely being behind a stranger's gun.
It's all a circle everything gets returned.
There's a key that'll unlock your soul to everything it needs to know;
it starts with a prayer and goosebumps on summer nights by the window,
while the sky consoles our psychosis.
Still I find you near me;
you found a new owner.
Will I find peace in this loneliness?
Will I be fast enough to hide behind its light?
Dead flower nights; swallow me whole.
How romantic was our subconscious trance.
What a dance;
standing ovation,
I spilled my guts
laughing until God finally ask:
"What is all the commotion?"
As he sends cold rain and thunder.
"It's a celebration!"
I'm loving this,
you k*now*.

our blueprint burns black

It could get worst sometimes,
you can't heal,
the human longing
nonexistent,
you can't
feel.

You just need a little break, that's all;
from all the little changes
and thoughts of evil
fascinating to
you like roadkill.

Keep going on,
keep going off;
it's beautiful to realize
what you've been through.

You're moving on,
you're moving off;
flowing like a river runs
into whatever, till
our blueprint
burns black.

It would be best if you master your madness,
the happy feeling relies on you not being a slave to your fist.

You just need a little push, that's all; from all
the odd phases and hard-headed miracles.

This disturbance stops the flow
like when the waves merge with the Saturn soil;
your tears dry just as fast, awaken by
a lightning in the process
of being
born.

my one lie

Daffodils in the desert of my past.
A rainstorm on its way but
I know that it won't last.

A lily on the ocean of my youth,
burns from the heat of the sun;
a fire that burned everything
I have said to protect with my one lie.

It took a day of tired pain to see the happy life
that I always dreamt of living.

It took only a second to go back
to the memories that lack attention.

Meaningless abuse that are sent my way
comes back to me; a funeral for the happy.

Daisies in the middle of the street.
A rainbow tattooed on my feet;
a two-faced weather forecast
sends bruises canyon deep.

A sunflower in the center of my heart
starts to fall apart, petals landing on
my cold sheets mixing with shards
of your finest glass memories.

A vision I can't take, the beauty
I missed so well. A beautiful memory
I've promised to protect; with my security lust.

The day has gone again, the moonlight shines down with pity;
it's my only friend. I rather live this boring fantasy,
than see the flowers in my life
abused by me.

my testament

You smile at me,
I perk up curiously;
we're a genderless tragedy
we are meant to let love be.

I see you with your sparkling eyes
and kind demeanor, remembering
the last moment we saw each other.

I see that the smallest touch can save
a lever from being pulled down with surrender;
when will I get down from our summer fever?

You've been there,
under the heat of a July morning.

Your gorgeous smile painted a beautiful image;
we are meant to let love be.

Heaven is only a nickname for the home we live in;
Hell is a fantasy unless you get to know the *real* me.

I see you with your sparkling eyes and kind demeanor,
forgetting slowly, the last moment we saw each other.

I see that the smallest touch can save a lever
from being pulled down with surrender;
my misfortune teller ask about my will
and here's my testament.

Winter can't come any faster,
I found myself unsatisfied;
I hide our lie and drive
the memory out of town.

may I have your disapproval?

Forever is a fantasy's foe,
what is yours to take
is also yours to throw.

What's ours is something
we built with clean intention;
this moment now is our resolution.

You've got nothing to lose here,
we are yours to keep twenty-four seven.

I made a playlist for us
to sing tomorrow;
*may I have
your disapproval?*

Yesterday was all blurred and hazy,
let today's sunlight have its way with you.

Forever becomes a topic of dismay,
what is now is
yours to mistake.

But the seed grows and has grown,
but the feeling falls
like ice cream
snow cones.

What's ours is something we built
with desperation;
this moment now,
our causal destruction.

One day the alarm
will be set off,
the next day chaos
will swallow us
whole.

What's in the final hour
is something we built
through years of
evolution;
this moment now our
devolution.

the lowest source of hope

Found you,
among the other things
that found me;
a memory
I cannot seem to forget.

Around me,
a field of three-leaf clovers,
a field of crazy lovers;
our first sweet nightmare.

I'll do it again,
until we finally discover the truth.

The fruit inside us
that keeps us longing for more;
the mystery becomes our fall.

Seasons, amongst other things
that changes,
a rainy night that keeps
us awake.

Found me once more,
keep me from leaving
any generous clues.

Shooting stars are the lowest source of hope,
their mystery becomes our fall.

You shot pass me in routine,
leaving a scented remedy;
healing me as you come and go.

I'll do it again,
until we finally recover
from the hail love weathers.

What a killer invite to a party,
I don't own you anything honey.

The mystery sour grapes just the same;
my smile died in an instant
as it innocently meets
your arsonist themes.

the biblical end

Turn me on and switch my channels,
sit on my lap and whisper in my ear.

On the gifted road of lollipops and free gold,
on a mercy overdose of a killer's train of thoughts.

You strike me as a good thing,
expand your arms like this
when we're dancing,
step on my foot,
I'll cut your pretty
white legs off;
violent passion
keeps the story going,
we're an interesting read.

Turning another page;
burning another page.

Turn me off and go on ruining everything,
the lower winds have taken us hostage,
I miss when you were beside me.

On the miserly road of rejected smiles,
being an intrusion to a psychos daydream.

Turn, turn, turn, turn another page;
until we reach the biblical end.

Turn, turn, turn, turn another page;
until each page burns like hell.

Showcase
how we misbehave.

Showcase
how we're feeling dead.

Showcase
our manic
en*ding!*

unapologetic insults offered towards the *morning light*

Two different cards reveal
two sets of pictures;
contrasting and reciting hymns
sang by angelic vultures.
Redeeming themselves
with every nibble of the feed;
scaring off Seagulls peacefully standing on seaweed.
Lingering upon the horizon line waiting for twilight to arrive;
hoping, ever so hopeful that tonight the moonlight
shines on our good side.
That's when I find a knife on your bedside,
missing from where it was sheltered
underground to make sure our past crimes
don't return; seeking to haunt us
and unravel the blindfold off our infected eyes,
am I the best witness the court can provide?
Seeking to know you despite the resounding
"no" and apologetic grins
offered towards tomorrow,
and unapologetic insults offered
towards the *morning light*.
As it shines with defeat turning as gray as the field of sky,
looking down with pity at a crowded space; fueled by people of
different nature
growling danger upon danger just to be immune to fear as it snows
through their summer plans.
Abusing the chorus; *just to end it by repeating lines, just to end it by repeating lines.*
A set of lips dirty and dry as ours,
with a brave soldier's voice is
withholding information
with chapped wisdom;
we're nervous mouth breathers

silenced by death saying:
"I don't know."
"I don't know."
As we saw the moonlight appear
through our curtained view
of what we thought we knew.
"Farewell sweet memory."
"Farewell spontaneous energy," I said.
As I let my cards bleed,
fall like angel feathers to the floor
in a single heartbeat I lost it all.
"Death takes away your voice," she would say.
"-without an echo," I would utter with contempt.
As the shovel sang with violence to the violin,
to the orchestra of: *"What could've been."*

in a dopamine trance

An empty nest on the tallest tree in the Savannah forest,
is caught amidst the frightening breeze of Hell's fire;
this orchestra of unfathomable despair fell upon their mortal heads,
as the cries of a mother eagle awoke them from their beds.
His whispers are louder than the dreadful sound of falling buildings
birthing hurricanes with featherless wings.
Poor fallen angel swings on a noose made by hopeless beings
lacking amusement,
conquered by their stack of heroes;
not sufficiently withdrawn from their sorrows.
Leaving the mass after the chorus,
after the holy statues fall on their starving
demon-possessed manifesting egos.
Always in the middle of a history lesson
awake while a dream caves in.
Whilst torture succumb to pleasure and twinkling stars
after a session with a stolen guitar.
Driving too fast into the country road
on a middle finger stretched till the eye could see;
on both sides now, I rather be near the smell of manure,
and horses, my ideal fantasy.
Sleep I cheated on, days I bleed too long,
words I force too strong, digging more tunnels to piss on.
I love the scented failures;
kisses on the envelope of letters.
Pictures of a smile after reading words you signed
in a dopamine trance.
Pillows know more than you give them credit for;
an ally to our hard skull after a long day's work,
while our cells inside endure labor,
caged in a war between repair
and at times diseases thrive
even after we wake up,
and try out there to survive.

Our dance with death is
a sensual choreographed ballet.
A decadent array of loving arms,
with a winter cold embrace;
meant to freeze out,
meant to dictate
when to seal shut
the insanity parade
caused by suicidal days.
Refrain from repeating his acts.
Unchain from every prize you've won
under his tutelage,
under his prideful smile;
duck too late from the direction
of his smoking gun.
Sacrifice another minute
to add more coal into the fire,
be inspired by the red of the sky,
the twilight eyes behind a lover's mask;
every fresh deceit destroys a man.
Paint a portrait of black and white;
blatant affairs of a young heart.
Never mind the visual temptations,
spit on the performance of the mime.
The chill from outside grabs hold,
awaking fibers of stories untold.
The music store I went to yesterday,
fell apart like the bridge of a song,
so emotional are these train of thoughts;
the rails even curved just to make it even more so.
Water doesn't hydrate your type.
It pleases your soul to write about things that died,
of a unhappy tale, where no one survived; where smiles
fade on characters that are livid as much as they're vivid.
The curtain falls, unscrew my precious mind to reveal
what I've lost in you. In a world so cold, since I let you down;

breakaway from the final act, much truer
than any fact that are lacking to last.
Good morning
my sunshine,
my buddy,
my only choice.
My fatal smile,
only hangs there a while
convinced that death confides in me,
more than the most delicious of lies.
Have a great day, she'd say twice;
I'll gift you with power hugs,
keep tabs of how many on a tally chart.
For when the time comes,
we meet again
my one
and
only
sweet...
he-
art.

you're beautiful

You went too far
into a foreign direction,
my eyes went blurry,
I am tearing up,
I saw it coming;
what a *beautiful lie.*

I couldn't have done this
without you,
kill the thought of a life so good.

I couldn't have loved the way I do
if it wasn't for you and
you're beautiful…

You were my virgin light,
now you shine away from right.

High and mighty; you'll remind me,
she felt like summer; what a *beautiful…*

lie.

Couldn't have done this,
the way I loved you;
what a lie.

I couldn't have done this without you,
kill the thought of a life so good.

I couldn't have loved the way I do
if it wasn't for you and
you're beautiful…

fascination elsewhere

My fire is almost out;
but there are lovers
left to burn.
I am not the first spark to arrive;
I am the last fallen leaf
on the charcoal's ash.
Under my eyes you sail away,
sway with the unfriendly waves
in the night's donut light.
Goodbye for now my unfair lady;
find fascination elsewhere.
What my eyes were to meet are boats
already sunken happily.
I am a tiny pebble,
an insignificant ripple,
a mere pixel in your screensaver;
a situation gleaming
with the most delirious
presuppositions.
Arrangements so doomed
to prove any certainty of emeralds,
I am sullen with my sapphire insults,
scabs bleeding on ruby scented roses;
you're a *stone*
cold killer.
The absence of one in your finger.
Where are we in a couple of months?
Will I even consider the calm turquoise blanket under your shade?
We sing about our future days,
conversations are the *air*
to these *wings*.

so sweet, *yet are we?*

Sleep disaster away;
it awakened with decisions
manifesting past
our method
solutions.

Our method of fascination is so tranquil;
so polluted with movies.

Honey, so sweet, *yet are we?*

So full of butterflies when free-flowing,
when paired with a nice
weather and a stolen
sweater from
an unnamed
stranger.

Betrayal is nameless.

Our faith is to taste the bitterness,
during illusions of fun
on blue fluorescent evenings,
and joyful pastures burning whitest;
trying to convert introverted stars.

Meet you on the core of this sunny *betrayal!*

My favorite gravedigger, *"have you found any gold yet?"*

A library book is passed from one hand to the next like a whore.

Compensated
with plastic cards,
she dances
to the wind
sometimes,
pitied
under
sunlight
and
lamplight
eyes.

worshipers of unconscious heartbeats

I need to wake up with more than a craving for hot food or cold water.
I need to wake up holding onto gospel from many dead nights ago.

I am chasing you through a trail forsaken by a blanket of spring flowers
in a petal position amidst a crossfire of wishes; it must be dandelion season.

I am staying trustworthy to our hopeless remedies
ignited with similarities
so cruelly inviting.

Our subconscious finally learned something,
we worshipers of unconscious heartbeats.

I am never going to pursue watching a rerun of our episodic moments,
I am letting myself be reduced
to forgetting you;
never
returning,
always
leaving.

not so inno*cent* anymore; my white coat

A single spark is all it is
in a formless laugh
so overcome with insecure
deliveries.
Heavy was our chances;
somebody
light,
light my cigarettes.
Our undiscovered pearls shine
at the endless seconds of a long restless
night,
under a moonlight
depraved
a visit from
depraved
stars;
a comet flat-lined
in the South.
Gray was
our beautiful days.
Blue was
our grass those nights.
Colors don't matter
to eyes that left
love
hanging with
a rope,
an empty chair
and
no note.

Not so inno*cent*
anymore;
my white
coat.

every passionate release redefines love

Is happiness a sickness too?
Sleep doesn't come easy because I was led through *the other door.*
Heroes are dropping like flies so suddenly.
Tonight we say *"welcome"* to the madness.
No breath or Heaven *or some shit…*
Just another halo under
diamond nightlight.
I'll be waiting
for you,
for fireflies
to demonize
our friendly fire,
for when you are ready
to love me
again.
It's surreal that I can't yet
muster
a tear.
It was too soon to navigate
a way out of center stage,
how we sang with defeat
after each stanza;
after every passionate release
redefines love.
I needed that, and you provided
unreturned glances;
so lovingly absent was the embrace
we did not get a chance to take for granted.
My pillow doesn't allow me to escape into the confines of comfort,
or the healing measured in mutilated hours; life without you would
be sad.
It hurts my selfish plans that you were already found by *somebody else…*
Even as we synchronize what it meant to us
every song sang under the rainy night.

The singing forest, with dark branches extending as high as it could
finds the courage of a thousand moonlight.
Am I under arrest for the value I placed under your summer branches?
Towering hedges, under grey weather raining with waves of gasoline
fumes.
Promise me that tonight the flames would be our savior.
Bring birth to new manifestations,
infectious lessons bouncing off my cold cut corners
inside a heart vacant for days;
suddenly it places your name
under a date.

the moments that break before d*awn* even w*aves*

I won't forfeit
what battle with myself
has started to race;
my stamina is just
recharging.

I faint before the music,
leave me to it to learn how
to get back up from this.

Letting another body pass without any hardwire attached,
despite the high voltage of electricity catching fire
from every exchange of innocent smiles.

Select me from the gathering herd as your one and only prey,
I pray that I make a safe getaway.

Still I am killed
with uneven
laughter
partaking;
the moments
that break
before d*awn*
even w*aves*.

dusty forgotten books in a low shelf

The sunset curls up ashamed that we didn't share its welcome,
instead we had the rain and our unzipped thunders.
"Loveless quotes bled through every silhouetted sweats."
Around her neck was a grey scarf for the winter chill,
we drove uphill to our house, then a runaway passes by,
riding a flat bike as best he could on the uneven slope.
"Should we give the struggling man a ride honey?"
I would say, parking in front of the boy.
"No, it only reminds me of where we are, let him get used to it while he is young."
Thunder cues the bended windshield wipers wiping at what we've failed to produced;
we became dusty forgotten books in a low shelf of an abandoned bookstore:
Who the fuck cares anymore?

obscuring paranoia valleys

You've left our conversation hanging
like the last leaf of a burning tree,
see to it that you dream of me;
I obligate your heart to flee
into a guiltless regimen,
let us overdose with sin proudly.

We're joyless customers in our *mind buffet*,
eating away the greens and rotten childhood
memories so bleak with the aftermath of monsoons,
who pilots these train of thoughts anyway?

By the creek, we're throwing knife-edged rocks;
aimed at mystical frogs
obscuring paranoia
valleys, trying to wake
up sleeping heartbeats
keeping a beautiful
secret.

Shush, someone
is coming,
teach me how
to m*ou*rn
properly.

en*try* by en*try* by en*try*; eternal

So I can rejoice with inspirations after all,
direct my energy far away
from my ego and
lay it freshly baked on the table
for another angel.

The lens of my glasses aspire
beyond the clearing rain,
to see clearer and think about you
other than dancing with hurt;
aging so quickly.

I start to think these are tears
from my past pains,
so I can regenerate
the soil within me.

But I missed my chance to say: *"No."*
Oh, you cowardice float,
get caught hanging in a balcony
of a damaged home, break a leg
on the dinner table,
she won't notice.

This can't be real,
I can't be sent off to journal,
en*try* by en*try* by en*try;*
eternal.

Burning
white spaces
for her…
for him…
to never forget
and immortalize
the *pleasure;*
my *pleasure.*

ever-changing tarot card readings

We inhabit
the words
we say,
interrupting
voices
liberated and clever,
infusing fabulous
madness;
*how does
it feel?*

The ever-changing
tarot card readings
are telling me
your part in
my life is
more;
*is any
of this
real?*

I am recollecting
chances
I didn't take,
I need to return
your glances
my broken Parakeet.

I repeat
I did not ask
for agony
this sweet.

My very own
shipwreck,
taking months
and days
and nights
to sink down properly
into the deep green sea
of such
limitless
clarity.

tears, illusively tranquil

I learned that there are lessons
we avoid for the sake of avoiding
hurt.

To love is to
burn
a finely written
promise
to yourself about
what did
and didn't
work;
in ink made of our shadow's
tears,
illusively
tranquil.

Burnt;
second chance to lay down
the hurt.
I am stunned
by the sudden
change
in our alibi
as I am once more
under arrest
by your restless
eyes.

a list burning like sin

See this through as if a dream,
tear from the seams
like the Titanic in the seas.
Leave a mark in my history,
brutally carved with feelings
decayed as they may.
Shouts of prayers were redeemed
after false worship
to accompany this hopeful message.
I'll wait, I'll analyze this predicament
with a sigh and a list burning like sin.
As I pursue this steep emotional trail
and in every step of the way,
I will surrender to the bitter breeze,
and envy serenity in that stone
rolling down the hill.
Most of my daydreams are born
in overcast shells by the window sill,
designing a will profoundly ill
and misshapen still like clay.
You're that little gray in my sunset tonight,
that little green in my sunrise.
This moon looking down
at me will be my cover
from the impending ruse
in these yet hollow hours.
Meet me halfway I would say,
imitate a statue while
I wait out by the hidden staircase.
While the sound of a gorgeous waterfall
sounds to the heavens near us.
Without longingly deserving its view
to renew what is still thriving with fondness.

The stars are nowhere to be sought,
there's no blanket of solace to hug me,
despair,
waiting to be unsung.
Resounded with a missing gun.
Seasoned with a cycle of win or lose,
I am halfway right or so I thought.
After all in this fight there comes a break
and mine would be when my sanity wakes
to create more envious binge
confined inside a white room
without corners.
Sighing
in torture with
a throbbing
conceited
humbling
desperation.
To return
to that first
hint
of spring
of summer heat
in your winter.
In our loving way, in our complex way.
Our compositions of insanity
that erotically clashes
with forbidden fantasy.
Here my dear where
I last met you giving me
despair
never shy
to let me care.
Now with shame in the mix,
I might just burn the messenger alive
at the stake.

While I am not afraid,
yet still shaken from
this act of moving on.
I hope your light finds its way back home.
Still the thought seems foreign
like everything.
The concept of forgetting what you
simply can't.
It seems unknown to what is available.
Left in the heart you disposed of like
leftover meat.
Let me be, let me sleep on the dead grass
as we speak.
While my mind alters what remains.
What do our remaining lessons endeavor anyways?
I am enlightened temporarily.
This stubborn maze of our everlasting search for peace.
Find it clean and make you feel wealthy
even as I blink in disbelief
from acquainting with the illusion of it.
It's the bliss felt for invisible kisses
from someone far away.
Not knowing her feelings were dancing
its own battlefield.
Unaware of what's around,
oh how darling the sound of all of it was.
My wanderlust of false hope,
filling my cup with fine wine
by the river shore.
Flowers in this field of dead grass
becomes just another
selected finality.
Let it be,
let me flee,
send a beam of light

my way and
I will follow
it.
Stranger, stranger
on the phone
always unknown,
I am ready
to know you:
Whoever you are.
I am tortured and flawed,
I'll step on your feet it will hurt,
I won't ask if you're ready
if you do the same for me.
Laugh instead at knowing
how unprepared
I am as well.
I can already feel the shine of your first smile
directed my way:
Whoever
you
are.

I fell for

I only had one day to prove my worth,
to be a daydream that you can hold.

I only came as a slave to my curious soul
and to fulfill the empty spaces in my changing world.

But it's now time to pack my bags,
it's now time to take my blindfolds out,
to meet with the same sad truth;
to say goodbye to you.

I catch your hand fully intertwined with mine,
but soon enough you're letting go.

Time to shout and plead guilty for once,
that the only star in my night sky is you;
but sure enough we lost track of time,
so before it's too late I admit,
I fell for you fast.

I only had one day to make this last more than a while,
to play it as innocent as a child playing outside.

I only came as a slave to my heavy heart
and to regain my faith and trust in what I got.

Did you ever regret meeting me?
You don't feel any different it seems.

I am merely a small wave in your ocean of repair,
if only you knew my boat can take you anywhere.

Did you ever think how rare it's been to feel the way I do,
but soon enough I'd be an iceberg in your sea
and freeze you out taking you
under with me.

My bags are packed,
my blindfold is gone,
I am following your light.

Met with a hopeful truth
tonight;
my reason to return
is *you*...

the hymns of *our* longing

The stars leaned in for a sweet kiss;
we closed our expectant eyes,
cancelled the sensation of sight
and connected the softest part of your soul
with the hardest part of mine.
The city lights of *SoKor*
is ameliorated by our graceful attendance.
Your face lit up brighter than a painting by *Monet*.
I wanted your untouched purity all over my dreams.
I tended to your tears,
and stitched your scars
with angel hair.
Then Sunday morning came,
I am bedridden with honest dread;
thinking our forbidden love,
is not worth
the wait.
The pain emanating from my skin
is giving-in to full spiritual decay.
I guess, I was selfish in yearning for a heart
too incompatible with my musical taste.
I guess,
it's *blind* love,
again.
I was *deaf* of hearing
what's actually
t*here*.
I guess,
I am easily
disconnected,
wildly
distracted, and
disdainfully
dissatisfied,

I am
disgusted
with myself.
"You're the talks of HEAVEN
and I am the *beast*
from HELL."
It's hard to remain
true;
to play at showing you
I *still* care.
Yet,
your beauty
your mind,
your innocence,
still
color my days.
I was truly hypnotized.
Our drama
with its suffering
melody,
became remedial
at times.
Our harmonious exchange of emotions,
were merely
fantastical wars,
mostly fought using
fabricated words.
Still,
I find comfort
in knowing I was there
for you when
your loss
became
our loss.
I took your dreams
under my *red* wings.

I took your *presence*
as what it'd feel like to attain
complete
peace of being;
peace, despite myself;
peace, despite a tainted spirit;
peace, through unreturned love;
peace, through irrational clarity;
peace before routine sleep;
peace before
a loveless,
luckless,
death.
You were my farewell to youth,
burning in a plough of flowering sins.
You were my farewell to dreams hoaxed
under sunlit streams of lying hopes.
I want a divorce from my incessant feelings,
but your colors explode yet again,
excreting a golden sunset.
Are we able to pursue a mode of detachment
from the uneventful *past*
with the complimentary *future?*
I guess not.
When the *present* gets off at the wrong stop
we shout:
"This is us!"
I want the silent pain to rain elsewhere,
I want no longer to be its submissive
participant,
client,
experiment.
Nothing can preserve the soul of a man;
even if he's encased in a barrel
of sodium.
Letting go isn't an easy release;

a few letters sent sincerely
don't always leave one smiling;
from d*ear*,
to d*ear*.
It's the irrevocable memories that are first
to fry inside the ovens of a fiery
delirium.
Ours will die
the quickest
behind a firing squad
of deleted
messages.
This choking sensation
kills indiscriminately,
and has taken
billions of living casualties
each day.
NOW,
we are stardust
on a forsaken
poet's
bass drum.
And that
concludes
the idea of a living
you,
or a living
me.

Epilogue

Here we are, inside a blue room in the basements of drowned memories. Somehow, all the bedcovers remain kempt, and the dust coated the roses a fine shade of abalone. The screen windows are busted in, with shears from rats who knew how to use them. There are cracks in crevasses where cables and electric wirings used to breathe life into a fat TV. I counted about twelve ominous nails, a slave to no canvas; paintings of landscapes or attempts to recreate Monet's lilies. Those were childhood feces left behind, by shadows of an easier time, leaving a smell of orange juice freshly squeezed and bread finely toasted with a cold thick layer of peanut butter spread to the edges. What a warmer time it was, to be a subject to care from a parent, without wanting provisions from the ego to start contending. We'd delight on the springs of these old mattresses, with such dangerous euphoria, as we reach our hands under, trying to uncover runaway marbles. Losing count of the many cuts our innocent dreams provided, for the future body to rid of with a smirk of denial. These tortured scenes crystalized our tears in the succulent darkness of adulthood. Here, the nights are pleasantly spent begging for mercy, from love, from religion, from our parents, from our friends; until our ambitions to court greater change, is devoured entirely during the attempts at manifesting it.

    We now enter the cabinets with clothes that were forced to cover our young skins; styles we are yet to condemn, flipping through neurotically sequenced photo albums. Those times when our unconsciousness was such joy. Being too aware, made the later years a devilish fabrication. Help me carry in buckets of white paint; the shade of liquid cocaine and farm-fresh milk. We'll do our best to make windows out of these blue wall enclosures. Let the light penetrate the room's unmolested surfaces, and flirtatious molds, making the air a lethal shade of *slow death*. Here we are, asking *it* to help us with the lid.

What now? But to wipe the stone chimney clean of dead wood, and ashes of loved ones, beloved pets, and letters to lovers that made it to heaven's secured safe. There is a bluebird that made it inside, fluttering its beady eyes and blinking its bellflower wings. It relaxed its shining shadow on the clock radio, it is forever 0:00. Here we are in the timeless, with this agent of kindness, supervising our return to a pure and dazzling renewal. Its curious foot fumbled with the buttons, making a funeral pyre of tonight's parachute into an endless dread. Here we are dancing, so sublimely fascinating to our core audiences, drawers with loose screws, memorabilia with forgotten origins, a sweater from a friend who betrayed you, a lightbulb about to give-in to announce our rhythm's timely demise. The devil's mice came out, as soon as blackness snapped with such ineffable precision. Their secretive and murmured vocals mastered control over our lucid dreaming, while the beast pressed the lid closed for a thousand years.

And now, we use our heavy hearts as pouches, for uncuddled remarks. Let's regard ourselves as victims of lust, valor of souls, blankets of sun over a tornado, doves listening fondly to a wet kiss shared by newlyweds. The sensitivity of those eyes, and the morbidity of those loud velvety lips, made the red wine sing inside my lungs with such livid compassion. The gradual aim for a definitive love awoken the comatose heart as a Goddess from the East blessed it with star particles. Friendships have sailed away with my dignity offended and caused my affinity to the monstrous to intensify. True love's unwavering pendulum parks on the paradisal corners of Eden's shallow ponds; a love uncompromised by even one asymmetrical pebble. There finally comes an end to the counting of our emotional currencies. The receipts feed the embryonic fires, blackened by layers of pulverized charcoal, drenched in liters of petroleum. We celebrate the musical embarkments of each spark; awed by the ebb and flow of the oscillating flames. We nurture the glow, as it nourishes the blue room of its intruders, installing a mass of incredible forgiveness their natures found without a conceited response for. They've vanished, these tax collectors, these impatient corneas, behind the branches of our irises, filtering the goodness out of our eyes. No more will they deprave us of feeling alive, feeling enriched, feeling enlightened by the most molecular happiness a single moment inspires.

And so, we finally know.

A modicum of solace is achieved in knowing just plenty enough, from the nothingness that we are, that we came from, that we inevitably return back to. There exists a divinity inside the spacious newness of a life mastered; after investigating each posthumous epiphany, and posthumous declaration. We sigh with the spring and glorify in the winterized version of our summer prayers. The tones of a remarkable love are yet to fill the souls of our little ones. Everything is good for now. Our days are colored-in with scrumptious sunshine, as our hearts found the last traces of HER *melody*.

Exit

www.ingramcontent.com/pod-product-compliance
Lightning Source LLC
Chambersburg PA
CBHW060346080526
44583CB00012B/201